Great Tim

Dublin and Belfast to Dungannon, Cookstown, Omagh, Strabane, Letterkenny, Stranorlar, Donegal, Killybegs, Glenties, and Londonderry, via Portadown.

Miles from B'fast	STATIONS.	Week-days.												Sundays.
		a.m.	L.R. Exps a.m. *	a.m.	a.m.	a.m.	p.m.	L a.m.	L.R. Exps p.m.	p.m.	p.m.	D p.m.	p.m.	
	DUBLIN ....dep.	..	6 40	..	..	9 15	..	11 30	3 0	3 0	..	6 40	..	.
	Drogheda .... ,	..	7 17	..	..	9 55	..	12 11	3 8	3 8	..	7 20	..	.
	Dundalk ..... ,,	..	7 46	..	..	10 25	..	12 51	4 6	4 6	..	7 52	..	.
	Portadown ...arr.	..	8 36	..	..	11 19	..	1 47	5 3	5 3	.	8 53	..	.
..	**BELFAST**....dep.	8 0	8 25	..	..	10 45	..	1 30	4 25	4 25	5 35	9 10	10 45	.
7½	Lisburn...... ,,	8 14	8 38	..	..	10 58	..	1 43	4 38	4 38	5 48	9 23	11 1	.
20	Lurgan ...... ,,	8 37	8 55	..	..	11 16	..	2 8	5 1	5 1	6 12	9 48	11 25	.
25	**Portadown** ...arr.	8 45	9 3	..	..	11 24	..	2 16	5 9	5 9	6 20	9 56	11 34	.
..	**Portadown** .....dep.	8 48	9 9	..	10 10	11 28	..	2 22	5 14	5 35	6 24	*10 2*	*11 40*	.
31¾	Annaghmore ...	9 0	..	..	10 21	11 39	..	2 33	..	5 47	6 35	*10 13*	*11 52*	.
34¼	Vernersbridge .. ,,	9 5	..	..	10 26	11 44	..	2 38	..	5 53	6 40	*10 18*	..	.
35¾	Trew and Moy.. ,,	9 10	..	..	10 30	11 48	..	2 42	..	5 58	6 44	*10 22*	*11 59*	.
40	**Dungannon**.....arr.	9 18	9 31	..	10 38	11 56	..	2 50	5 36	6 6	6 52	*10 30*	*12 7*	.
..	**Dungannon**...dep.	Stop	9 40	..	Stop	12 5	..	2 56	..	6 10	6 56	*10 31*	Saturdays only Portadown to Dungannon.	.
45½	Coalisland.... ,,	..	9 51	..	..	12 17	..	3 6	..	6 22	7 7	*10 42*		.
48½	Stewartstown. ,,	..	10 0	..	..	12 25	..	3 12	..	6 30	7 14	*10 49*		.
54½	**Cookstown** ... arr	..	10 11	..	..	12 37	..	3 23	..	6 42	7 25	*11 0*		.
..	**Dungannon**.....dep.	..	9 33	..	9 45	12 0	..	2 53	5 39	Saturdays excepted Portadown to Cookstown.	Stop	Runs to Dungannon on Wednesdays and to Cookstown on Saturdays.		.
42¾	Donaghmore.... ,,	..	..	..	9 54	12 6	..	2 59	5 45		..			.
49	Pomeroy ...... ,,	..	..	..	10 14	12 19	..	3 12	5 57		..			.
54	Carrickmore.... ,	..	..	..	10 31	12 29	..	3 22	6 7		..			.
57¾	Sixmilecross.... ,,	..	..	..	10 40	12 36	..	3 29	6 15		..			.
59¼	Beragh .... ,,	..	..	..	10 47	12 40	..	3 34	6 19		..			.
66¾	**Omagh** .... arr.	..	10 13	..	11 5	12 51	..	3 45	6 30		..			.
..	**Omagh** ....dep.	8 35	10 15	..	11 58	12 55	1 58	3 58	6 35		7 52			.
70¼	**Mountjoy** ...... ,,	8 41	..	..	12 4	..	..	4 5	..		7 58			.
76½	Newtownstewart ,,	8 50	..	..	12 14	1 11	2 13	4 17	6 49		8 6			.
80¾	Victoria Bridge . ,,	8 59	..	..	12 27	1 20	2 23	4 32	6 58		8 16			.
82¼	Sion Mills ...... ,,	9 5	..	..	12 34	1 24	2 29	4 37	7 2		8 22			.
85¾	**Strabane** ....arr.	9 10	10 40	..	12 42	1 30	2 35	4 43	7 7		8 28			.
..	**Strabane** .....dep.	..	11 0	..	..	..	4 23	..	7 15		..		Stop	.
105	Letterkenny ..arr.	..	12 8	..	..	..	5 28	..	8 15		..		Saturdays only	.
..	**Strabane**...... dep.	..	11 0	..	1 0	..	4 23	5 50	..		..			.
99¼	Stranorlar....arr.	..	11 50	..	1 40	..	5 8	6 35	..		..			.
117¼	Donegal ..... ,	..	12 57	..	..	..	..	7 30	..		..			.
136¼	Killybegs .... ,,	..	2 15	..	..	..	..	8 45	..		..			.
123¾	**Glenties**...... ,,	..	1 45	..	..	..	..	8 0	..		..			.
..	**Strabane** ....dep.	9 13	10 42	10 53	12 52	1 33	2 39	4 46	7 10	..	8 31		*11 58*	.
88¾	Porthall........ ,,	9 20	..	10 59	12 58	..	2 46	4 53	..	..	8 38		..	.
93	St. Johnston ... ,,	9 29	..	11 7	1 6	..	2 56	5 1	a	..	8 47		..	.
94¾	Carrigans ...... ,,	9 35	..	11 12	1 11	..	3 2	5 6	..	..	8 53		..	.
100¼	**LONDONDERRY**arr.	9 45	11 0	11 20	1 20	1 55	3 15	5 15	7 30	..	9 5		*12 20*	.

* Breakfast Car, Dublin to Portadown. **L.R.** Light Refreshments served on these trains.
L. Luncheon Car Dublin to Portadown.
a Stops at St. Johnston on Saturdays. **D** Dining Car, Dublin to Portadown.

These had been the standard timings for many years and pertained until June 1932 when very enterprising accelerations were put into force, some of which lasted until 1940.

THE GOLDEN YEARS OF THE GREAT NORTHERN RAILWAY

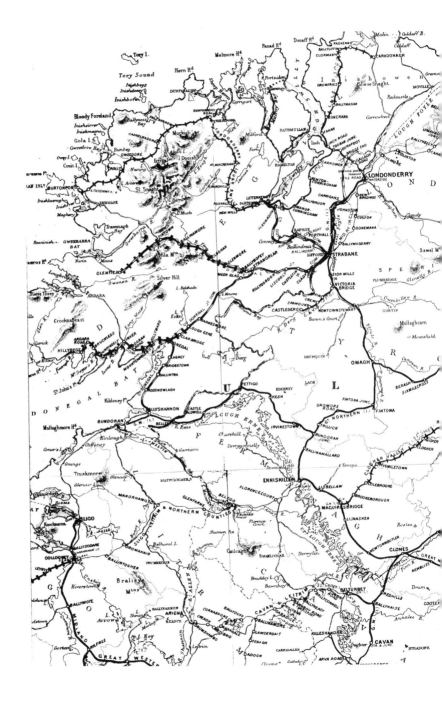

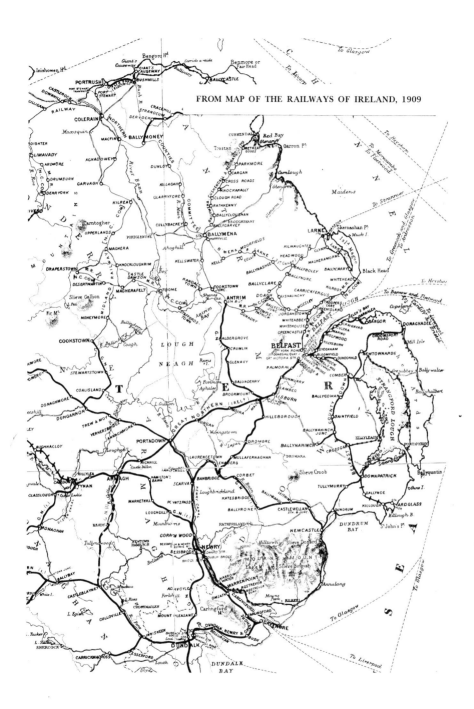

FROM MAP OF THE RAILWAYS OF IRELAND, 1909

Certificate presented in 1917 to driver Dan Sweeney of Enniskillen shed (see page 115)

THE GOLDEN YEARS OF THE GREAT NORTHERN RAILWAY

R.M.Arnold

Blackstaff Press Belfast

Published by Blackstaff Press Limited, 3 Galway Park, Dundonald, Belfast BT16 0AN

First published 1976
New Edition 1979

ISBN 8 85640 182 X (hardback)

Printed by Belfast Litho Printers Limited.

CONTENTS

ACKNOWLEDGMENTS

The personal recollections of railwaymen can often be just as convincing as the official documents and a satisfactory aspect of my research has been how often the one has corroborated the other. So I am very grateful to the following retired GNR men for their help with Part I, this in many cases taking the form of long letters: S. Adams, W. Bateson, T. Campbell, J.V. Collins, W. Donaldson, W. Jackson, J.J. Kelly, F. Lambert, J.J.K. Love, L. Macauley, W.J. Marshall, B. McGirr, S. Nelson, W. Stewart and T.E. Thompson as well as three who did not live to see this book: William Gillespie, John Holland and Sam McCague. I should perhaps make special mention of Irwin Pryce, former Station Foreman at Great Victoria Street, Belfast. His interest in this book seems to have been on a par with his attitude to the railway. It was said that during his early days when employed as number-taker he invariably had the correct carriage numbers noted down before each train had stopped at Belfast, so well could he identify each vehicle even in the distance. Many of those who came after him and are employed by NIR today tend to regard their GNR days with mixed feelings, but I must mention those amongst them who have helped: J. Gibson, A. Gribben, F. Reid, J. Scallon, J. Shannon, T.N. Topley and P. Wray, as well as two with non-GNR backgrounds who dug up useful information, Noel Craig and Frank Dunlop. I must also express appreciation to George Hanthorn and his staff, exiled by bomb damage to caravan accommodation adjoining the 'motor' platform, for courtesy which had much of the warmth of their old railway.

I have had excellent co-operation from CIE, from the staff of the Belfast Public Record office and Mr. R.B. Beggs of the Ulster Folk Museum. The vast majority of amateurs in railway matters could not have been more helpful. I must mention especially amongst them C.P. Friel, who, amongst many activities, was, with Wallace Gamble and John Richardson, responsible for most of the diagram material, the Ordnance Survey Office supplying the remainder. J.D. Fitzgerald's fine collection of GNR photographs has indeed been an inspiration and once again R.N. Clements has been most forthcoming on locomotive matters. Others who have helped in various ways include: G. Beesley, R. Carlisle, H.A. Frazer, D. Grimshaw, J.N. Hamilton, D.T.R. Henderson, M.A. McMahon, I.C. Pryce (junr.), H. Richards, Sir Cecil Smith and D.J. Veltom.

Last but not least come the photographers, whose work is reproduced on the following pages:

H.C. Casserly   12, 19, 21 (t), 54, 82, 92(b), 93, 107, 123, 126 (b)
the late F.C.G. Chapman 124
D.G. Coakham   10, 20, 28, 46 (t), 50 (b), 51, 74 (b), 88, 94, 110, 111 (b)
N. Craig   5 (b)
M.D. England   9, 48
N.R.S. Foster   77 (b), 89, 97, 104, 126 (t)
the late A. Johnston   3, 7, 8, 21 (b), 42, 46 (b), 47, 52, 79, 81, 115, 117
S.G. Nash   83 (b), 106 (b)
W. Robb M.B.E.   5 (t), 18, 24 (b), 30, 45
Major General Sir Cecil Smith 1, 6 (b), 14, 49, 53, 78, 80, 83 (t)
Also Real Photographs 15
Locomotive & General Railway Photographs 58, 74 (t), 92 (t)

Joe Magill, of British Railways staff at Newton Heath, Manchester, painted the cover picture.

INTRODUCTION

This is not a conventional history of the growth of a railway, with all the political
and economic overtones; Dr. E.M. Patterson has already dealt with such matters
in his book. My purpose rather is to present the Great Northern Railway well established and at work in the years of its finest achievements.

The organisation behind a major railway stands as one of the most impressive
accomplishments of the first half of this century. A detailed book on the services
of any major English railway would be a daunting if not an impossible undertaking,
but the GNR, the second largest network in Ireland, presents a tempting challenge.
No doubt the steam locomotives and other engineering aspects have in themselves
a tremendous appeal, but here I shall be more concerned with a system that organised men and machines in such a way that the traveller could stand confidently on
any station platform and find his train, warm and clean, at the time stated.

I have tried to present this railway as a live unit—dealing with the motive power,
the rolling stock and the lines they travelled only as they served the public.
Similarly I feel that the railwaymen who helped to give that service have much
more interest than engineering or financial statistics. These days, especially, we
should remember that the GNR was, like rugby football, one of the great levellers
across Ireland's political divide. Men of different creeds and political opinions often
shared a footplate—and a genuine affection. They may have been nearly all
Armstrongs at Enniskillen, Campbells at Derry, Reillys at Dublin and Thompsons
at Belfast, but the bond was considerable and unusual in Ireland. Lastly, I have hoped
to show how the various tentacles of the GNR, though in several cases never entirely
justified, made up a splendidly logical jigsaw of public services.

The GNR usually had a stud of about 200 locomotives and 500 carriages, but by
1938, despite staff economies after the railway strike five years previously, they
also had 5,330 employees which by 1943 had grown to 7,000. Its route mileage at
its maximum was about 560, roughly one fifth of Ireland's total railway and exceeded only by the Great Southern & Western. Though one or other of these two
railways appeared in twenty-nine Irish counties, they met only in the North Wall
yards in Dublin.

Fate has been kind in enabling me to observe the GNR from an early age. Nearly
fifty years ago I was just starting to segregate in my mind the three railways that
served the city where I was born. The NCC clearly was as exciting as it was eccentric;
the BCDR handled an immense suburban traffic in a way that has left me ever since
trying to find anything so well done. But the Great Northern was obviously the
most far-reaching, a sane and organised structure that would take years to unravel.
The first link in the chain of circumstances came when I went away to school in
Tyrone; the railway was, of course, out of bounds but with the help of a timetable—soon better known than anything else in my desk—I could before long identify
the departure of most up trains as they gave their mournful whistle prior to entering the tunnel. And since travel is really what a railway is about, soon I was visiting
with various teams places like Armagh, Milford, Derry, Enniskillen and Dublin.
Subsequently, I had a job which often involved being sent to the back of beyond
for years. Besides weekend trips home from Newry, Carrickmacross, Lisburn,
Oldcastle and Newtownbutler, I now had a further opportunity to familiarize myself with the daily railway routine at these stations.

Thanks to an early habit of recording most of the railway activities I saw,
writing an operational book on the GNR posed no great problem. I could not go
back much before 1930, it is true, but as it seemed a pity to kick off in the middle
of the GNR's greatest days, I enlisted the help of those named to explore at length

the World War I period and after. There will be those who claim that the GNR reached its finest hour further back, in 1913, but that view is prompted by financial considerations which should not be paramount in respect of a public service, and, besides, ignores the remarkable achievements of the 'thirties.

The golden years, as I see them, lasted approximately from one World War to the next. In this interval the GNR suffered more than other Irish railways from events which endangered revenue and profits. There was the advent of the 'eight-hour day', with the considerable intake of staff this required; the creation of the Border and the costly delay to train services it brought; and a railway strike which destroyed much of the goodwill that had existed between the staff and the public. Yet, despite such a series of handicaps, the progress the GNR made in giving a fast, comfortable, frequent and reliable service remains most impressive. Even in face of 'bus competition, only 19 of a total 560 miles of track were lifted. And during World War I, when British railways deteriorated, the GNR improved by leaps and bounds. It is for this reason that I carry my story through to the third year of the second war, 1941; which found the GNR again operating the fastest trains in these islands. Never again was it to reach such heights.

During this period, for those who had a taste for and could afford travel, the GNR catered magnificently. For those with an eye for scenery, several lines snaked and stretched through mountain and lake terrain to the sea. Sportsmen of all types received splendid co-operation. Special trains conveyed horses to hunts and race meetings and catered of course for the racegoers as well. The railway listed and published over thirty golf courses it served and regularly ran excursions for the supporters of the three styles of football played in Ireland. It also owned hotels and was specially enterprising in the meal facilities it provided on trains.

But most interesting of all was the criss-cross of connecting services for those who had to travel other than for pleasure. The sheer organisation behind this daily routine, and that of the goods trains, is fascinating when one studies the various routes; passengers from Londonderry, for instance, the GNR's most northerly point, could choose at Omagh to go either to Enniskillen and the West, or to Portadown for Belfast, or to Armagh; or they could take the main line south, where at Scarva, Goraghwood, Dundalk, Dromin and Drogheda services could be had for the other towns in their area. Was there not something especially intriguing about stations like Dromore and Glaslough from which the Dublin-bound passenger could take a train *in either direction?* This choice also offered at most 'Irish North' stations, if someone were en route for Belfast.

To study in detail when and how such services were operated requires a large book, so I have divided the work into two parts. Part I confines itself to the north of the GNR system and does not touch at all on the Portadown-Dublin line, or its branches, and Portadown-Cavan is also more suitably left for Part II. I segregate the areas according to the various engine sheds responsible for their train haulage. The GNR had nine major depots, and some small sheds. As Belfast was easily the dominant depot, Part I begins with it and then considers three others in the north.

Of that splendid system which in the 1931 timetable required 159 pages, little but its main line now survives. Its 59 miles in the Republic belong to CIE, as does the Howth branch and two branches at Drogheda—a short one to the cement works, opened in the 'thirties, and part of the former Oldcastle branch (to Navan Junction). In Northern Ireland only those 53 miles of main line and the 18½ mile Antrim branch remain. And by the time this book appears the last GNR terminus in the north will be closed; trains which formerly arrived at Great Victoria St will be diverted to a new Central station at Maysfields.

R.M. Arnold

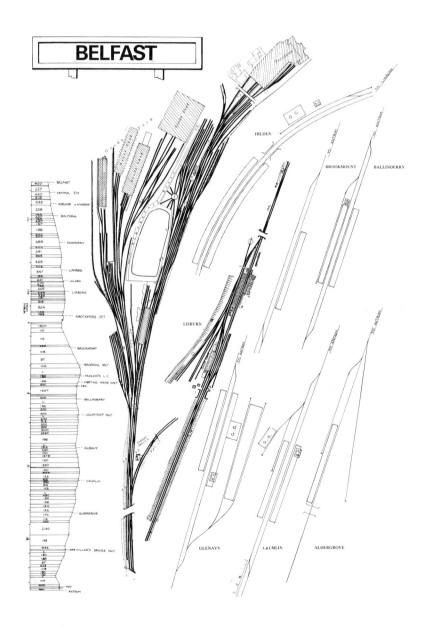

BELFAST

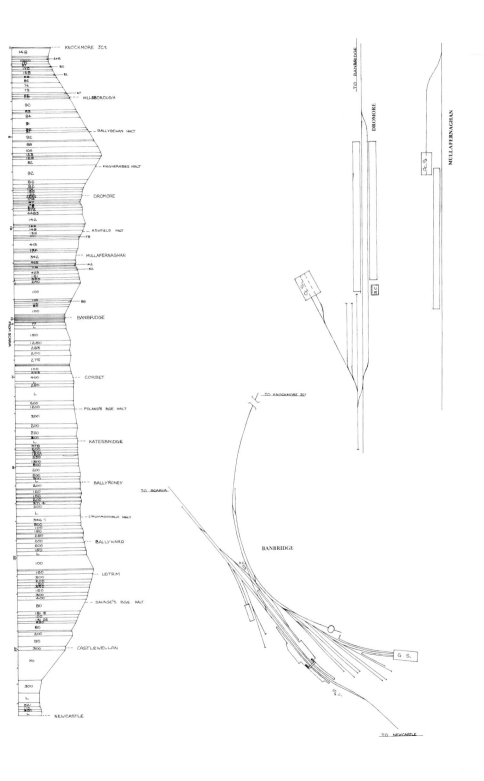

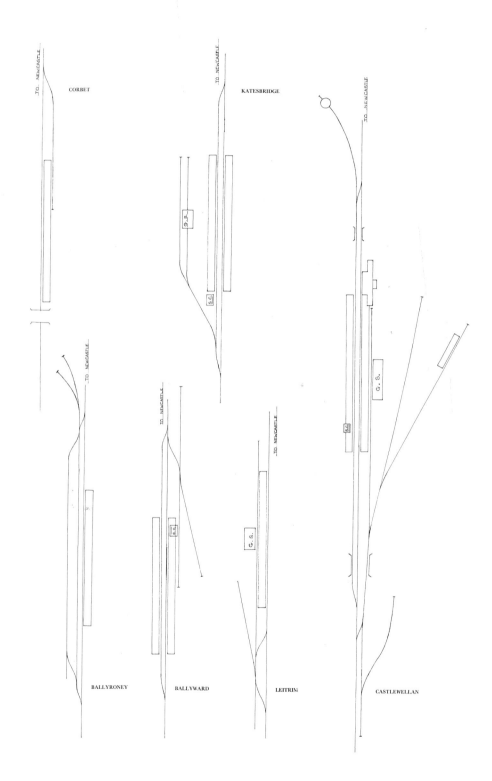

BELFAST

In 1911 the eleven-road locomotive shed in the bog meadows at Adelaide, 1½ miles from the GNR's Belfast terminus, replaced the Ulster Railway's shed, only a stone's throw from the passenger station in Great Victoria Street. Around that period the engines were referred to more by their names than by numbers. Of an evening just prior to the old shed's closure *Juno* or *Neptune* or *Diana* could be observed quiescent after an express run to Dublin, alongside some of the largest goods engines, *Pomeroy, Culloville* and *Banbridge,* ready for a night journey.

The Blackstaff river, that 'foul stream', flowed past the northern side of the depot and bordered Grosvenor Road goods yard. But the real barrier between the passenger and goods areas was 'the pond', a constant irritation to the management who could have made very good use of this space. 'The pond' was the property of the Ulster Spinning Company, its water being pumped over Murray's wall, the bulwark of railway property on the up side of the line. Adjacent was Murray's Tobacco Factory and its very unrailwaylike odour. Long after the old shed had disappeared, its seven roads retained their numbers and became the 'loco yard' sidings.

In 1900 the passenger terminus had had four platforms and little or no suburban traffic, though Belfast's rapid growth to 350,000 meant that by 1904 the horse trams could record a total of 28 million passengers. The following year, when the trams were electrified, the railway saw a challenge to benefit from such traffic. So a shorter platform, called to this day the 'motor platform' but officially known as No. 1, was added for a new frequent local service and, in the same year, hydraulic buffers were erected at the main arrival platform. Thus each of Belfast's three railway ter-

Saturated LQG 160, with name Culloville removed, passes Knockmore Junction with down main line goods about 1913

1

Great Victoria Street terminus, Belfast, showing Murray's Tobacco Factory . Ex-railmotor trailer 210 is in the passenger yard

mini came to have five platforms, though except in summer the GNR had probably the most traffic.

It was just possible to have four operations going on simultaneously if one included the 'third line', which ran under the permissive block system to Adelaide and through a large marshalling yard, built with the new shed. The main line was rejoined at Balmoral when a new signal cabin nearer Adelaide opened in 1913. Here a group of very short sidings dealt with seasonal traffic for the Royal Agricultural Show.

By 1920 Adelaide was arguably the most important depot in Ireland and, even though no new enginemen were recruited between 1925 and 1932, in the latter year it had still 70 drivers and the same number of firemen. This was double the numbers at the next largest shed, Dundalk, and represented about 30 per cent of all the enginemen employed by the GNR. Until the railway strike of 1933 country sheds tended to be smaller than those which survived latterly, and in the 'twenties in the Belfast area one rarely saw more than ten engines daily which did not belong to Adelaide; perhaps three from Dublin, one from Derry (or Omagh), one from Clones, two or three from Portadown and four from the sub sheds, Banbridge, Newcastle and Antrim. This chapter is almost wholly concerned with the services to those three last-named points, as well as the local traffic to Lisburn.

BANBRIDGE & NEWCASTLE (including SCARVA)

At Knockmore Junction in 1870 only one branch went off, but on the opposite side from today. The Banbridge line had always more traffic potential than the one to Antrim. Around 1910 a scheme to make a third line through from Knockmore to the city came to nothing, as bridges 280 and 281 still testify with their double arches (a curious form of which has recently been revived). Likewise a move to build a new locomotive works at Knockmore in 1920 never got off the ground; one of several objections to the GNR, professed by Unionist politicians, being that its repair works were in another state. The Banbridge branch reached that town after the line from Scarva, as was obvious from the layout there. Because the Scarva branch was first operated by the Dublin and Belfast Junction Railway, it subsequently became part of the GNR's Southern division though always worked from Banbridge.

Between Knockmore and Banbridge the only places of importance were Hillsborough and Dromore, but this steeply graded line provided neither town with a very convenient station. From the small station—a very nasty spot to try

7 with the standard two-coach set at the 'motor' platform, Belfast. The bearded figure is Inspector Johnson who represented the GNR at fairs until about 1920, and whose camera covered GNR engines thoroughly at that period

to stop a heavy goods train—to Hillsborough's Georgian houses was a lengthy climb. The station from the Market Square, Dromore, lay a good half-mile along Church Street. A seven-span brick viaduct over the Lagan, a little beyond its platforms, was the most impressive piece of civil engineering on the line. It still stands today in awesome majesty, one of the few reminders that this stretch of railway ever existed. Mullafernaghan, the only other station in 1915, was an irresistible piece of railway nomenclature, though not quite the GNR station with the longest name. On a line where speed rarely exceeded 45 mph, the only restriction of note was one of 25 mph between mileposts 4¾–5¼.

The main Belfast-Portadown county road climbed steeply over the Banbridge branch at the 'Burnhouse' bridge. The railway then crossed both Lagan river and, a mile further, the Ulster canal, during its steep climb into County Down. Just beyond Hillsborough station was, unusually, an aqueduct (bridge 13) and before Dromore station the road to Lurgan passed under the railway at the 'Maypole Hill' bridge. The last bridge before Banbridge (No. 50) crossed the Bann (two 60ft girders) just prior to meeting the Scarva branch. In 1921 a lengthy renewal operation was performed on this bridge and for this period goods trains, and even some passenger ones, ran via Scarva.

The charming village of Scarva is, of course, still there, as indeed are the station's twisting platforms, with, at the Dublin end of the down one, the hedge in the shape of a seated man. Trains still pass through but the station itself is closed and gives no indication of its place amongst GNR junctions for just short of a century. During the 'twenties Scarva had a good main line passenger service, including several of the inter-city expresses. The signalmen there were M. Gavin and W. Burrell and on Scarva's big occasion, 13th July, it was traditional that both men worked in the cabin all day. Burrell was renowned for strict adherence to every rule. Everyone who knew this savoured to the full an episode whereby Cyril Retalic, a Newry guard and a most experienced railwayman, made a mockery of the signalman. Passing through Scarva on an up goods, the tail-lamp of Retalic's van was missing but phone calls by Burrell to both Tandragee and Poyntzpass told him everything was in order.

Burrell became even more puzzled when the same thing happened several times—but Retalic carried the joke too far and an inquiry was held. Scarva's Head Porter for many years was the cheerful Aaron Minnis who for a period lived in the stationmaster's house.

From the bay platform the branch went off north-east, crossing the Newry canal by the 'Wash' girder bridge. The fifth bridge on the 1/98 bank at milepost 1¼ was known as 'Martin's', latterly a stopping point for the railcar. Towards the summit of this 2-mile bank the line became slightly steeper and the old 0–6–0s in charge of the branch goods during the 'twenties often backed some way up the main line to take a good run at the climb. There was then a fall under 'Brown's' bridge, down to bridge 13 at the Banbridge end of Laurencetown station. Just beyond the platform stood the three span girder bridge over the Bann, after which the line climbed, much less steeply, all the way along the river to Banbridge. With its industrial atmosphere, this stretch of railway had an unique appeal, more like Yorkshire than Ireland, but softened with much rich woodland.

The Scarva branch had more than its quota of level crossings, the first being Drumhork, near milepost 3¾. Next came Uprichard's, a half mile on the Scarva side of Laurencetown, where W.J. Olds was the stationmaster until the line closed, temporarily, during 1933-4. His porter Bob Anderson, who lived in one of the gate houses, was in charge of the station by 1939. Chapel Row crossing was on the other side of Laurencetown station. One morning as the first train approached, the gateman apparently remained asleep, despite repeated whistles from the 0–6–0. At the last minute a priest appeared in full regalia from Tullylish chapel a few yards away and proceeded to open the gates like a man who had been doing it all his life. Gatekeeper Marr had been killed at Chapel Row on 18.6.19. Some 150 yards further came Hazelbank crossing.

The line crossed the river again at Lenaderg on a girder viaduct and yet again at 'Hayes' lattice girder bridge. An incident at Lenaderg level crossing belongs to 1935, after the line's reopening. The 12.50pm goods Portadown-Banbridge, with only a few wagons, was running early and the gatekeeper, Mrs. Ewart, attempting to open the gates in a hurry, injured her arm. As a full-time gatekeeper her wages were five shillings (25p) per week, but even that was precious at that period. The long siding at Lenaderg was mainly for the use of Geohegan's foundry and opened, like the other two sidings on the branch, with the key on the Scarva-Banbridge staff. Jack Bleakley began as a boy porter at Lenaderg. A guard during World War II, he was killed at Castlewellan shunting tank wagons. The final crossing and the last siding was just outside Banbridge at Millmount, near the bleaching firm of Cowdy, whose name was always given to bridge 20 over the Bann. All traffic into the firm's siding had to be worked from Banbridge direction, the wagons being hauled over the bridge and then backed into the siding.

The Ballyroney extension passed under Banbridge's Bridge Street, with a 37 yards tunnel. As an eventual route to Newcastle from Belfast, this was obviously a very long way round compared with the BCDR—though reasonably direct from Dundalk or Dublin. The lovely Bann valley was followed for 9 miles and the railway crossed the river several times, notably at the 'Black' bridge at milepost 8½ (from Scarva) and at lattice girder bridge 51 before Ballyroney station, the railhead for Rathfriland four miles away. During the 'twenties the crew of the goods, leisurely shunting, became aware of the fascination their operations had for an old man watching with a donkey from the bridge. One day he ventured down to the platform and proceeded to amaze them with a learned discourse on the difference between Walchaert's valve gear (not used on the GNR at that period) and Stephenson's link

*5pm with PPs 4—4—0 about to leave Newcastle No.2 platform. As the date is June 1933,
carriages have obviously been detached to help with later heavy return traffic. Note BCDR
six-wheeler*

motion. For a place which had once been a terminus with an engine shed,
Ballyroney's situation was rather unusual, for after 1906 it was not even a block
post, ground frames operating sidings at both ends of the station.

As the railway now cut across due east to avoid the high land, by Leitrim, near
the line's summit, one felt really in Mourne country, and when the staff was handed
up at Castlewellan a BCDR tablet was received in exchange. Indeed the station's
BCDR origin was apparent in the roof style and the use of a subway—where the
GNR would certainly have produced a weather protected lattice girder footbridge.
In the 'twenties, I had never any doubt that the agent at Castlewellan, J. Barr, was
a BCDR official, but it seems now that he had joint BCDR and GNR status.

At Newcastle one side of the engine shed was used by BCDR engines and the
other, until 1933, by GNR, adjacent to a 50ft turntable. The other active turntable
on the line, besides the mysterious one Castlewellan seldom used, was 42ft 3in at
Banbridge, altered to 45ft in 1936. It was the practice for the BCDR to use
No. 1 platform at Newcastle, with its side door to Golf Links Road and the Slieve

QGs 152 leaving Newcastle, with the Mournes and the Slieve Donard Hotel in the background

4—4—0T 6 at Ballyroney about 1900

Donard Hotel. Both were 650ft (most BCDR platforms were twice the length of GNR ones) but the up-platform at Banbridge, across from the Scarva dock, ranked as the longest on the GNR's Northern division, 660ft.

By 1890 there had been enough 4—4—0 tanks for a couple to be sent to Banbridge, one, kept in a small shed at Ballyroney, for driver John Murray and the other in charge of 'Barlow' Herd at Banbridge. Those used over some twenty years include *4, 6, 7,* and *8*. When the two extensions to Castlewellan were completed in 1906 Murray was transferred to Newcastle. The two P class 4—4—0s of 1905 were said to have been specially built for Newcastle traffic and every now and again appeared there, though not as often as sister *89*. Certainly as soon as *44* arrived in 1911 she became Murray's engine, sharing the line's workings with another of that year (*129*) manned by driver Barney McGee and fireman Jack Campbell of

Leinster, with extended smokebox, at Dromore. Next to the engine is a brake third of type L.4 introduced in 1911, the same year as 44

6

Adelaide shed. Each crew made the double trip twice a day (186 miles), the fireman remaining in charge while his driver went home for dinner. With no mileage allowance such men spent most of their life in the company of their engine. Other 4—4—0s appearing at Newcastle from time to time in those early days were *45, 46,* and *106,* displaced now from the Derry road by the Q class.

About 1918 another class of 4—4—0 was tried out on Newcastle trains while still new, U class *198,* much more familiar at Dundalk. Beattie and Carlisle had replaced Murray and his fireman Beckett, when it was decided that *198* should be tested on the BCDR which had never had a 4—4—0 of its own. There is, sadly, no record of the performance of either *17* or *198* on strange territory, but a log of one run by *198* is interesting, especially since the appendix reveals *198*'s extraordinarily low coal consumption. On this occasion (15.2.19) schedule seems to have been 5 mins more than the 105 mins of the 1.50pm, and *198* took 108 mins 20 sec. With probably about 80 tons the sectional times from Newcastle to Banbridge were 8 mins 5 sec, 10 mins, 3 mins 40 sec, 6 mins 15 sec, 4 mins 30 sec, 6 mins 25 sec, and 6 mins 35 sec; then to Lisburn 7 mins 45 sec, 7 mins 5 sec, 11 mins 10 sec and 8 mins 35 sec before running nonstop to Belfast in a steady but unexciting 12 mins 10 sec. This was all child's play for *198,* regarded for years after as the best engine the line had ever seen. By that period the early enthusiasm which had prompted a nonstop time of 70 mins had abated and the ambitious staff-exchange apparatus at Dromore, Katesbridge and Ballyward been abandoned.

To connect with main line goods, the Scarva branch prior to 1923 ran a goods at a rather unusual hour for such a minor line, 2.45am ex-Banbridge. In 1918 a 2—4—2 tank was in charge of the branch for old Herd and W. Wallace. *90, 94* and *95* seem all to have had a turn on a job for which they were not ideally suited. Mixed trains could be quite heavy and during a morning spell of 80 mins at Scarva a special goods often had to be run, after which the tank returned light for the 9.58-mixed, off the 9am ex-Dundalk. Officially the JT load up the 1/98 was 24

U class 198 outside the old loco shed at Belfast

Scarva branch engine about 1915. The guard with the watch chain has been identified as Bob Brown; the engineman behind is George Steele, appointed driver in 1909

wagons, or 15 wagons if the carriage set of 4 six-wheelers was attached. The fireman's job was no sinecure for at the end of each day he had to coal the engine by shovelling from a wagon alongside. The eight-hour day ended this arrangement, and the early morning trip to Scarva soon ceased also, making life more pleasant at a shed which had now no night turns. Big Billy Stewart, a fireman here, was soon to be a most reliable partner for Joe Beattie at Newcastle. Dundalk seems to have decided on the various Banbridge workings as a suitable employment for non-standard 0–6–0s, and during 1919, for instance, *37, 193* and *194* could be seen there with either Belfast or Banbridge drivers. Even more were the D class used and it implied a certain historical aptness to see them on the Scarva branch, just about the only off-shoot the old Dublin & Belfast Junction could boast. During the 'twenties *41* in particular was often in use on the branch, and with her sister and the three Clifford 0–6–0s proved much more popular for passenger trains than standard A and AL class engines. The resemblance between *40, 41* and the GS&WR J15 class in their saturated state has often caused comment and the building date, 1872, is only one possible common feature in addition to 17 in x 24 in cylinders and 5ft 1½ in in driving wheels—unusual on the GNR until 1913, when they fixed on something similar for their future mixed traffic engines.

Of the A class, *33, 61* and *146* were the most used around Banbridge, grand little engines, with the first-named, especially, a terrific steamer. AL class engines, such as *56, 58* and *140*, were mainly used on the Belfast-Newcastle goods, often manned by that splendid looking big man, Sam Glass, whose brother was, until reduced, a permanent-way inspector. After commencement of the eight-hour day, this crew from Adelaide would find the passenger engine for the 7.30am to Belfast already prepared, the one Newcastle crew coming on duty later to take over the 0–6–0 for the return goods. When the 1.45pm ex-Newcastle, with Banbridge crew, caught them up (usually at Banbridge, except on Rathfriland fairdays), footplates were exchanged and the Newcastle crew then had the passenger train through to

PPs 77 on Newcastle train at Belfast, with driver Joe Beattie

Belfast and back with this engine, on the 4.45pm to Newcastle. This proved a neat arrangement for most of the year, the Newcastle engine being coaled at Adelaide for the 11am, usually with six boxes of 9 cwt each, until the next day. In the summer months the 6.15pm went through to Newcastle, so an extra pair of men were drafted in, leaving Newcastle workings more like the old days when Banbridge men usually worked the goods in and out of Newcastle.

Jack Gracey and fireman Hugh Malone, the first of these additional men, were still based at Newcastle in November 1919 when Gracey was killed at the Adelaide coaling gantry. The cause of this tragedy is of interest. GNR 4–4–0s with the 4ft 6in boiler, such as the Q and S classes, were reversed in the opposite way from U class engines, almost unknown at Adelaide at that period. Some shed man, in an attempt to move *198* forward, in fact did the opposite and Gracey was crushed. For a time Jack Tinman took his place and then 'the boxer Smith' had a spell at Newcastle, working the 4.45pm ex-Belfast and the 7.25am ex-Newcastle. Overnight Smith used a home-made bed in the shed, scorning lodgings. Each morning his fireman, Tommy Thompson, would find a mass of magazines of the 'Gem' and 'Magnet' type in the shed, for Smith was an industrious reader, but the driver himself would most likely be away for an early swim. One morning Billy Lloyd, the cleaner, began to look anxious. It was after 7am and there was no sign of 'the boxer'. So Thompson whistled a few times and then brought *198* against the train. At the last moment Smith appeared at the non-platform side of the engine. 'I was at St John's Point when I heard you whistle,' he declared. The fireman smiled to himself. He guessed Smith had probably been somewhere around the hotel, not more than five minutes away.

When *198* went back to Dundalk *72* became the Newcastle engine, the Belfast-based workings usually being by the small-wheeled version of this P class, or PP class, rebuilt with 4ft 6in boiler. Joe Beattie spent over ten years there till the shed closed in 1933, when his fireman was Johnny Lynch, various men taking the other turn during the summer months. Two firemen of those days who still survive are big Frank Little and Sam Mehaffy, who succeeded him in lodgings with Mrs. Quinn at Causeway Road. Not blessed with the most conciliatory temperament, Mehaffy later rather surprisingly (or maybe not so) became shed foreman at Adelaide. During his Newcastle days he was firing for Ned Jennings on 75 when Harry Ferguson from the Dromore area—since recognised as one of Ulster's foremost motor specialists—requested a footplate run. Knowing this engine's capacity for disconcerting bounce, it was suggested he might be happier standing on the tender, but Ferguson wanted more speed and Jennings, the right man for such an occasion, obliged him with a race down the bank into Newcastle. The occupant of Newcastle shed during its last GNR year was invariably either 76 or 77, now superheated, splendid Victorian relics rebuilt for many more years of service.

Apart from excursions, it was possible to see only two sets of carriages in Newcastle. Both were basically three bogies and usually crossed each other at Banbridge. The 7.30am ex-Newcastle of the 'twenties possibly gained an occasional extra passenger (despite the lengthy journey) because, except on Mondays, it reached Belfast 25 mins before any BCDR-routed train. The set had always a brake 3rd (all trains were compartment stock, like the BCDR), a compo and a 100-seater 3rd, often 191. For years the 'superior' class coach was 102 and the brake 417, later 76 or 112. A regular Banbridge clientele was catered for each morning. The engine would come off there and collect three extra vehicles from the short siding between the platform and the engine shed. 2nd class six-wheeler 129 was for years one of these, as well as a bogie compo of modern type such as 368. The third coach was the only one of the trio to have any 3rd class accommodation and 17 and 71 alternated on this duty. All returned as far as Banbridge on the 4.45pm, except 368 which waited for the 6.15pm. The regular guard on the 7.30am was Alec Wolseley, also in charge of the 2.25am goods ex-Belfast. Always carrying his basket with appletart inside, he was an avid conversationalist, especially on the merits of Linfield Football Club.

In 1921 the other set had been six-wheelers (all six), but by 1924 a bogie set had been got together for duties less concerned with season ticket passengers. No doubt the happy medium of supplying sufficient accommodation to suit the traffic manager without overburdening the loco department was responsible for several interesting rebuildings during the early 'twenties. One of these involved coach 7, previously with only 36 (1st class) seats, but in 1921 altered to include 2nd class

L.2 type 417, with brake compartment 30⅓ft.

10

accommodation, seats being arranged that passengers faced inwards and each other in a very sociable manner. However Adelaide driver Jack Richardson, very tall but often in poor physical shape, was accustomed to use 7 for the opposite season, seclusion, and many a day at Banbridge he would step into the 1st class and remain there until Leitrim, leaving it to his fireman to do what was required. That wily old engineman Bob Fletcher, finishing his days in the same link, recorded during a week with *105* in 1925 a coal consumption of 31½lbs per mile, as against over 40lbs with Richardson 'in charge'. Fletcher's comment was that the 'company' would be better advised to pay 'that man' to stay at home, as his wages would cost less than the extra coal!

The Banbridge guards were Bob Ryan (brother of the well known Dublin driver), Jack Spain and Davie Jardine, later to become foreman. One of them was in charge of the 6.15pm ex-Belfast, always hauled in the early 'twenties by a small 0−6−0, often *137*. When Billy Lindsay of Adelaide was in charge of this train, no one had any need to travel to Bangor or Portrush for a fireworks display. The banks in the cuttings were alight, and departure from each station an occasion for dense smoke, Lindsay's big red nose shining through it all, and fireman Black apparently quite oblivious of the opinion of either passengers or railwaymen. Though an authority on house property, owning some in the Botanic area, Lindsay just had no flair for locomotives. Eleven six-wheelers would not have been considered an occasion for special effort on the BCDR, and in fact four of his were usually detached from the 6.15 at Lisburn. The smartest train of the day was the 8.45am Belfast-Banbridge, usually four six-wheelers (later 2 bogies), which with six intermediate stops made the 24¼ mile run in 51 mins. When the crew on the late Scarva turn came on duty they took this engine for the day, the first run being the 12.45pm goods to Laurencetown. On Mondays and Saturdays the branch passenger set was attached, providing a connection on Saturdays to the 2.5pm to Belfast. The engine which had worked the early Scarva turns went off to Belfast (for coaling) with the 1.25pm passenger. From 1923 its first duty of the day, after shunting, was the 7.30am to Corbet, conveying workers to the bleach greens convenient to this tree-bedecked station. The four six-wheelers which included guard's van 310 were then propelled back over the 3¼ miles to Banbridge. On Saturdays at 12.30pm this operation was managed in the opposite direction but on other weekdays the ordinary 5.37pm (5pm ex-Newcastle) sufficed. By 1933 this special working ceased as the linen industry floundered. Ballievey siding between Corbet and Banbridge (capacity 45 wagons) served, until about 1939, a factory nestling in the river valley, wagons of coal being propelled from Banbridge at 10.45am as required.

Until 1920 one of the firemen at Banbridge had been big Owen Finlay, quiet and well-spoken, whose father was stationmaster at one of the nearby stations. In June of that year he became yet another of the men to be appointed to the extra driving job at Newcastle. That area has long been rather sensitive on political matters and many considered Finlay to have IRA sympathies. The crunch came one afternoon when he showed himself reluctant to take the 1.45pm out of Newcastle because a party of British soldiers were aboard. It seems that for several months after this incident Finlay was 'on the run', Joe Beattie being only too pleased to work both early and late turns at Newcastle during his absence. In 1922 Wallace was transferred to Omagh, where he was to be senior driver for over twenty years, and a year later Herd retired, so Finlay was now driving at Banbridge. Jack McWilliams was his fireman, and on the late run he could have got home to Belfast in the van of the 9.30pm goods had not Finlay deliberately kept him working. Yet when a

PPs at Banbridge

relief man was on the firing job, Owen showed himself more than helpful in assisting him to catch that goods, but McWilliams spent most of his spell at Banbridge cycling through the darkness.

All the year round, Banbridge had quite a good Sunday service to both Belfast and Newcastle and I have an account of one such journey around 1920 with 0–6–0 *58* and a train of six-wheelers. That nondescript-looking Adelaide driver Sam Welsh was in charge, and for most of the journey a young man had his head out of the window a few compartments from his engine. He looked very festive indeed in a straw hat, and there it was every time Welsh looked out from the footplate. After Lisburn there was a nonstop run to Belfast and Sam could restrain himself no longer. He lifted the bucket, half-full of dirty coal-dust water, threw it past the tender, and caught the fellow full side on. At Belfast the passenger staggered from his compartment, his hat and shirt soaking and filthy. He glared at the men on the footplate but Welsh's wizened face was expressionless, as the foreman took the victim away for a clean-up.

Undoubtedly Welsh preferred a goods train for a fuller expression of his personality and on a summer morning the 2.25am Newcastle goods was ideal as it strolled gently towards the Mournes. On such occasions he invariably had a shotgun on the footplate. After bagging a rabbit or pheasant he would halt the train until the victim had been retrieved. Altogether the whole line was rather a sporting one and just prior to a hunt, 1925-30, the 11am to Newcastle provided evidence of this. Archie Willis of Ballyfinaghy was just one of several who used the railway to transport his horses to a Co. Down hunt. Well in advance each animal's experience and suitability for rail travel had been carefully weighed and as many as a dozen horseboxes placed against the buffers of No. 2 platform, with a few others in the Spion Kop (q.v.). A phlegmatic. confident horse could be trusted to pass along the platform and into its box, but the more nervous ones were brought round via Glengall Street to the Kop platform, where gravel had been sprayed to prevent a slippery surface. With the coaches backed down against the boxes in platform 2, the 11am pulled out and then down against the remainder in the small yard. The first horseboxes of the full stud (Nos 601-700) were withdrawn in 1930 and by 1941 forty-seven had ended their days. However, during 1939-40 eight new ones were built and these and 643, 693 and 699 of the older ones lasted until UTA days. GNR men tended to admire more the occasional BCDR make they saw, only one example of a respect they had for this railway.

Gradually the older 0–6–0s were withdrawn and 4–4–0s became more common on Banbridge (and Scarva) trains. Due to the gradients, the practice was to run tender first out of Banbridge on the branch, and this was blamed for a derailment of 74 by S. Dawson at the canal bridge. In the other direction Joe Gibson, generally very cautious and one of the few drivers who invariably took water at Banbridge, the only column en route between Lisburn and Newcastle, crashed through Drumhork gates. The most likely occasion for a carefree exhibition by the enginemen was on the return trip from Warrenpoint on a summer Sunday night. The other two drivers were now Ned Boland, who had fired for Malone on the Dublin express, and Billy Beckett. Many a wild run the latter man produced, his fireman Rodgers, probably almost as drunk, being under the impression that it was he alone who enabled the stops to be made approximately at the platforms. At Belfast most Banbridge drivers relied upon the advertisement for Palethorpe's sausages near the buffer end of No. 5 platform to estimate the best point for applying the brakes.

Billy Bateson fired at Banbridge for much of the 'twenties, usually to either Dawson or Gibson. His predecessor was McCausland, something of a dandy. An incident which suggested his duration on the railway might be short occurred one afternoon when J.C. Gordon, the stationmaster, met him coming down the yard with a bucket, the contents of which he had just obtained by boring a hole in a beer barrel. Old Gordon's reaction to this was more that of a sportsman than of a disciplinarian and he confided to Gibson, 'The nerve of him! Now if I had been ten years younger...'

Some years later, when Archer the stationmaster proposed going off in a hired car to a Masonic spree in Rathfriland one evening, Dawson arranged to go with him. Though on the late turn, the driver appeared on the footplate already dressed; having kept as clean as possible, he had only to wash his hands before joining the stationmaster. A few days after the superintendent at Belfast passed Dawson at the shed and inquired if he had enjoyed himself at Rathfriland. Dawson took this very ill and concluded that Archer and Hill had been discussing his going off duty early. He never spoke to Archer again.

Shortly afterwards big Mick Magee was the Banbridge shunter and like all true men in this department was mainly concerned with saving time for himself and the railway. On Saturdays there ran a late 11.15 from Banbridge to Ballyroney, really the 9.45pm ex-Belfast, which after 27 mins at Banbridge went on to Katesbridge, where the engine ran round, propelling over the final 2 miles. Mick grudged that 27 mins of wasted time, for after the empty train came back the engine would have to be turned for the following morning, before being put away in the shed. So he suggested to Joe Gibson that they turn the engine before going to Ballyroney, but Gibson would have none of the plan as steam heating to the carriages would not then be possible. Magee, no mean psychologist, quickly gave his views on the passengers involved. 'Thon boys,' he said, 'will be in no state to know the difference.'

For a time in the early 'thirties one of the 4–4–2 tanks, now in superabundance, began to be stabled at Banbridge and another at Antrim. 148 was a regular one at Banbridge and worked the 6.30am to Lisburn where a connection was made with the workmen's train (6.40) ex-Portadown. The tank then ran light to Dromore for a spell of shunting or, for a period, to work a local to Banbridge at 8.32. Before taking the 9.45am Banbridge-Belfast it might have to work a special goods to Laurencetown and it seems that on such occasions the 15.2 tons axle load limit was ignored. This was also now the engine for the heavy 6.15pm ex-Belfast, except

13

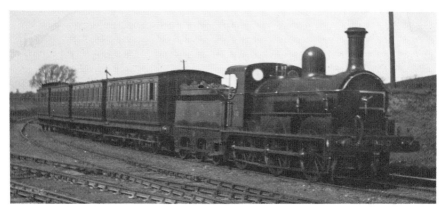

D class 40 approaching Knockmore Junction with train from Antrim. The leading coach appears to be of type R.4, with two first class and two second class compartments. Next are two thirds, followed finally by a guard's van of type W.2 with roof lookout.

in summer, and on Thursdays and Saturdays the tank would make an additional trip to Belfast and back. I never knew of a 4—4—2 tank stabling in Banbridge after 1933 though this type could still appear on the 8.40am ex-Belfast.

The ANTRIM Branch until 1933

Though this characterless line had some reasonably pleasant scenery, high hedges tended to obscure the passengers' view whenever a cutting was not already doing so; and until World War II, its operations also could rank as about the least interesting on the GNR. Had the junction with the main line been at, say, Broomhedge, with a route nearer to Lough Neagh as well as Ballinderry village, it might just have had some tourist possibilities. As it turned out later its two major stations, Glenavy and Crumlin, suffered from not being as convenient for Belfast passengers as 'bus routes built up by the NIRTB. Antrim itself had a good and, after 1934, an extremely fast service to Belfast by NCC so it was traditional that the last departure by the GNR route was about 5.40pm, which crew handed up the staff at Knockmore each evening just a few minutes before the last train entered the branch from Belfast.

Prior to the eight-hour day, the Antrim based crew took charge of the first departure each morning at 7.55 for a 65 mins run to Belfast. They were back at Antrim around lunchtime and then made another return trip. At that period the morning goods left Antrim again about 10.30am, this and two passenger departures Belfast-Antrim at 8.45 and 4.25pm being in charge of Belfast crews. For years old George McKinley, short and stout, had 2—4—0 *121A Dalriada* for this passenger job. His daughter would bring his dinner up the platform before the afternoon run and at Antrim he'd be ready to wash it down at the pub, leaving his fireman in charge. He liked everyone to have the same easy-going life as himself and would, at times, save the cleaners from the fury of Foreman Cleaner Sam McIlveen. After the old UR engine had been retired he usually had a P class 4—4—0 for this job or even *118*, one of the few J class to work at Belfast. His successor was another old man, Charlie Hunter, who usually drove *82*.

During Antrim shed's last thirty years its drivers, in succession, were J. Henderson, W. Davis and D. Gray. When old Johnny Henderson had trouble with an A class or even older 0—6—0 he found one method infallible—the guard, Christy Anderson, would be sent to track down Bill Gaynor's wee mare, horse dung being highly regarded for its ability to seal up a leaking boiler. In July 1920 the BCDR 4—4—2 tank *17* arrived at Adelaide for an exchange with *198* but the BCDR fireman sent with her refused to oil the engine as not part of his job, though the tradition on the GNR. Henderson was ending his career on odd jobs there, so he made his last contribution to his old branch and did the oiling himself. The tank engine seems to have done most of her GNR work on the Antrim line. Davie Gray fired to Davis for some years at Antrim before being appointed driver.

The carriage set they had at Antrim had been, for years, made up of six-wheelers, but in 1924 some of the GNR's best suburban stock was provided for the commuters, in the shape of two handsome F.2 'superior' compos. There was also a brake 3rd and two K.1 3rds to complete a 136-ton set of 422 seats, which also made a lunchtime trip to Lisburn. The other three passenger services from Antrim were all with the same set, the 'wee Antrim', made up five six-wheelers. *267* was the guard's van for several years and there was *70*, one of the longest lived compos, two 3rds, and that rare sight, a 2nd/3rd compo, the only two, *56* and *111* having been tri compos prior to 1919. McKinley always had the 'wee Antrim' set and one day about 1915 his engine was *40*, 0—6—0 with tall chimney and boiler squatting low on her frames, already mentioned as a popular type at Banbridge. A coupling rod broke and, swinging round, sliced the top off the splasher. Until Dundalk could take it for repair, this engine continued in service as a 0—4—2 but with adhesion so reduced that it was scarcely able to mount Adelaide's coaling gantry to haul away empty wagons.

For the eight-hour day the Belfast crew on the 4.10am goods changed at Antrim to *74* 'Davie Gray's engine', to work the 7.45 to Belfast. When Gray, soft of speech but with a heavy hand on the regulator, came on duty he took the 4.10 engine (around 1930 invariably 0—6—0 *9*) for the 2pm goods to Belfast, getting back *74* for the 6.20pm passenger to Antrim. His fireman was W. Jackson and, as a 4—4—2 tank was often in use for the other passenger turns, the 42¼ft turntable at Lisburn gradually went out of service.

For its 18½ miles the branch had forty-three bridges, less per mile than the

QLGs 9 at Antrim shed

Banbridge branch but more than the Cookstown. The only notable ones were (and are) at Crumlin and across the Sixmilewater outside Antrim, near a point where, in 1900, a halt had been proposed for Masserene Park. There was seldom any sprightliness about the running on the Antrim branch but I have recorded 54 mph with SG2 0–6–0 *181*, considerably faster than I ever experienced between Knockmore and Newcastle. Until the mid 'thirties Antrim trains had only five intermediate stops after Lisburn. Aldergrove was the last of these, existing long after the advent of the aerodrome.

Local Traffic

Most Antrim and Banbridge trains called at intermediate stations between Lisburn and Belfast, thus adding to the local service. In view of the Belfastman's disposition for going home for lunch, this proved very popular. Over the years such a generous lunchtime service to Lisburn must have cost a lot in fuel—though not in wages, as the runs could be fitted into most men's early turn. When in 1905 Belfast's tramways dispensed with some 1,000 horses in favour of electrification, the GNR countered with unlimited-travel tickets and introduced the North British Railmotors, which were expected to have as rapid a turnaround as the trams. As well, three new halts—identifiable for many years by their wooden platforms as Finaghy, Derriaghy and Hilden—were opened to tempt people to live even beyond the tram terminus.

As often as not it seems that a railmotor ran alone, without any of the nine trailers supplied by Pickering in 1906. It seems also that on a service as frequent as every half hour, even at non-peak periods, the steam motors were even more unreliable than recent attempts to replace the engine and carriages system. A chalked announcement at Belfast would, at short notice, indicate cancellation, usually because of leaking tubes. On most all-stations services 26 mins were allowed to Lisburn, the same as some of the diesels were taking in the early 'seventies, though 4–4–2 tanks for many years kept a schedule of 22 mins. The position of the guard, exposed behind metal expanding gates in a partition between 1st and 3rd class, seems to have been less than ideal. Doubtless even at that time the 'superior' class accommodation was occasionally empty and the guard could rest his legs there.

A 4–4–0 tank sandwiched between two trailers meant that its driver had no footplate work in either direction. Built for light branch work, these little engines came to be known as the 'Daisy Bells'. From the driving compartment in the trailer a control gear opened and closed the regulator and the engine whistle could also be sounded by a connecting wire. Later this was discontinued and a klaxon horn placed in the trailer cab. After 1913 all GNR steam motors were withdrawn and the Lisburn local had just two trailers, hauled or propelled by a 4–4–0 tank. Eight such trailers were in service. Next to the engine would be one of the four F.12s; in its centre 58 2nd class seats in the usual airforce blue. A sliding door at each end led, after the passage for the door, to 1st class compartments, one with ten seats in red upholstery with antimacassar, and the other with nine. The driving vehicle had 78 3rd class seats in the usual brown pattern.

In 1914, Glover, coming to grips with motive power availability in his new job, ordered that the pressure of the six best engines of class BT be increased to 160lbs for the local traffic at Belfast. *1–6* were selected. A minimum of three with a fourth as spare could have kept the service going so I doubt if *1*, for instance, ever did work on the Lisburn locals after 1913. On the other hand *97* certainly did, despite pressure of 150lbs, and 21,705 miles in 1916 shows constant activity. *3* appears to

16

have had a minor mishap at Belfast in 1917, *92* getting her boiler, so *5, 6* and *7* after that time were active at Belfast, the latter running no less than 24,475 miles in 1917 —on 7½ mile trips.

'The boxer' Smith, of the 4—4—0 tanks, had been one of the best known steam motor drivers also, an earnest, enthusiastic personality. Well-built and proud of his physical fitness, Smith always carried a piece of string in case a rival should boast superior chest measurement. A teetotaller and non-smoker, he was reputed to have a house full of clocks. He used to tell how he had set the fashion for the young men of Portadown, who would ask the draper for a 'Smith' tie, collar or hat. Smith saw no point in using a short word when a longer one would sound better and Stevie Hill, the Adelaide Locomotive Superintendent, was given many anxious moments on matters of vocabulary. One morning **early in January 1919, he left Lisburn in charge of a local train in a heavy snowfall. He risked leaving Dunmurry and Balmoral against adverse signals but near a well known landmark, the *Cats' and Dogs' Home*, *93* ran into another local, propelled by 4—4—0 tank 7 and halted at the home signal. Although the two tank engines suffered almost all the damage (the opposite of the BCDR accident of 1945), about a dozen passengers were treated for minor injury and Smith was reduced for six months. 7's boiler was afterwards used to heat the old railmotor shed where six-wheelers were repainted, *384* being one of the last to be turned out resplendent by Billy McIvor.

Shortly after the accident a vacancy arose for Locomotive Inspector. With his recent record Smith saw no point in applying, but he could not resist having some part in the issue. Aware that Hill would recognize his handwriting, he enlisted the aid of a fireman to concoct the following application, purporting to come from one, Sam Welsh: 'Sir, I apply for the position of Locomotive Inspector. I have over forty-five years' service and during that time have been mixed up in more smash-ups, pitch-ins and run-offs than any other driver. So I know all about enquiries and investigations and how they should be conducted.' Hill read this application back to Welsh who was nobody's fool, and quickly replied that he would accept this job for five years only (he had but two years left until retirement).

Another incident of note occurred on 9.2.18 when Alec Balmer, ticket collector at Gt. Victoria St, was severely injured in the head by a rifle butt for refusing to permit a soldier's brother to accompany him onto the platform. Later this man was promoted to guard and was one of the best known characters in the Belfast area. A devout Baptist but very absent minded, he was also quite bald and his colleagues used to smile at the split-second change he made from his civvy cap to his railway one, so that no one would know. All trains had a 2 mins ticket inspection at Adelaide, except those which ran nonstop from Portadown, when collection was made on the train; and a few which missed out local stations and had theirs collected at Lisburn.

One of Adelaide's foremen during the World War I was old 'Romiley' Robinson. His nephew, Billy, was one of the best known firemen there by 1920 and was to become a top link driver of the 'fifties. He loved to tell a story about a foreman, Jimmy Brennan, whom he observed one day going off in his bowler hat and leaving Ned Jennings in charge of his office. Robinson got to a phone and rang the shed in an apparent state of excitement, requesting the breakdown train for a derailment of the Antrim goods at Moira, not, of course, on its route at all. Ned was just getting it all organised when Brennan returned to restore sanity.

During 1919-20 the working of the propelling trains to Lisburn had been taken over by 2—4—2 tanks. But a few of the peak-period locals were considerably

**I heard of this incident from a reliable source but have been unable to trace the record.

17

heavier, and usually in charge of 0–6–0s. The 7.20am workmen's train ex-Lisburn had 11 six-wheelers thirds in 1920, for instance, a useful set for a football special. A more interesting set of six-wheelers worked the 8.40am down local, which had the only brake 2nd *339*, three other seconds, including *30*, three thirds and the oldest first (type P.3) on the railway. Jack Norton's regular engine was *90*, whose control apparatus worked so well that when he blew off the brake in the driving trailer the engine's regulator automatically opened. But after an instruction from Glover in 1920 the fireman opened the regulator, the driver's function being merely to apply the brake for adverse signals and station stops.

W. Robinson has a long period on the locals, firing to Bob Gill, who had an accident at Lisburn with one of the saturated 4–4–2 tanks, *186*. This occurred when propelling had ceased during a dispute about a driver's responsibility for the engine, even when in the trailer, later resolved by giving the fireman driver's pay on the propelling job. Gill was in trouble for striking his train when he was supposed to be running round it and the guiding hand of his fireman (probably having a quick refresher in the 'Robin's Nest') was obviously missing. At Derriaghy of an afternoon one could sometimes observe two schoolgirls, set down from Robinson's footplate, being joined a few moments later by a dapper gentleman from the F.12. Hand in hand, the trio would go off down to the public road. They were J. Milne Barbour, a GNR director and a leading politician, (for whose family Hilden siding had been opened in 1877) and his daughters.

A regular guard on the 10.15pm ex-Lisburn was Pat McAleer—with his cap on the back of his head. Thin, eccentric and a devout Catholic, he was a stern enemy of S. Hobson, a driver to whom he would never speak when handing over the journal sheet. As he leaned out at Dunmurry on 11.2.24 to ascertain if a man was getting on or off, the 10.15 gathered speed and his head was severely injured. This was the year Adelaide got its large allocation of superheated tanks, so Norton and Hobson had their regular *187* and *189* replaced by engines such as *30* and *139*, with a train of at least three bogies.

The 4.58pm local ex-Lisburn at Balmoral. A K.1 type (100 seater) carriage, next to the propelling 4–4–2 tank, strengthens the 3 coach set

At that period anyone could walk unhindered about the area which made up arrival platforms 4 and 5. No.4 had one booked departure, however, the 'pay' train, which each Friday brought the wages to Adelaide. In May 1922, when in charge of Joe Donnelly and Jimmy Gilkinson, it had been stopped en route and the cash stolen. The story that the sum was £10,000 seems a little excessive and I would not be certain that the IRA was responsible either. It was certainly a period of unrest, but railwaymen may have planned the raid. At the end of No.5 platform two short sidings went off, called the 'Spion Kop' and mainly used for unloading perishable vans that were shunted off the rear of arriving trains. Later in the day the observer got relief from the standard passenger types when a 0—6—4 tank or an ancient 0—6—0 arrived to remove the vans to the goods yard. At the 'kop' fruit from Co. Armagh, geese from Strabane and bacon from Derry were transferred to lorries and carts.

Nearby were lines of low wooden platforms which gave the cleaners access to the carriages in the sidings. Amongst these women the best known was possibly Mary Ann Hewitt, with a posture like Queen Victoria and the latest news about everything. Another charwoman, Annie Reid, happily chewing aniseed balls, would listen to her friend as they took a break in a first class carriage! When the head shunter, 'Count' Johnny Moore, was promoted to guard at Antrim he left behind a legend of escapades, including one where he was found about 6am frozen in the ice below the water column, after partaking too liberally of 'John Jameson'. Moore had an able assistant in Jimmy Bradshaw, surely an apt name for one of the GNR's best railwaymen. By his expertise, tact, charm of manner, Bradshaw could persuade even the surliest of drivers to perform miracles. On a busy day his shrill finger whistle and penetrating voice dominated the shunting area. Later Jack Rickerby spent many years shunting there, after entering the GNR at Dunmurry in 1923. To-day he is the oldest 'conductor' on Northern Ireland Railways.

Displaced from the locals, Belfast's passenger shunting engine for the rest of the 'twenties was invariably a 2—4—2 tank, most often *93* but both *92* and *95* saw their

PG 0—6—0 sets back from platform 5 to the 'shunting pad', passing over the points to 'Skion Kop'

19

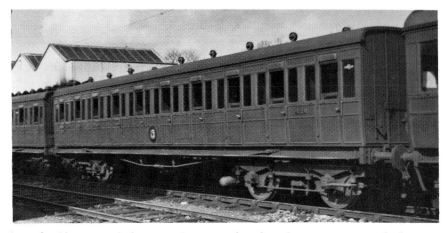

last of Belfast on such duties, and my own first footplate trips were on the latter engine at that time. It seems that Inspector Blemings was convinced that for most of the day an engine specifically for shunting was not really essential in the passenger area, so a gadget was fitted to 93 to record the number of shunting movements. Adelaide men were not to be defeated by a trick like this and they managed to disconnect the apparatus—recording a complete blank, which, although not far from what Blemings suspected, could not be said to prove anything.

Until around 1927, when he retired, John Irwin, Belfast's stationmaster, kept in touch with every operation in a manner difficult to conceive on the modern railway. Always known as 'Neighbour' Irwin, from his habit of addressing a miscreant with that title (and also to distinguish from a later namesake in the same job), he would not have been fooled by excuses from any quarter. Belfast always liked to have as many 100 seater 3rds as possible for strengthening on busy days and the shunters were considerably impressed one day when 'Neighbour' informed them that he had written to Dublin for 429, which he had tracked down there—where they were only supposed to have the more attractive (but marginally less useful) K.3s.

For the less regular observer, unaware of what was going on behind the scenes, the shunting at the passenger station had considerable fascination. In those days arriving or departing trains were very seldom signal checked due to a link of good judgement between shunter, enginemen, and signalmen. Some years later I was to learn that one man, especially, in the North cabin had his career made a misery by various shunters and even by some enginemen. For every time he pulled a lever he was harried with criticism, apparently so that by the time he went off duty he would feel guilty enough to stand drinks to make amends. A group would then wend its way to the nearest pub, 'Skelly's', near the old Coliseum cinema and known by railway men as 'The Glue Pot' (because it was so difficult to get out of). On the counter there the day's shunting movements could be retraced in porter to settle the argument.

Billy Lindsay, who had been so boisterous with the 6.15, ended his career on this shunting job. His heavy hand might have served a useful purpose now, but unaccountably Lindsay began, at this late stage, to treat his engine with delicate restraint and became extremely unpopular with the shunters—who, despite Lindsay's openhanded attitude towards subscriptions and the like, thought him dangerous.

At this period his fireman was Bob Surgeon whose father, Andy, had been the regular driver of 0–6–0 tank *204* of non-standard (Hunslet) origin, regarded as a very powerful machine, used for ballast and construction work. At one time that department had had its own driver (Tommy Spence) but when some locomotive men objected Jonathan Courtney got the job—to be crushed to death some time later at the Gas siding, Maysfields.

At another period the passenger pilot's link consisted of W. Mercer (thirty years later a top link driver), T. Ballantine, dapper, punctilious and interested in neither alcohol nor tobacco, H. Gillespie, an avid womaniser, and Jack McGettigan, with firemen who were to become well known to enthusiasts of the 'sixties: J. Shields, H. Gribben, E. Thorpe and R. McBrien. The disinterested McGettigan was most unpredictable in his handling of a class which had the lowest adhesion weight on the railway by 1925, 25 tons 16 cwt. Some days he amazed everyone with his speedy expertize. Other times a train would be held up while he carried out a most prolonged job.

A popular engine at Belfast, A class 150—with cut-down chimney for working to Donegall Quay— at the one-time passenger terminus of the Belfast Central Railway

At that period about ten shunting engines were in steam, a motley variety, from the powerful QG tanks and the lowset RT tanks with their huge buffers, to various old 0—6—0s. Most had had a spell in the country at some time, except the 0—6—4 tanks whose 4ft 3 driving wheels seemed to keep them permanently on Belfast yard shunting, mainly in the dock area. Even visits to Dundalk for repairs were rare. *98/9* usually worked in Adelaide marshalling yard and *168/9* at Grosvenor Road. *34*, which had a bark like a small cannon, or other small 0—6—0 banked the heavy night goods to Balmoral, or even Dunmurry if the load was over 65 wagons. A few old Ulster Railway 0—6—0s such as *144* were also still about; or *139*, still in green livery when in 1920, with driver Jack McBurney, she killed a shunter. Shunting drivers were either old men whose eyesight had failed to satisfy Doctor Foster Coates (the men considered his impossible standard required them to see Bangor from his premises at College Gardens, so they tried to learn off the test card), or others knows as 'Red Label men' who had disgraced themselves. For a period Welsh, usually on *66*, was one of these. Few 0—6—0s ventured down the Central line for shunting duties unless their chimney's height had been reduced. In fact most Donegall Quay work was performed by the RT class tanks, but such a precaution may well have been due to a foreman's nightmare in which Sam Welsh challenged Queens Bridge tunnel with the standard height chimney.

John Anderson was one of the signalmen who worked the Central Junction cabin. Most days old Frank McDonald, who had once been a ganger on the track, came along for a game of draughts. Half blind with a patch over one eye, he would go off in a huff if he wasn't allowed to win. 'There's George Henry,' he would say, as his son passed on an engine. During the early 'sixties, before this box was closed, one of the best amusements for young hooligans was to stone excursion trains returning from Bangor. Like most vandalism, this behaviour is not exclusive to modern times for I note, in the records, shunter W. Moore being badly injured while travelling on a light engine from Maysfields on 28.9.29 by a stone thrown from Lisburn Road. Maysfields itself was a dangerous enough spot for a different reason, kicks from cattle being a constant hazard.

POST-STRIKE PERIOD

In 1932 7,000 engineering workers were out of work in Belfast. Such was the

GREAT NORTHERN RAILWAY (IRELAND).

From	To
RUNNING SUP.34/196 Dundalk. 31st Jan. 1934	Ex-Fireman W. Bateson, Banbridge.

Re-employment of Redundant Enginemen and Cleaners.

Kindly note you will be re-employed as Cleaner at

Belfast on and from Monday the 5th February, and you will require to

report for duty at that Depot 6-0 AM on that date.

As already advised no guarantee can be given that

your re-employment will be of a definitely permanent nature.

desperate unemployment situation which all Adelaide's cleaners and some firemen faced when they were dismissed as a result of the strike in 1933. Their gradual re-employment seems to have been handled impartially, but the letter reproduced above hardly reflects how eager most of the men were to return, at almost any price. It was 1940, then, before the list of redundant men was swallowed up.

Bitterness remained the keynote of the men's attitude to management and towards those of their colleagues who remained at work and accepted the 10 per cent

SG2 0—6—0 arrives at Magherabeg

SG 0–6–0 with goods at Ballinderry

cut in wages. A typical case was a man who after some trouble earlier at Clones had been transferred to Belfast as a shunter. During the strike, though previously a most militant agitator at the outset, he volunteered to fire on the engines. So while former cleaners and firemen walked the streets, he became Tinman's fireman, eventually leaving the locomotive department to finish his days unlocking 1st class carriage doors on Belfast platform—a peculiarly apt occupation.

Apart from the closures of sheds at Antrim and Newcastle, services on these lines continued as before, but the Scarva branch was not reopened until October 1934. This was begun cautiously with a new railbus which often ran to Poyntzpass and Goraghwood as well. A wintertime gap on the Newcastle branch was thus solved, for the 11.20am railbus ex-Goraghwood (a connection of sorts, off the 9am ex-Dublin) ran through to Newcastle, also taking passengers out of the 11.10am ex-Belfast. New rural stopping places, in 'bus style, were introduced, as railbuses

Foreman J. McDermott awaits the arrival of the Scarva branch train, with U class and J.19 replacing railcar A

SG3 97 on Hillsborough bank at Ballygowan

could be easily entered from the trackside, these on the Scarva branch being Drumhork Cross, Uprichards Cross, Chapel Row Cross, Hazelbank Cross and Millmount, previously a mere mill siding. E was the vehicle most often used but F also had a spell.

On the Knockmore-Banbridge line platforms had already been erected in 1929 at Ashfield, Magherabeg and Ballygowan Halt. The title of the latter was explicit, to distinguish from the BCDR station some 20 miles over the Castlereagh hills. Boy porter Ernest Scott was one of several employed at such places, lighting lamps and collecting tickets for the princely sum of 10/- per week. Of these three halts, only Ashfield could accommodate more than two bogies and passengers were asked to travel at the front. A much more short-lived idea was a platform on the Banbridge line at Knockmore in 1932. After 1933 the area beyond Banbridge, already well served with stations, was given extra stops at Poland's Bridge, Drumadonald and Savage's Bridge; only the last had a platform, entraining usually being by means of steps carried in the guard's van. At about the same time Brookhill became a new platformed halt for the Antrim branch, followed on 2.3.36 by Legatiriff, with its platform on the other (down) side. Passengers were expected to travel in the first carriage to this halt, which was given a destination board 'Legatiriff' instead of 'Antrim'—quite an honour for the few school children, or those returning from Lisburn market. Miller's Bridge (2.5.38) and Meeting House (11.12.39), both without platforms, were the last new halts on the Antrim branch. The siding (trailing) on the down side beyond Crumlin viaduct to the mill, had now been abandoned and on the Scarva branch Martin's Bridge had replaced Chapel Row.

TRAINS TO BELFAST from NEWCASTLE & ANTRIM Lines.
Also LISBURN Locals 3 Oct. 1935

		Crew	No.
7am	Lisburn-Belfast	J. Norton/W. Mercer	116
6.30am Banbridge-Lisburn		(B) H.Malone/W.Wylie	51
7.20am	do	do	51
7.33am	do	S.Kelly/R.Dudgeon	65
8am	do	J.Norton/W.Mercer	116
7.40am Banbridge-Belfast		(B) J.Gibson/S.Dawson	202
7.40am Antrim-Belfast		G.McDonald/H.Hanna	183
8.35am	do	T.Irwin/W.Marks	77
7.25am Newcastle-Belfast		J.McDonald/J.Crawford	52
9.03am	do	J.Norton/W.Mercer	116
10am	do	do	116
9.25am Antrim-Lisburn		(B) H.Malone/W.Wylie	51
9.40am Banbridge-Belfast		R.Smith/W.Richardson	65
10.35am	do	(B) H.Malone/W.Wylie	51
9.40am Newcastle-Belfast		J.Hodge/L.McAuley	105
11.30am	do	J.Norton/W.Mercer	116
12.12am	do	R.Smith/W.Richardson	65
1.15pm	do	J.Norton/W.Mercer	116
1.30pm	do	R.Smith/W.Richardson	65
1.40pm	do	J.Hodge/L.McAuley	183
2pm	do	J.Blakely/W.Dawson	105
1.25pm Banbridge-Belfast		T.Irwin/W.Marks	77
1.40pm Antrim-Belfast		J.Young/R.McBrien	63
2.53pm	do	R.Smith/W.Richardson	65
2.45pm Banbridge-Belfast		(B) J.Dodds/G.Reid	51
3.28pm	do	M.Thompson/J.Nelson	183
3.50pm	do	L.Kyle/R.Tweedie	21
3.15pm GOODS Banbridge-Belfast (Maysfields)		E.Jennings/J.Boland	100
4.58pm	Lisburn-Belfast	J.McKeown/T.Ballentine	116
5.50pm	do	do	116
6.05pm	do	(P) W.Spence/W.Jackson	148
5.40pm Antrim-Belfast		J.Young/R.McBrien	63
5pm Newcastle-Belfast		J.Gilkinson/A.Boreland	72
6.50pm	do	D.Kelly/H.McDade	151
7.20pm	do	J.McKeown/T.Ballentine	116
8.05pm	do	(P) W.Spence/W.Jackson	148
10.45pm, 9.45pm & 8.50pm	do	J.McKeown/T.Ballentine	116
8.43pm Banbridge-Belfast		J.Tinman/J.Hanna	21
7.40pm GOODS Antrim-Belfast		M.Thompson/J.Nelson	183
7.15pm GOODS Newcastle-Banbridge		(B) J.Dodds/G.Reid	51
9.30pm GOODS Banbridge-Belfast		D.Kelly/H.McDade	151
10.20pm	do	(B) J.Shannon/E.Boland	72
11.35pm	do	W.Arneill/W.Robinson	65

(B) Banbridge crew   (P) Portadown crew

BELFAST DEPARTURES of 3 October 1935 against those on opposite page

ENGINE		TO
4–4–2T	116	Lisburn 6.40am, 7.25am, 8.30am, 9.35am, 10.35am and 12.50pm
4–4–2T	65	Lisburn 6.55am, 11.45am, 1pm, 1.55pm Banbridge 8.40am
4–4–2T	63	Antrim 12.15pm, 3.45pm
4–4–2T	21	Lisburn 3.30pm Banbridge 6.15pm
4–4–2T	116	Lisburn 4.30pm, 5.28pm, 6.20pm, 8.15pm, 9.15pm and 10.15pm
4–4–0	77	Lisburn 7.50am Banbridge 11am
4–4–0	105	Newcastle 7.10am Lisburn 1.10pm
4–4–0	72	Newcastle 1.40pm Lisburn 9.45pm Banbridge 10.50pm
0–6–0	183	Antrim (goods) 4.15am Lisburn 1.5pm, 2.35pm and 5.45pm (thence to Antrim 6.35pm)
0–6–0	202	Banbridge (goods) 2.15am
0–6–0	100	11.20am goods to Banbridge via Portadown and Scarva
0–6–0	151	Lisburn 6pm Banbridge 7.35pm
4–4–0	51	Antrim 8.05am Lisburn 12.35pm thence to Banbridge at 1.12pm Newcastle 5pm
4–4–0	52	4.55am goods Banbridge-Newcastle

OTHER WORKINGS BY BELFAST BASED ENGINES				OTHER DEPARTURES WITH ENGINES NOT BASED ON BELFAST			
4–4–0	85	8.15am	to Dublin	4–4–0	192	7.40am to	Portadown
4–4–0	133	8.25am	Derry	4–4–0	136	9.30am	Cavan
4–4–0	84	10.30am	Dublin	4–4–2T	148	12 noon	Portadown
4–4–0	130	1.30pm	Derry	4–4–0	123	2.20pm	Portadown
4–4–0	122	3.10pm	Cavan	4–4–0	173	2.45pm	Dublin
4–4–2T	65	4.15pm	Portadown	4–4–2T	148	5.10pm & 6.45pm to Lisburn	
4–4–0	133	4.45pm	Derry	4–4–0	192	5.20pm	Portadown
4–4–0	135	8.35pm	Portadown	4–4–0	86	5.40pm	Dublin
0–6–0	138	SHUNTING at Queens Quay (BCDR) S.Walker/W.Bingham H.Gillespie/H.Gribben		4–4–0	156	6.10pm	Portadown
				0–6–0	177	6.40pm	Portadown
				4–4–0	191	7.10pm	Dublin
0–6–0	150	SHUNTING at Donegall Quay A.Lyttle/E.Stewart W.Deane/J.Mason		4–4–2T	148	9.40pm	Portadown
				4–4–0	132	10.45pm	Portadown
						NIGHT GOODS	
0–6–4T	22	SHUNTING at Donegall Quay J.Owens/T.Thompson W.Smith/P.McIntyre		0–6–0	78	2.30am	Clones
				0–6–0	48	5.25am	Portadown
				0–6–0	202	10pm	Enniskillen
				0–6–0	110	11.15pm	Derry
0–6–4T	23	SHUNTING at Maysfields Cattle Yard P.McGee/W.Dobbin		0–6–0	161	12.55am	Portadown
0–6–2T	98	SHUNTING at Grosvenor Rd. Goods Yard					

J.Beckett/J.Willis, J.Corr/G.McCullough, W.McElroy/R.Jones

P.Hoey/A.McMurray relieve 110 (Derry goods) at Adelaide yard and shunt.

Three other crews on shed duty.

Railcar A in branch platform at Scarva

Apart from sheer volume of activity, the connoisseur can note many aspects of interest in the engine workings, as shown in my summary of an average winter day. *116*, known as 'Hodge's engine', was by no means a regular for the propelling job, but Jack Norton and his noiseless handling of the locals (usually with *139*) was very much a feature of the push-pulls for over twenty years. By now the Antrim goods engine is also working the passenger turns on the branch, *183* and other regular engines such as *15* and *16* being genuine mixed traffic engines (GNR style), unlike those previously used. That somewhat erratic character, George McDonald, was in charge of the up goods one morning when it ran away with him, the engine, in spite of that adverse 1/106 near milepost 18, smashing into the wall beyond the turntable. Everyone was wary of Antrim's turntable, Joe Beckett being one of the few drivers capable of getting the correct balance at the first attempt. Stevie Hobson is remembered for a departure when only a premature change to 'danger' by the advance starter warned him that he had left his train behind. On this occasion, Hobson, even more surly and disagreeable than his brothers, for once did manage to smile! Stevie cared nothing for the feelings of fireman, inspector or shunter. Absorbed in his newspaper, he countered any request for extra shunting with, 'I'm at my tea'. However, on the stopping trains to Lisburn and Antrim where he was mainly employed, Hobson was an excellent timekeeper.

The extra power of that SG3 on the Newcastle goods (as far as Banbridge) was partly the reason for only one goods up the Hillsborough bank. Here, where the A class were restricted to 24 wagons, the bigger engines could cope with an extra 15. The circular tour of the 11.20am goods, a handy innovation, provided the Scarva branch with the goods service formally managed by the branch 'mixed', not now possible with the railbus. It also gave Tandragee a useful goods service and then provided an engine for the 3.15pm goods ex-Banbridge, run mainly for shipping traffic. No one could complain of lack of engine variety at Banbridge and, apart from an occasional visit by *40*, the smallest 0−6−0 was likely to be a PG. However, a sur-

LQGs 0—6—0 and 0—6—4 tank busy at Maysfields

prise was 60 on the 9.45pm to Banbridge two evenings running, quite possibly some Banbridge man's last opportunity of travelling behind the once familiar A class. The 6.15pm was now usually 7 bogies as far as Lisburn, the rear portion continuing to Antrim at 6.35pm.

Railbus F had the Scarva workings at that period and it is interesting that fifteen years later the two drivers involved were amongst the first to work in the diesel link at Belfast when AEC units arrived. One was Sammy McCready, whom the Banbridge stationmaster always consulted if he had problems; a man for all seasons, who really enjoyed driving the first NCC 2—6—4 tank to arrive at Adelaide in 1952. The other was Billy Jones, three months senior to McCready but surviving him by many years. Nearly twenty years after those early days on the railbus, Jones was appointed diesel instructor at Belfast.

By 1935 one seldom saw a six-wheeler on a regular train in the Belfast area, apart from an occasional strengthening job on a busy Saturday. This was not due to the building of more suburban coaches, for nothing of the kind had been constructed since 1926. What had happened was that additions were being steadily

SG3 48 passes Central Junction with coal train for Adelaide yard

Qs 125 leaving Portrush with return special for Portadown, in 1937

made to the corridor stock for placing in Derry and Cavan trains, thus releasing compartment bogie stock for suburban traffic. In fact the only new compartment coach of the 'thirties was, strangely enough, built specially for the Scarva branch, not considered even worth reopening in the summer of 1933. This was *3*, of class K19, a modern looking vehicle, only 22 tons, but with 60 seats. The reason for its construction was the thriving state of the branch traffic. Then Banbridge shed was altered to accommodate railcar A (later B) which took over most of the services the railbus reinstated. On very busy days a railcar was capable of hauling the new coach and in the event of breakdown a passenger vehicle was now on hand for a replacement steam locomotive. An example of this occurred on 22.7.37 when *71*, with small 4ft 3 ins boiler, worked the branch all day, the regular railcar men firing, and drivers Jack Owens and Sam Strannix coming from Belfast to drive.

Opposite Grosvenor Road goods yard's entrance, the old Belfast Central Railway went off on a curve, restricted to 15 mph. After a ¼ mile there was a short downhill stretch at 1/130 to the short tunnel where the Lisburn Road, Bradbury Place and University Road meet above the former site of Windsor Station. This was 0.6 miles from Central Junction; the other station, Ormeau, was where milepost 1 might have been, there being a short rise from here to Maysfields. At the bridge at Botanic Avenue, between the two abandoned stations, your author was fifty years ago wont to view the double track for sign of activity, and occasionally was rewarded by engines such as *80*, *149* or *167* making sober progress. Here one could see short goods trains without brake van, for this 1½ mile stretch worked under the permissive block system and speed was not supposed to exceed 15 mph. My first journey can only have been in 1930 when the crew of *65*, still in her maiden coat of paint, suggested a trip to Maysfields from No.4 platform with wagons off the tail of a Derry train. It was on such duties that 4—4—0T *6* ten years before had ended her days. Propelling with up to five wagons was permitted from Central Junction to Maysfields. In 1939 an official letter to driver Willie Godfrey asked him to explain the 11 min late departure of the 3.45pm to Antrim—which had been due to excess time with one of these transfers. Having to run round at the junction would certainly have taken up more time but I never observed this.

Each weekday about twenty movements in each direction along the Central line were booked, but in addition to shunting engines to and from the yards on each side of the Lagan, special coal trains from and livestock trains to the dock area could appear. This was also the route for an occasional passenger train going through to Ballymacarrett Junction on the BCDR, 2.4 miles from Central Junction. In such a situation the Absolute Block system had to be adopted to East Bridge Junction, with single line beyond and a stiff adverse grade of 1/85 after the Lagan bridge, the line then falling at 1/95 as it crossed over city streets to parallel the BCDR yards. At first BCDR engines usually worked such trains on their own territory but as excursions to Bangor became more popular GNR engines (restricted to an axle load of 15.2 tons) worked through. On 17.7.35, for instance, *100* worked a 9.5am excursion from Banbridge to Bangor and, on the following Sunday, 21 July, *37* worked the return of a Dublin-Bangor excursion as far as East Bridge Junction, where *131* took over. But traffic wasn't all into the seaside town, for on several Thursdays (the Bangor half-holiday) summer residents and holiday-makers were given a 6/- return trip to Dublin. On this 8.40am special another old warhorse, *40*, appeared on 15.8.35, *192* taking over after the Lagan bridge. Inter-railway specials of an even more interesting nature occurred on 31.8.35 and 11.12.36. On the former the invaluable *40* conveyed 'Blackmen' from Comber to Ballyward but exactly what kind of train *89* had to handle at Donaghadee remains an intriguing mystery.

1937 became the first summer for the GNR's last 0–6–0 design; the UG class was to dominate foreign workings into Bangor for over twenty-five years, until the decade when all such traffic ceased. It seemed sound mechanical policy to use exist-ing parts (U class boiler and cylinders and SG driving wheels) for this mixed traffic class, whose axle load due to better weight distribution, seems to have been less than the 4 ton lighter QG 0–6–0s. So in the UG class the GNR now had an engine permitted to go anywhere a small 4–4–0 could and with much more adhesive power. It was thus able to handle bigger trains (theoretically anyway) if steaming well. More economical than a SG 0–6–0, which had a grate area 4.6sq ft larger, the new engines usually seemed under-boilered for the 8 bogies that would have been easy for the 1913-15 engines. *78*'s first passenger job was the 6pm local on 28 April and she regularly appeared on this and the morning Antrim goods for about a month. Her large D2 tender bore the usual G.N.R. in small lettering, which had replaced GREAT NORTHERN about 1930, but the next to arrive, *79*, had simply GN in large letters, in the style of the blue compounds and well lined out. The same treatment was applied to *80–2*. Like the last batch of 4–4–2 tanks seven years before, the UG class had, for a time, 200lbs pressure. Unless we consider the numerous rebuilds from 1919 onwards, *78* was the first Dundalk built engine since *25* in 1911. During her first seven months she ran 32,723 miles.

As the 'thirties progressed, every effort was made to produce more non-peak traffic by offering cheap fares. For instance, any Sunday passengers from stations Crumlin to Ballinderry could make a trip to Belfast and back for 1/7 (8p) thus using the two trains in the timetable (the 9am on its return trip and the 8.5pm ex-Belfast). Apart from a very occasional winter when Lough Neagh produced enough ice to encourage 'skating specials', there was little on the branch itself to attract excursionists but occasionally, in the summer, interesting specials traversed the line for Portrush. For instance on 15.7.35 no less than three Q class 4–4–0s made in-triguing comparison with NCC engines at that resort. *134* worked the first special out of Lisburn, followed by two more ex-Belfast, hauled by *123* and *125*. About this time *122, 125* and *133* were fitted with tablet catchers for NCC single line work. At the other extreme, the early hours of 13 March of the same year produced Ulster's heaviest snowfall for some years. As there was no chance of the goods reach-ing Antrim to time, *139* went off, light engine, to work the 7.40am passenger, but stuck in a drift at Crumlin, and was hauled out later by *100*.

Newcastle had no Sunday GNR trains during the prewar winters but there were three in each direction for Belfast-Banbridge services. The day trip Sunday fare from Banbridge to Belfast was 2/10d but an advertized afternoon fare of 2/6d was offered in December for those wishing to visit a pantomime, even a few pence being significant in the 'hungry 'thirties'. During the summer, 90 per cent of the excursion traffic was in the other direction and on sweltering days Banbridge folk must have been attracted by a 'bathers' excursion' of one shilling (5p) on several Thursdays to Newcastle, by the 1.40pm, 5pm or 6.15pm—extraordinary value for a total 44½ miles (the return 'bus fare in 1976 is £1). In the summer any day 3/6d brought one from Belfast to Newcastle, better value per mile than the BCDR route, though still behind the best the NCC could offer. When Dromore had its general holiday on the first Monday in August a day out to either Belfast, Newcastle or Warrenpoint could be had for 1/9d.

A class *28* was an interesting engine working a passenger special out of Newcastle on 9.6.37; excursions like this, returning to Portadown by the Scarva branch, had appeal. Nothing heavier than a U,P or PP 4—4—0, or a UG or PG 0—6—0 was permitted on this branch and the same applied between Banbridge and Newcastle— except that a QG was allowed there. So seven bogies was about the limit for Newcastle trains, though an extra one could be taken by a 0—6—0. During 1938-9 when 'mystery trips' were popular, some such half-crown excursions from Dublin, loaded to eight bogies, did not appear to unduly tax *102* on the 1/98, even though the 14 min schedule from Scarva to Banbridge was exceeded by 1¼ mins on one occasion (15.10.38). Such specials were one of Banbridge's rare opportunities to see catering vehicles.

The afternoon of 20.7.35 gives an impressive glimpse of the Great Northern's share in Newcastle traffic on a busy summer day. The 1.45pm ex-Belfast arrived with two 5ft 6in P class 4—4—0s, *51* piloting *89*, the train engine, as usual, returning with the 5pm to Belfast. This train crossed at Banbridge the 5pm ex-Belfast, headed

RT coming off Lagan bridge at East Bridge Junction

by *72* which returned with a 7.25pm special less than two sections behind *77* on a 7.5pm return special. *151*, with the 6.15pm ex-Belfast, managed somehow to find a path through all this and later worked the 9.30pm Newcastle-Banbridge. Prior to that, *51* left on a 8.5pm special and then *71* on the ordinary 8.20pm. Yet twenty years later the authorities, in their fever for closures, could not delay even a couple of months for such summer traffic, but on the first day of May wiped Newcastle off the railway map.

On the other hand, even in the 'thirties, the line couldn't pay its way in winter and by 1939 signalmen at Katesbridge and Ballyward were no longer considered necessary outside the summer months, a long section staff Banbridge-Castlewellan being used. In case of shunting, the guard of the 2.15am goods carried the keys of the two unmanned cabins as well as those of waiting rooms en route where goods could be deposited. Against this there was a new siding at Newforge, near Knockmore, and thenceforward the rattle of windows being upraised acknowledged a nasty odour permeating the vicinity of the factory using the siding. At first wagons to it were propelled at 5am from Lisburn, but the traffic may not have come up to expectations for by 1940 this operation was being performed around 7pm, and not every day.

And so we come to 1941, with operations around Belfast still very little different from what they had been since 1934, despite three years of war. But from 1936 a railcar had been appearing at Belfast and E was not only working the former push-pull trains as well as the Antrim branch on Sundays, but was reaching Banbridge most weekdays with the lightly patronised 8.40am, now booked to take 54 mins with eight intermediate and five conditional stops. None of the four very similar railcars, *D–G*, had as much accommodation as the minimum push-pull train of the 'thirties, which even before the war was often strengthened to four or even five bogies. First class passengers, especially, had their accommodation reduced from 19 to 8, and even the 3rd class was cut by over a third. In 1938 *E* performed a new operation when the 1.5pm local was cut back to Dunmurry, the railcar then having 3 mins to run forward empty and then traverse the crossover for a 1.18pm back. With the war an even shorter run was seen, 6.3pm to Balmoral, returning empty just ahead of the 5.20pm ex-Antrim.

Banbridge train passes Newforge siding with Qs 121

33

The air raids of April soon made such reductions in seating intolerable and rail-car D, which had replaced E, like most other railcars soon disappeared to the south where coal problems were already in evidence. By May 1941 the Banbridge line timetable had considerably expanded, as it catered for working folk who now preferred to live safely in the country and for those already there who were finding well paid war work in factories. New trains to Banbridge were at 2.50pm and 9.15pm and the 7.35pm went through to Ballyroney, from where there was now a train to Belfast at 6am—an hour previously unheard of. Changes on the Antrim branch were rather more due to troop trains, both regular and unexpected, and soon the new branch to Gortnagallon would further contribute to this once quiet line's traffic. Already there was a new 6.30am to Antrim, and new trains to Aldergrove at 5.50pm and 10.50pm.

Extracts from traffic observations during 1941 reveal an occasional engine rarely seen at Belfast in the 'thirties. Things were not yet so tight that Adelaide was sending out engines as quickly as they came in, but most of the predictability of the 'thirties had gone. The 7.40am ex-Banbridge of 1936 (due in Belfast at 8.39) was now 7.35 due 8.38 and during August and September of 1941 it produced *27, 52, 79, 102, 151/2/3* but *89* was easily the most regular. On the next train from that direction due in Belfast—the former 7.25 ex-Newcastle due just ahead of the mail at 9.5, but now 7.20 due 9.8am—*53* made the most appearances, but *74, 80, 81, 151, 153* and *199* also turned up. For the Antrim line I have selected the 3.50pm of 1937, 4.25pm in 1910 but by 1941 3.35pm. During the post-blitz period the engine was still usually a 4–4–2 tank, as it had been since 1925, but *147* was now the most regular engine though never noted at Belfast in the 'thirties. Others which appeared during that period of observation were *62, 64, 116, 142* and *143*.

The great decline in speed and punctuality had still not, in the war's third year, set in. For the next three years GNR passenger and goods mileage were to reach record proportions, in an excellent effort to deal with the emergency. Many will recall those days at Lisburn, for instance, where a passenger awaiting a down train, especially, would find, not once but several times, that after the signal came off, it would turn out not to be the expected train at all, but a goods out of path or a military special. Soon one came to know that if old Joss Chambers or his fellow foreman, Bob Orr, did not appear on the platform the train approaching would not stop. Though we did not know it we were getting a better service than ever again.

It seems apt to close this chapter with a final reference to the Lisburn local, which after a few altercations with the buffers of the motor platform, followed by a period when propelling was changed to the Belfast end, ceased to run in push-pull form towards the end of the war. Once, when an evening local was about to leave Belfast, fireman W. Bateson observed a woman and two American officers pass under the archway from the ticket barrier. The smartly dressed woman headed straight for the 4–4–2 tank and stepped up beside Bateson, who instinctively began to wipe a seat clean for her. But she was already busy at one injector and beckoning her companions to join her. Suddenly, as he recalled Robinson's story about Milne Barbour and his daughters, Bateson had no doubt as to who she was. Since her childhood days the railway had experienced a devastating strike and was now pressured by war, but to this girl a GNR engine would never lose its lure. Bateson's pipe-smoking driver on this occasion, Matt Thompson, also provided a link with earlier days in this chapter for he had been Murray's fireman in the little shed at Ballyroney during the pre-1906 period.

PORTADOWN

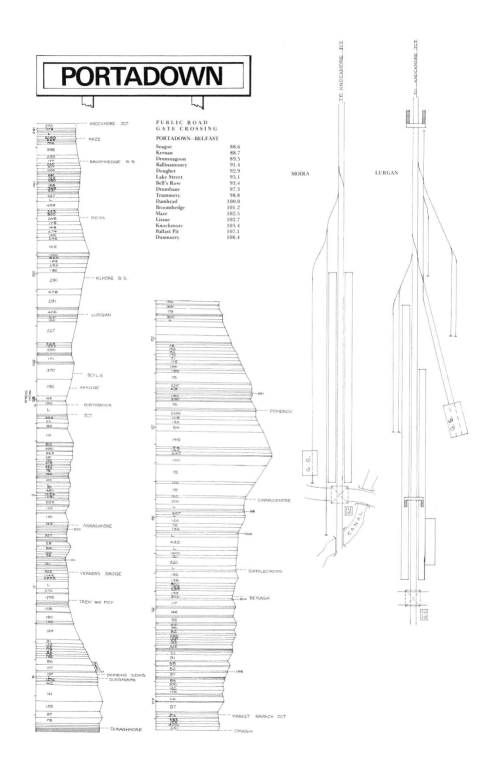

KNOCKMORE JCT

MAZE

BROOMHEDGE B.S.

MOIRA

KILMORE B.S.

LURGAN

BOILIE

SEAGOE

PORTADOWN
JCT

ANNAGHMORE

VERNERS BRIDGE

TREW and MOY

DICKSONS SIDING
DUNGANNON

DONAGHMORE

POMEROY

CARRICKMORE

SIXMILECROSS

BERAGH

MARKET BRANCH JCT

OMAGH

PUBLIC ROAD
GATE CROSSING

PORTADOWN–BELFAST

Seagoe	88.6
Kernan	88.7
Drumnagoon	89.5
Ballinamoney	91.4
Dougher	92.9
Lake Street	93.1
Bell's Row	93.4
Drumbane	97.3
Trummery	98.8
Damhead	100.0
Broomhedge	101.2
Maze	102.5
Lissue	102.7
Knockmore	103.4
Ballast Pit	107.1
Dunmurry	108.4

MOIRA

LURGAN

TO KNOCKMORE JCT

TO KNOCKMORE JCT

G.S.

G.S.

CANAL

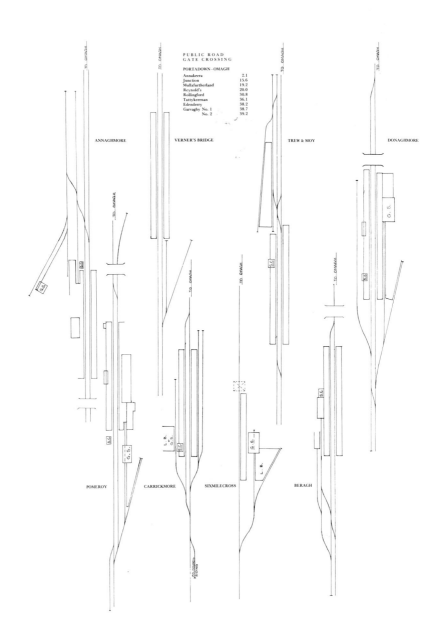

PUBLIC ROAD
GATE CROSSING

PORTADOWN—OMAGH

Annakeera	2.1
Junction	15.6
Mullafurtherland	19.2
Reynold's	20.0
Rollingford	30.8
Tattykeernan	36.1
Edenderry	38.2
Garvaghy No. 1	38.7
No. 2	39.2

ANNAGHMORE

VERNER'S BRIDGE

TREW & MOY

DONAGHMORE

POMEROY

CARRICKMORE

SIXMILECROSS

BERAGH

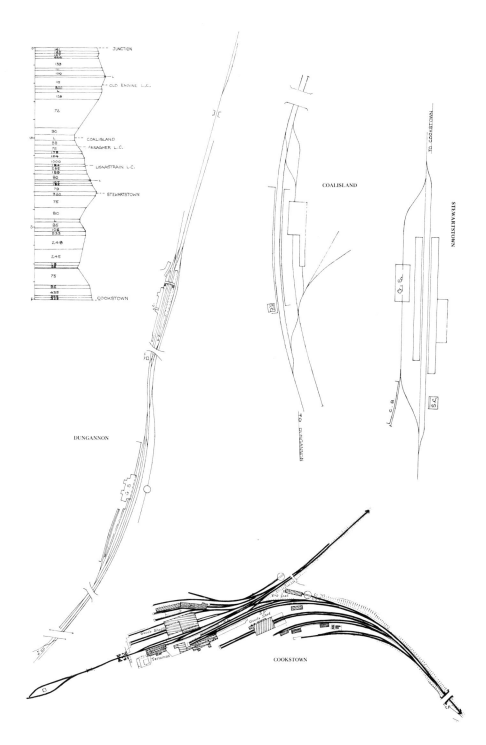

JUNCTION

OLD ENGINE L.C.

COALISLAND
ANNAGHER L.C.

LISNASTRAIN L.C.

STEWARTSTOWN

COOKSTOWN

COALISLAND

TO COOKSTOWN

STEWARTSTOWN

Gₛ Sₛ

C₊ B

S.C.

TO DUNGANNON

DUNGANNON

G₊ S₊

Goods Shed

Eng Shed

S₊ Shed

Goods Shed

Terminus

COOKSTOWN

PORTADOWN

Today scarcely a week passes without large compensation being paid after a fatality. Over fifty years ago, however, the GNR did not part with cash so lightly. There was the case of permanent way inspector W.J. McDonald, for instance, who was killed by a train at Seagoe about 5pm on Boxing Day 1918: because the territory he was responsible for was from the *other* side of Portadown (limit Castleblayney and Tynan), it was decided that he was not on the company's business. At the more humble end of the scale, a horse employed by the GNR at Lurgan on 5.4.17 was so angry (or so hungry) that he bit the top off carter John Finden's finger.

All this seems to tie in with an attitude of resentment in the Portadown area against 'the bosses', rather more vehement than I have sensed elsewhere on the GNR. Certainly at times it does not seem to have been the ideal district to work in. On Christmas Day 1914 Portadown goods-porter J.G. Martin was shot in the eye by a toy pistol, pointed by one of two boys he found trespassing on the line. On 13.5.22 the foreman at Lurgan's passenger station, Frank Metcalfe, was beaten up by three men from the town so badly that he was never able to resume work.

So much for the twin towns, but they are, of course, quite pleasant places in their different ways. By the period of this book both Portadown and Lurgan, one mainly a busy railway junction, the other a major linen town, had outstripped the county town Armagh in population. Lurgan's modest station was a little more centrally sited than Portadown's fine structure, trapped by the Bann in the cul-de-sac of Watson Street, and I expect figures would prove that Lurgan folk supported theirs better, especially when a decline in the linen industry caused many to travel daily to Belfast for employment. Portadown's traffic was much less local, more that of passengers changing trains and wagons being marshalled in the large goods yard. One Portadown driver told me that he was always glad to get away from Lurgan and I'd say there was little love lost between the two towns.

This chapter is intended to cover the Dungannon route to Omagh, the Cookstown branch and Portadown's local traffic to Belfast. After 1933 Portadown was the shed mainly responsible for these services but prior to that Adelaide had the

UG 82 arriving at Lurgan with up train

major share. As Portadown advanced from a position little more important than Armagh's prior to 1920, a new roundhouse-style engine shed was built in 1925, which in turn became too small for the 1945 Portadown, with over fifty drivers. To assist in clearing the site for the new shed, at least one of two small tank engines, *203–204* (previously the property of contractors building the Keady line), was in daily use up to 1925 and gave several enginemen their first footplate experience.

PORTADOWN — OMAGH

Until 1936 Portadown-Donaghmore was all double track, apart from the section through Dungannon tunnel. The line from Donaghmore to Omagh was single, in four sections, once the Market Junction cabin at Omagh had been closed about 1924. For a period Dungannon Junction was the only cabin with switching-out apparatus, put into effect each evening at 7pm when the last Cookstown train had gone, the box opening again for the goods next morning at 6.30am. Later in time Annaghmore and Donaghmore could also be switched out. Due to the important night goods the line was in action throughout the twenty-four hours.

The main feature of operating, which also applied to Omagh-Derry, was staff exchange apparatus, the only line on the GNR after 1933 where this applied. What it amounted to in practice was that instead of the 10 mph regulation exchange by hand, nonstop trains could pass through at 30 mph if using the apparatus. It was rarely required by more than four trains in the day, the up and down mails between Derry South cabin and Trew and Moy, the 12.45 between Omagh and Dungannon, and the 4.15 between Trew and Moy and Pomeroy, from which point it was booked to stop everywhere to Strabane. To achieve the saving of a minute (at most) at each passing point the public had to be kept clear of the platforms, in case of mishap with the heavy staff (in pouch for the exchange), even though the exchange position for each cabin concerned was at least 100 yards from the station. At night in the winter a white light marked the exact position of the apparatus. Tenders of engines likely to be used on such trains had the net fitting, on the driver's side, to collect the staff from the lineside apparatus.

Having surmounted the summit of the 1/110 bank at Annakeera crossing, the next half-dozen miles invariably produced the only lively running in the first ¾ hour from Portadown and I know of few GNR stretches of track where sitting over the bogies was more stimulating, even though the actual speed might not touch 60 mph.

SG3 14 with down goods near milepost 8 (bridge 19)

There was usually a slight slowing for Annaghmore curve, followed by brown boggy rather deserted country. Just beyond milepost 7½ was the steepest, though short, bank on the GNR, one of the three nasty spots for a driver of the Belfast-Enniskillen goods. Their instructions here were quite simple, to keep steaming the engine, but the guard was expected gradually to increase his brake pressure, from post 7½ until canal bridge 20, so that couplings would be taut. After the Blackwater bridge the engine had to be eased for 'the Moy' which made it impossible to build up speed for the long bank to the tunnel.

Certainly working a heavy goods train up through Dungannon tunnel was one of the GNR footplatemen's least agreeable assignments, even though it was less than a half mile long. This was especially the case for elderly drivers or men with chest complaints, such as Tommy Godfrey, who used to cover his face with a handkerchief and lie on the footplate, hoping to obtain some air from between engine and tender. As the fireman worked away at the sanders it was sometimes difficult with a heavy train to be certain in the darkness if progress was being made. For comfort in the tunnel the best method was to give the engine a hammering before Shaw's crossing (milepost 14) to burn off all the smoke, then put her on the small valve with reduced damper, flap open and blower on. The best story I have heard about Dungannon tunnel concerns driver Sam Welsh, already introduced.

During World War I, Welsh, who was regularly being suspended or having his turn changed, had a spell on the Cookstown goods. One night, stalled in the tunnel with a very heavy train, they adopted the usual procedure of backing out carefully, dividing the train and taking the first part to Dungannon station. As they reached the platform there the young relief signalman approached with his bucket for coal (any allocation of coal they got was small so signalmen judged most drivers upon how generous they were with it). Welsh, noting that he was in his stocking soles, his boots in the cabin, invited him for a novel experience, a footplate run through the tunnel. All went well until they re-entered the tunnel with the goods, in an atmosphere of smothering smoke and steam. Welsh shouted 'She's leaking' and at the same time flooded the footplate. As the unfortunate lad 'slapped' about in his stockings he could hear the driver hammering the cab sides and shouting 'We'll never get out alive'. After setting down the signalman the rascally driver could hear shouts of 'Never again' as he proceeded towards Dungannon Junction.

After a stiffish start the fireman got a few miles of a breather before Donaghmore, in pleasant, lush countryside. Goods traffic there, mainly to the soap works, soon declined as did passenger support, though the station was convenient enough to the village. Beyond stone overbridge 55 at the Omagh end of the platform, which style Pomeroy had also (No. 69), came the first of seven restricted curves in 16 miles. In this direction most of them were of no account whatsoever, in the other a clear test of a driver's nerve or patience. At Pomeroy all the passenger could see of the village were backs of houses high above; and then one was really in the scenic part of the line, with progress usually slow enough to savour it to the full. At the summit-cutting the Pomeroy-Omagh road, far above, crossed on a dangerous bend.

It was not much benefit to be running through Carrickmore, for one of those 30 mph curves was about a mile before the station and immediately before an old ballast quarry. The village here lay about a mile away towards the Sperrins in the north. Three quarters of a mile beyond the station came the Peat Moss siding, in decline even in the 'twenties. Probably the most dramatic part of the journey was leaving Carrickmore in the up direction, the grades here dictating a maximum load for a Q class, unpiloted, of 'eleven', about 7 bogies and a four-wheeled van. A 0—6—0 of SG3 type on a goods was expected to take 40 wagons.

40

A steep fall from milepost 30 through Rollingford level-crossing usually produced the first speed in excess of 50 mph for 22 miles, and then came Sixmilecross, considered by many as the best village between Dungannon and Omagh, but not even a block post as far as the GNR was concerned. It was also the only station between Portadown and Newtownstewart (51¼ miles) to adjoin a level crossing, though they were certainly common enough between stations. The GNR did not approve of fly shunting, but here, because of the facing sidings on the single line, this had to be resorted to by down goods trains. After the twin village, Beragh, there was a possibility of 60 mph by passenger trains. For goods, however, the switchback could cause a breakaway and there was a 5 mph restriction over the Camowen river bridge, a fine three arched structure. This river was crossed once again 2 miles from Omagh by the 'Asylum' bridge (No. 100) and drivers who concentrated along this stretch upon keeping the couplings taut were not missing any high quality scenery, the bog now being superseded by the even more monotonous Tyrone bush. Willie Godfrey, elder brother of Tommy, asked once to explain a loss of over 10 mins on this section, gave a reply that was a terse comment on a railway whose partiality for rules may have defeated its own purposes: 'I was working the train with safety,' he asserted.

Prior to the eight-hour day, Portadown drivers Peter Lawless (with *122*) and George Gillespie shared the working of two passenger trains to Derry, the 7.30am mail and the 5pm ex-Belfast, these returning from Derry again at 12.15pm and 9.30pm—the night mail. From 1916 the goods, though not yet the passenger, had the benefit of superheated engines, *176* being regularly on the Omagh goods with such Portadown drivers as Dan Kelly and the Willis brothers, Ben and John. The through goods from Belfast to Derry also meant lodging over and on this service Adelaide drivers, whose careers all took very different turns subsequently, included Blemings, Boland, Lindsay and Lisk. SG2 type 0–6–0s replaced the NQG class on these trains, Blemings having *180* and not seeing too much of his home in Newcastle. W. Boland produced such low consumption figures with *181* that the hapless Lindsay accused him of stealing coal from the wagons in the train. Presumably this was never substantiated, for Boland soon got the foreman's job at Adelaide. Prior to that he had had his moments of fun, a favourite prank while shunting at Lisburn being to insert a hammer in the points and then complain about delay to the night signalman, W. Connolly—who would come padding out in his carpet slippers to correct 'the fault'. *181* soon came off the Derry goods to act as standby for the Ambulance train, and on one occasion, 8.1.17, conveyed 142 soldiers from Dublin to Belfast.

But the Belfast name best remembered for driving to Derry must surely be that of Tom Macauley, from about 1909 in charge of the 3.30pm mail ex-Derry with PP 4–4–0 *106*. Prior to that, as recalled by his son Louis, then a schoolboy but over fifty years later an Enterprise driver, also at Belfast, old Tom had 0–4–2 *Liffey* for the goods to Banbridge, returning with the morning passenger. When the first PP with extended smokebox (*50 Donard*) came to Adelaide, Macauley had to have her for his Derry job, and each evening an army of fitters would await his return, so particular and indeed knowledgeable on mechanical matters was the red-bearded driver.

From 1912, due to the strengthening of bridges, Macauley could have a Q class for his run to Derry, and during the next seven years was invariably driving either *134* or, latterly, *123*, with firemen such as Bleakley, Walker and Keary. When *134* burst a tube beyond Beragh, Macauley and Bleakley escaped round the sides of the 4–4–0 as it ran on at speed, but managed to stop it near the Market Junction by pulling the vacuum bag off its spud. Cheerful Sam Walker (still alive in his eighties) spent several happy years firing to Macauley, despite some anxious trips after Tom had encountered a few of his cronies in Derry. Macauley would often take young Billy Donaldson, son of Frank, the Omagh carriage examiner, for a footplate trip to Derry. After a ramble round the city with Abie Keary (one of the best and tidiest of Adelaide's firemen), they would bring a noggin of whiskey back to Tom and, as a reward, young Billy would be permitted to start the mail out of Derry, than which there was no greater honour.

With the end of the war the night mails ceased and also, for a few years, the 11.10am to Derry, so Portadown lost for a period its share in such passenger workings. Lawless, with failing sight, became Portadown's foreman cleaner and Gillespie was transferred to Adelaide, sharing the Derry turns with Macauley. In 1921 they were both living in Roden Street slightly nearer to the old shed. It was then, compared to its sorry state today, a street of shining doorknobs and brightly painted woodwork, behind which also lived other senior Adelaide drivers such as J. Hegan, C. Hunter, W. Morton, T. Speers, J. Tinman and S. Welsh. Glover's first superheated rebuild was Q class *133* and this became Macauley's engine in 1919, a situation not to the liking of George Gillespie. In the circumstances it was a tactful move to pacify him with *128* of a class much more used on Dublin express passenger trains than the Q class had ever been. *128* was, however, still in saturated form and was transferred to Omagh when the next rebuilt Q, *136*, reappeared.

Gillespie was a large stout man whose handling of an engine had none of the science of Macauley, and during the next few years he managed to get *131* and *124* while his partner still held *133*, regarded as the best engine on the Derry road. When the Derry services came back to four trains in each direction in 1924, a Portadown engine *120*, with driver W. Leake, had charge of the mail but later McBennett of Adelaide came into the Belfast link, which now worked the 8.25 and 10.45 through to Derry and the 4.40pm as far as Omagh. Gillespie was in charge of *124*, with W. Richardson firing, when he received a knee injury from the engine step at Strabane.

Saturated Q 123 at Dungannon with up mail

Already over retirement age, it was said that he had been demonstrating his continuing agility to Glover, on the footplate, but he never drove again and Macauley also retired about the same time. To pass his retirement Sam Walker gave him a fox terrier.

Those who fired to Paddy McBennett, and this included Macauley's son, Louis, did not have their sorrows to seek. Pat was a martinet on locomotive matters, especially as regards coal economy, and his engine, *135*, had the largest blastpipe on the GNR. While *122* with Hobson seemed invariably to be full of steam and ran an amazing 63,686 miles in 1929, every shovelful *135* received had to be expertly placed or the needle would go back. McBennett regarded the use of the picker as quite inexcusable. He used castor oil for running in ex-shops engines and his style of driving approaching a station was unmistakeable. It was his view that all piston valve engines should be worked with open regulator, with no coasting, right to the moment of stopping. Possibly he regretted the rapid demise of the slide valve passenger engine and certainly he applied for the post of Locomotive Inspector, which was filled by Blemings, and considered that it was his religion (it could not be his ability) which had prevented his appointment. With some property and, it was said, considerable wealth, there was little doubt that he felt superior to most of the railwaymen but he never showed this to the lower ranks. During 1933 John Dudley, later a driver at Adelaide, was walking the streets of Belfast as a redundant fireman. He recalled to me meeting McBennett at this period, and the elderly driver shook him warmly by the hand, in so doing passing him a pound note.

Some details survive of two journeys by the late Col. H.T.W. Clements during the 1919-32 period over the Portadown-Omagh line. They indicate the remarkable superiority in running of a superheated Q class compared with the saturated QL, but it should be remembered that the latter engine had the slower timings of an emergency period. Both trains were much lighter than was afterwards normal on Derry trains, *128* on 12.3.19 having 3 bogies and 2 vans (one six-wheel and the other four-wheel) and *136* on 8.10.32 the same, apart from the four-wheeled van. On an incredibly slow timing between Portadown and Omagh of 98 mins, calling at all stations, *128* lost 2½ mins but this could be put down to a special stop at Omagh Market Junction. The up mail that day, incidentally, was worked by saturated Q class *121*.

128's train in this example had been Hobson's old train, the 1.50pm ex-Belfast, booked out at 1pm in 1919, but *136* had the second train of the day, the old 10.45am altered in 1932 to 10.30am. Seven mins late out of Portadown, due to a special stop at Lisburn, *136* made the same stops but despite being allowed 14 mins less for the run than *128*, recovered nearly 4 mins. Every section was covered in a better time (128's time in brackets); Portadown-Annaghmore 10 mins 15 sec (12 mins 25 sec), Trew & Moy-Dungannon 7 mins 5 sec (9 mins 45 sec), Donaghmore-Pomeroy 9 mins 40 sec (14 mins 20 sec) and Pomeroy-Carrickmore 8 mins 20 sec (9 mins 43 sec) were probably the most notable sections. Earlier in 1932 *136* had been fitted with a special type of valve, usually called the 'floating kidney' valve, to assist coasting. It was removed after a few years and one wonders what McBennett thought of it. *136* seems to have been regarded as a special engine, not only on account of this valve but because she was chosen to be tested against the GS & WR in 1911. In her superheated state she seemed less lively than some of the exceptionally good Qs class such as *121, 132* and *135,* but had a good reputation for lasting well between overhauls.

Normally the Dungannon-Omagh stretch of line saw only five sets of carriages, two of them based at Derry and described in that chapter. Belfast also had two Derry road sets, used on the 8.25am mail and the 10.45. These returned from

Derry, in the 'twenties, at 3.30pm and 6.35pm but for periods in the early 'twenties and after the 1933 strike the 10.45 didn't run, so there was only one set for Belfast at Derry and this returned on the 4.40pm, the 1.30pm set forming the 6.35pm ex-Derry. In 1921, for instance, the mail left Belfast at 8.45am with a through coach for Cookstown, old six-wheeler mail van No. 2 (renumbered 482 in 1916) being added at Portadown for Derry. At that period the four bogies which went right through from Belfast to Derry included a brake 3rd at each end, one of which was 5, like the other corridor vehicles of 1913 easily recognised by a different style of panelling and soon transferred to Derry-Dundalk services for the rest of its useful life. There was also a tea-car and a clerestory compo, 352, regarded as a very comfortable vehicle. During the next few years the make-up of this important train, now firmly at 8.25, underwent considerable modernization. The mail coach added at Portadown became the splendid Royal Mail bogie 790 whose active life was prematurely curtailed by World War II, and 352 was transferred to the restored 10.45, a train possibly better known to the Duke of Abercorn than any other. A van which came to be associated with the mail was 434, constructed with the heavy salmon traffic of the up mail in mind, and at the other end brake 3rd 245 had a long spell. Another carriage I tend to associate with the mail around 1930 was 416, before its side corridor 2nd class was downgraded to 3rd like the other seating.

The 10.45, despite the Duke, had never the same standing and its 3rd class accommodation during the 'twenties was compartment stock, a couple of K.3s, with a bogie van such as 453 or 456. When it was restored in 1934 its clerestory appearance had gone. There was now a buffet car, 295, and usually another 3rd of centre corridor type. The superior accommodation was in the brake 311, doubtless also appreciated by the folk from Baronscourt as an elegant vehicle, despite a certain lack of privacy in its centre corridor, even in the 1st class.

While some of the bogies used on Derry trains were far from being the company's latest, they were luxurious compared with the six-wheelers which the country people of deepest Tyrone had to sample on the 9.40am Dungannon-Omagh. For a time a brake 3rd of type V.1 was attached to a four-door tri-compo catering for all three classes, but later the compo was replaced by a vehicle of type R.5 such as 81 or 97, with luggage lockers between two 1st class compartments which had each a 2nd class compartment outside. There was also, of course, a U.2 third (two on Saturdays, for Omagh market). Weary travellers off the cross channel steamers had to reach places like Pomeroy in this fashion after changing from the 8.25 at Dungannon.

A regular driver on the 9.40 was big Barney McCarthy of Portadown, always shouting. He had spent some years firing to Lawless but seemed to have learnt little or nothing about footplate work. When at length he did receive a driving appointment Joe Gibson, later for some twenty years a driver at Banbridge, fired for Lawless and he also had a spell with old William Frazer, father of the mail fireman between 1932 and 1950. Old Frazer had served in the 12th Lancers as his stiff, erect bearing and waxed moustache suggested. He must have been a 'bonny fighter', for on the goods he brooked no delay from signalmen even when there was already a train in the section. Eventually he was reduced to the shunting engine at Portadown—for leaving No. 3 platform there against signals and running into 108 on the Clones goods, driver W. Arneill, signalled through No. 4.

When driver Ben Willis, on the Omagh goods, was appointed shed foreman at Portadown, it was in the family tradition, for his father Sam had also held that position and his son Ted was in it when the GNR came under UTA administration in 1958. The Willis family seemed to do very well out of the railway financially but

4–4–2T 66 at end of No.2 platform, Belfast. Just visible is the head of W. McCabe, carriage examiner, and the Lister truck driver is W. Stewart. The bogie van in the background is 400, formerly a saloon of type A.2

Ben, for one, was not exactly popular with the men. Every night at eight he went round the shed area with his fox terrier. Many a time he failed to catch the cleaners playing cards because the animal ran in first and warned them. The set-up is well illustrated in the reports of the N.I. branch of A.S.L.E.F., which contain a complaint from Portadown committee about the foreman's rostering arrangements. Another complaint, that he had driven an engine from the shed to the passenger station, seems rather trivial but is nevertheless suggestive of the attitude towards him. The appointment of John Willis, Ben's brother, as successor to Locomotive Inspector Andy Moore was scarcely received with delight, or surprise. But now he would at least cease to have some of the 'plum' jobs at the shed, such as the 7.45am passenger to Belfast. On Sundays in the summer John usually managed to work one of the trains to Warrenpoint. His family would travel in the first compartment and John would then walk out through the barrier with them, leaving his fireman to attend to the engine until departure time.

As regards the local passenger service to Belfast, the through trains from Armagh, Clones and Derry seem to have provided all these prior to 1920; even in the 'twenties Portadown's share was quite small. When link working commenced the three top passenger jobs included, as well as that 7.45, taking over the 9am ex-Dundalk, after which two Lisburn locals were worked by the Portadown tank engine (for a time 115), returning with the 5.5pm Belfast-Portadown. On the late turn they took over the 4.20pm ex-Warrenpoint, shunted at Belfast and finished with the 10.45pm back to Portadown. For a period Billy Leake, an excellent engineman, whose idea of heaven was a 'pint', shared this turn with old Billy Carr who had had 87 on the Clones turn during the war years. 'The Masher' Leake had now 120 and Carr, who was succeeded by Andy Barbour, had 130.

The 6.40am passenger Portadown-Belfast was worked by the Belfast crew off the 11.50pm goods ex-Omagh, and usually comprised 7 six-wheelers and bogie

Splendid 80-seater second, with 8ft 10 brake compartment

van *400*. This was the set for Leake's train (the 10.45pm), apart from two of the small thirds which returned on the 6.10pm, and Leake and his fireman Bob Fenton found the shunting hours prior to this useful for quenching their thirst. The 6.10 was the principal business train, as it still was in the 'fifties, and the carriages used were basically those of the 7.45am—several bogie thirds of type K.3, two six-wheelers and an excellent new compo of type F.2, such as *224* used by the Traffic Manager's staff. Another handsome carriage, *320*, provided an adequate, if small, brake compartment as well as eighty 2nd class (season ticket) seats. The similar *377* also had a spell later on this low mileage duty.

But Portadown shed was at this period mainly concerned with goods work, with nine such turns, as well as five more on yard shunting. Drivers like Lowry Kyle, Dan Kelly, Jack Hoey, Fred Robinson and Tom Rodgers spent the 'twenties on such duties. Most of these were on the main line towards Dundalk so that, of all sheds, Portadown probably knew most about taking a heavy goods train over the Wellington bank. One turn, usually with *182* or *184*, took them through to Dublin at 3.35am, due in Dublin at noon. The return trip left at 8.17am so there was some opportunity for Robinson, a bachelor and endless talker, to indulge in his favourite

A class at Lisburn, driver Fred Robinson and fireman B. McGirr. Note 'ashpan' injector

46

hobby of admiring and deseeding the flowers in the Botanic Gardens. His fireman bore the interesting name of Oscar Sleith and lived in the Loughgall area. Frequent wettings en-route to the shed caused his early death from pneumonia. Later W. Wylie, a nephew of Lowry Kyle, also fired for Robinson.

That ideal team from Cookstown, McKean and Nelson, used to enjoy provoking Kyle. He would watch from his usual *14* in Dungannon goods yard while the branch 2–4–0 was turned at 2.30pm. Fireman Nelson would sit in his seat, apparently reading a newspaper, while McKean seemed to struggle to push the table round. Kyle would furiously point this out to his own fireman, Harry McQuaid, who several years later was in fact found dead by his fireman at the store road in Dungannon.

Between Beattie and Rodgers in seniority was John Smith, known as 'Pin Head'. One could scarcely distinguish his small thin countenance for his pipe, and despite the Puritan atmosphere in Portadown most of his pay went to the bookmakers. It was said that he had been kidnapped by the IRA about 1920 and this possibly explains why he always worked the same turn, to Warrenpoint, well away from the Clones area. Each morning he relieved the Portadown driver of the 9am passenger ex-Dundalk, and with this engine (*25* for a lengthy spell and then *199*) he then worked a local goods to Goraghwood and so to Warrenpoint in time to work the 4.20pm to Portadown, where a Dundalk crew took over the engine for the 5.35.

Two Dublin men, McKiernan and Kelsh, were also at that period stationed at Portadown as drivers and did not obtain a transfer back until after the strike. The brothers McKee were also Portadown drivers of the 'twenties. Big Bob was later transferred to Newry and Sam, a difficult man to share a footplate with, managed to get himself sacked for driving from Beragh to Omagh without the staff. Also worth mentioning amongst the more junior drivers were Billy Croft, gentle with an

PP 42 on Dungannon turntable about 1916, when fireman W. Deane, at the smokebox, was stationed at Cookstown. Driver is J. Long

E class 194, driver M. McShane, on Portadown turntable at the new shed

engine and father of two present day NIR drivers; Sam Strannix, Enterprise driver at Belfast later, and Matt McShane whose nickname for at least ten years prior to his retirement in the mid-'fifties could scarcely avoid being 'Hitler', for his black moustache seemed to have identical dimensions.

Few facial adornments could compare, however, with the heavy Victorian whiskers of Portadown ticket-collector Andy (or Andrew, as he preferred) Robinson, very partial to huge though harmless whoppers. He belongs vividly to my boyhood memories, calling over the 9.15pm (later 9.40) ex-Belfast near the top of the subway steps to Nos. 2 and 3 platforms. The carriages went through to Newry but every week-night there was a 3 min connection for Armagh. On Wednesdays a train for Dungannon would be waiting in No. 3 platform and on Saturdays the Cookstown engine after working up the 7.45pm returned from Portadown at 10.5pm. Such a personal service is almost a lost art but Andy gave it all he had, pronouncing slowly and distinctly each station name in full and ending triumphantly with 'and Dungannon'.

Probably even better known, for he searched for fare-dodgers everywhere, was Inspector Turner of Lisburn, who spared no man. He is said to have travelled with an off-duty guard from Clones, temporarily based at Belfast, on an excursion, going then to the match with him, but on the way home he tackled him for the return fare! For enginemen travelling home for the weekend the major problem was avoiding Turner's watchful eye. One man, aware that he was under surveillance, shared a horsebox for a lengthy journey, while Turner searched the train for him. When later the inspector saw him he said, 'If you tell me how you did it I'll not charge you'. Turner's approach was usually, 'Your ticket ye boy ye! I know ye have one but let me see it!'

Towards the end of the 'twenties the return working of the 7.45 engine was a pick-up goods. When the Cavan train left Belfast at 9.30, this goods followed from Adelaide yard; but in the summer when the Cavan train was faster and ran at 9.40, the goods went ahead at 9.20 as far as Hilden siding, where the passenger train over-

Rake of six-wheelers returning from the Maze races with Q class 125

took it. Hilden cabin was a block post but rarely switched in except to serve Barbour's siding. The goods then spent about 1½ hours at Lisburn, where the engine would, if required, leave its train and pay a visit to Broomhedge.

In 1921 the foreman at Broomhedge was John Adams, there since 1900 and the father of Portadown driver (by the 'forties) Sammy Adams. His busiest times at Broomhedge came with the Maze races, for which the GNR catered generously. A horse special usually left Dublin about noon, picking up horses at any station en route and wasting little time. Adams had made sure beforehand that the yard at Broomhedge was empty and here the animals were unloaded. No less than five specials were run on the following two days for racegoers, the sets of 13 six-wheelers being accommodated at Broomhedge, Moira and Lurgan. As many as twenty-four additional men would be on duty to prevent trespass on this busy stretch of main line. The horses usually returned on the Sunday and were loaded in about an hour at Maze, not Broomhedge, onto the special, invariably in charge of a 0-6-0 of SG type. Ordinary goods traffic, never very heavy, was dealt with, prior to the period of the 9.32 goods, by the Antrim passenger engine, driver George McKinley.

Lurgan's goods traffic tonnage in 1925 was about the same as that of Banbridge and the town has still those three level crossings (bridge 257 replaced a fourth), almost rivalling Newry. It must be one of the largest towns in Ireland never to have had either a turntable or water column. On 26.7.23 William McKinney, in charge of the station crossing, was killed by either the 3.40pm goods ex-Dublin or the 11.40pm goods Belfast-Clones. Another fatality occurred at Lake Street when the gateman there, John Donnell, was killed by the 8.25am Belfast-Derry on 3.4.25. Today Lurgan has lost its goods yard and even by 1935 Collen's brickworks siding at Seagoe (also served by that 9.32) and Broomhedge sidings were no longer mentioned in the Working Timetable. The latter yard, however, lasted for many more years and during World War II stabled an ambulance train.

COOKSTOWN

This branch had several interesting features, but as a passenger line it was probably unique in Ireland for having more colliery type sidings than stations. Amongst the many stations dealt with in this book, there were only eight where one could see

49

A stranger to Coalisland. QLs 128 in up platform

most days two company's engines at work. Cookstown was the only GNR terminus in this list. In Molesworth Road, convenient to its huge main street, the two stations sat side by side. The last stationmaster appointed by the GNR (about 1910), was George Roe Lavery. By 1923 Samuel Bryson had charge of both stations, though GNR and NCC continued to use their own platform, engine shed and turntable.

On this steeply graded branch, with Coalisland at the lowest point and Stewartstown near the summit, a route serving both had to be somewhat indirect from Dungannon. There was even a circular tour round Dungannon at the outset, so that although the pleasant walk from Trew and Moy station to Coalisland is but five miles, the journey by rail was twice as far. For its first five miles the line seldom lost sight of an industrial chimney. First near milepost 1¼ was a siding to a brickworks, trailing on the down side. Then within the next mile was the Tyrone Colliery Pipe and Brick Works, and after the line had crossed the road at the 'Old Engine' crossing, colliery sidings, both offshoots being on the up side of the line and best served by up trains. After a steep bank, which had often been almost too much for A class 0—6—0s on heavy goods trains, Coalisland was approached on the three span 'Flour Mill' bridge.

Coalisland station, like Stewartstown, was quite convenient to its village and had station buildings a little superior to those encountered on the main line through

Tri compo 69, used between Belfast and Cookstown in the 'twenties

50

Third brake 76

Dungannon. As the line climbed up out of the former, under double arch bridges, there was also a footbridge (No.15) to Byrne's sand sidings, which still gave useful traffic long after the other sidings ceased to function. Next,about a mile beyond Coalisland,was Sir Samuel Kelly's famous colliery, opened with great ceremony on 25.7.24 with two special trains, one hauled by Qs *124* which had worked a royal train only three days before. Described as having the finest machinery in the British Isles, the two 1,070ft shafts were expected to produce 100,000 tons per year. Extensive sidings trailed onto the GNR line, wagons being then propelled into Coalisland. Within five years the whole plan began to collapse due to poor quality coal. Though both engines were said to have used it on the opening day, this never became regular and in fact the old 'Congo' colliery nearer Dungannon, nearly abandoned in 1900, still produced a little coal for local needs fifty years later.

In earlier days the Congo and adjoining brick siding had been worked by propelling from Dungannon, but by 1925 the ordinary Cookstown goods was in charge of a big D 0−6−0, powerful enough to handle all this traffic of mineral type. At first the new colliery had a special working at 7.55am ex-Dungannon, which did not leave Coalisland for the colliery until the 9.40am passenger had gone through to Cookstown.

Leaving Stewartstown the road to Cookstown passed under the railway at the 'Chapel' bridge, near the summit of the bank similarly nicknamed. At the substantial overbridge at Tullyhogue there was a project in 1928 to open a halt but the plan was never implemented, though occasionally golfers for Killymoon were dropped off near the 68½ft bridge over the Ballinderry river. Finally the line climbed up under a three span arch (bridge 32) into Cookstown, certainly a friendly prospect each morning for any engine shy of steam.

Around 1910 there were four passenger services to Belfast, the 7am and 4.10pm going to Portadown, and the 8.55am and 1.30pm making their connection at Dungannon. Apart from a new 7.45pm in the mid-'twenties this was the general pattern until 1933, and indeed the year the station closed (1956) the mails were still leaving at 4.10pm. In 1931 its departure time was 4.20 and, with the 8.55, it was making the fastest ever booking of 28 mins to Dungannon, sectional times being, 9, 7 and 10 mins with 1 min stop at each of the two intermediate stations. At Dungannon Junction were signalmen Archie Collins and John O'Donnell and on 23.8.24, when taking the staff from the fireman of the 8.55, the latter man was injured. To keep even the 11 min booking of that period the engine would have been wasting no time slowing unduly for this operation, but I never managed to record anything as fast myself, despite timing five different classes on this branch.

For many years a set of four six-wheelers made up the 8.55 and 1.45, returning from Dungannon at 12.5 and 2.55. The 'superior' coach on this was usually *63* or *105* of type R.6, some of which were later demoted to third class with unusual black leather seats. One of the two thirds used in this set was devoid of the upper partition between compartments. The last of this type to survive was *132* and I recollect that it involved many overheard conversations as well as, at the less subdued period of the day, many pearls of repartee between compartments. The guards' van was for years one of the type which had steps inside to enable the guard to use the roof lookout. As one might expect, from the GNR's sound conception of priorities, the through trains to Portadown had bogie stock as early as 1921. *69* and *76* (both illustrated) made up the 7.20am set attached to a K.3 third. For years these three left Belfast on the tail of either the 5.35pm Belfast-Dundalk or the 5.30 Dublin express. On 21.9.33 Portadown shunter William Shanks was injured during the detaching of the Cookstown portion from the express.

Even the 8.25 Belfast-Derry had for a while a through Cookstown coach. This brake compo, which added still more to a splendid variety of types there, was *207*, the only one of the railmotor rebuilds to have a corridor connection. This J.1 formed, with two six-wheel thirds, the 9.40am Dungannon-Cookstown and the 4.10pm out again. The J.2 type shared with *207* the dignity of being the GNR's longest carriages. One Portadown shunter, Thomas McCormick, had his legs crushed whilst trying to enter *205* in motion on 26.4.33. A job was later found for him as crossing keeper at the Dobbyns between Portadown and Richhill. Commercial travellers and others alighting from trains at Cookstown could be conveyed to

Pluto, beside Portadown North signal cabin. The shunter is William Shanks and the tall fireman probably Derry's Paddy McDade

UR 2—4—0 of 1863 (GNR 127). The last of this quartet of double framed express engines was 129, withdrawn in 1912

villages with no public transport by Joe Tierney or Jimmy Neill, as taxi-cabs replaced the horse vehicles parked between the two stations.

In the days before Portadown's heyday, Cookstown was regarded as a sub-shed of Belfast, despite being over fifty miles away. Each morning at 2.45 the goods for Cookstown left Adelaide yard and for a number of years detached bread vans at Moira and collected wagons at Portadown for the Cookstown branch. Big Jack Petticrew was the driver for a period, but easily the longest on this job was hard-hatted Billy Morton who had *103* and then *10* for lengthy spells, until larger 0—6—0s became available, when he had both *9* and *109*. Most mornings the 6.35pm ex-Dublin goods passed them between Moira and Knockmore, but one morning it had not appeared when they hooked off at Moira and ran forward, prior to running round to remove the bread wagons. The signalman then made the crossover for them but fireman Tony McGettigan warned Morton not to proceed. Just then the Dublin goods was heard in the distance and the points were just put back in time for George McCann to go tearing through against signals. George was a heavily built man who finished his days sweeping up cinders at Portadown shed. He possibly may even have been glad to be taken off the footplate after a career of mishaps and de-railments. At Newry his engine finished up in the Albert Basin and in another incident Clones platform took the brunt of his carelessness. Reading the noticeboard at Adelaide one day McCann remarked to S. Hill as he passed, 'You'd hardly know me with my cap on'. He was indeed more often standing cap in hand in that worthy's office trying to account for some mishap.

Prior to 1920 the goods arrived at Cookstown at 8am, after crossing the 7am passenger at Coalisland. Later it was due at 7am and the engine would stop on the curve opposite the engine shed. Here the Cookstown engine would be ready to go to the station for the 7.20 and footplates were quickly exchanged so that the Belfast crew could work this train to Portadown. They then got back to Adelaide by travelling in the Dublin mail, and were also conveniently available to work the 'mail special' to Belfast in its path if the 6.40 ran late. In the vicinity of Cookstown shed was the carriage examiner's hut. Paddy Murray had this job, a civil man whose hours were cut down from 1922 by the appointment of another examiner, Jack Smith. A few years later they got a new hut beside the potato store, which had formerly been brake van *63*, a 10 ton vehicle dating back to 1893. A new 25 ton van appeared with this number in 1925.

Tommy Gage was the regular guard on the 2.45 goods and the 7.20 passenger. The goods guard at Cookstown was John Bell for the 12.5pm, the passenger guard there a small jovial Dundalk man, Sam Wright. At first he worked all passenger trains from the 8.50am but later, to avoid overtime, a Dublin man, Bob Carroll, shared duties with him, until 1933. Carroll was afterwards a guard at Portadown, sharing the working of the 2.10pm ex-Belfast with Mark Stratford, unmistakeable with cap down over his eyes. Carroll was an extremely friendly man to all and sundry, but possibly this was necessitated by very deficient sight which really should have cost him his job. So he was glad of all the help he could get in his daily tasks, and secretly carried a magnifying glass for paper work.

The earliest driver I can trace at Cookstown is George Cosgrove, appointed in 1887 and eventually Locomotive Foreman at Derry from 1920 until 1929. His successor was 'Cheeser' Steenson whose engine was *128 Leinster,* and then when this 2−4−0 was withdrawn he had J class *16* for a time. His fireman Jimmy Kennedy lodged with the Steensons and then, I understand, went off to Florida taking Mrs. Steenson with him. So old Romiley Robinson, foreman at Adelaide, had to find a successor and thought that young Steenson, a cleaner there, would like the job. But rather than fire for his father the lad left the railway and soon Steenson senior also resigned and followed his wife across the Atlantic.

By 1918 Jack McKean, tall, thin and gentlemanly, was the Cookstown driver, greatly respected and liked by all who came his way. The following year Sam Nelson, a native of the town, with brothers enginemen on the NCC, was transferred from Armagh for a splendid partnership with McKean lasting until the shed's closure. When the eight-hour day meant a second driver, Jimmy Gallagher was appointed, a brother of the Derry driver and of Mickey at Omagh, and he had a number of firemen over the years. The cleaners also tended to last but a short time. Possibly the best remembered are Bob Newell from Mullafernaghan and Hugh McIvor. Newell seemed at first a very religious type but his noisy behaviour in church was a constant embarrassment to fireman W. Swann. Most nights Newell slept on the footplate and possibly this hastened his early death from a chest complaint. McIvor, on the other hand, seems to have prospered after leaving the railway for he became a police sergeant. By 1932 the Cookstown cleaner was Billy Arneill, brother of Gallagher's fireman John who was to die five years later after an accident near Clones with *73.*

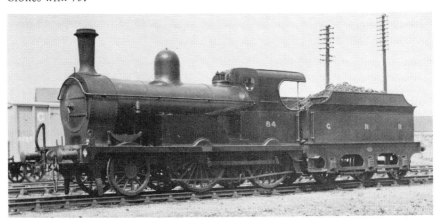

H. class in final form at Portadown in 1930

PPs 71 arrives at Trillick with down train

Until the late 'twenties the Cookstown engine was again a 2–4–0 (class H) so Cookstown saw more variations of this wheel arrangement than any other Irish town, as it was a favourite place for the NCC to use their various examples. During a spell of some ten years the GNR engine was usually either *84* or *87*, the former a great favourite of a splendidly free running class which forty years before had been in charge of the Dublin expresses. They were succeeded by *88* and then *53*, kept in immaculate condition by that engine lover, Sam Nelson, who liked to get trying out as many different engines as possible. He even experienced 0–6–0 *41* one day when *76*, replacing *87* for a wash-out, reached Dungannon with three tender springs broken and they had to wait until old Frazer arrived with the former D & BJR engine. But the engine they got in 1932, PPs 4–4–0 *71*, was probably the most capable of the lot and was still there in the shed during the 1933 strike.

One morning the goods was running late so the Cookstown crew took *87* for the 7.20 passenger. McKean had her going well down the 'Rectory' bank (named after Donaghendry church) when the engine gave a lurch and he saw to his horror that floods had washed away the ballast. But the 33 ton engine passed over the spot safely, though Nelson had to procure a glass of water for his badly shaken driver when they stopped at Stewartstown. So it was lucky indeed that Bryan, with his big SG3 engine, had not got any further. Normally Bryan would have worked *87* to Portadown. There a crew from that shed would have taken her for the 8.40am to Dungannon where McKean would get her for the 12.5. On another occasion with *87*, the brake leaked on in Dungannon tunnel and Nelson went down the train in the darkness pulling the cords. McKean then assumed he had got into the van but in fact left him behind; Sam, on his ½ mile walk to the station, being met by ticket collector Bob Dickson with lamp looking for him.

J.G. Wray was the agent in charge of Stewartstown for much of that period. On 11.12.25 he came rushing out of his office, to greet the 4.10, with the day's correspondence and cash bag, but fell on the slippery platform, twisting his ankle so badly that he was absent from work for twenty-five days, though receiving, as was the practice with salaried staff, his full £210. Charlie McMullen was his counterpart at Coalisland. A bachelor, he shared the station house on the down platform
55

with his sister, who complained incessantly to engine crews about excess smoke.

For some years McKean's eyesight had been uncertain so he had depended to a large extent upon his fireman. When Cookstown shed did not reopen after the strike a shed job was found for him at Portadown. Nelson was transferred there also and eventually received a driving appointment in company with other firemen of the 'twenties such as Bob Fenton, Issac Ross and George Pepper, one of four drivers bearing that surname and associated with Portadown.

THE POST-STRIKE PERIOD 1933-41

No longer was it possible to leave the GNR Cookstown at 7.20am for a 110 min trip to Belfast. The connection at Portadown had been an unhurried one of 16 mins until the arrival of the Dublin-Belfast mail, but after June 1932, when the 6.40 began to call at Lurgan, had been cut to 12 mins. The shed was now closed at Cookstown and the first departure 8.55am, but soon the new NCC loopline would make the 7.30am by that route a better train anyway; it was not until World War II that the GNR route became realistic once again for those clocking in at 9.30am.

The service to Belfast from Derry also suffered for a time, the second train of the day in each direction being withdrawn when trains began running again on 8 April. But the summer timetable of 4.6.33 produced some relief for Omagh and Dungannon passengers. A new 9.20am ran from Portadown to Omagh, doing the work of the former mixed from Dungannon and returning as a passenger train to Belfast from Omagh at 1.50pm, with a good connection from Enniskillen and, indeed, Sligo. I recall using this 1.50 on a couple of occasions, and very welcome it was after a period when there was no service up from Dungannon between the 10.20am railcar and the 4.55pm ex-Cookstown. During those summer months it was invariably hauled by either *120* or *123*, the latter's deplorably filthy state emphasizing indeed that the GNR's skilful cleaners were all now out of work, with only a few embittered ex-firemen doing their job.

The big D of the Cookstown goods was now based on Portadown and still worked the morning passenger train from Cookstown to Dungannon and back, finishing with the 11.45am goods—which still could have wagons from Byrne's sand siding at Coalisland and from the Congo siding and the brick works. The other two passenger trains in each direction over the branch were usually in charge of either *71* or *74*, which reached Dungannon by piloting the 1.30 from Portadown. To bring this engine back to Portadown there was the useful 7.45pm ex-Cookstown, which connected at Portadown with the 6.40pm ex-Dublin and so could have one into Belfast in a very reasonable 95 mins from Cookstown. This 7.45 took a neat 5 min connection from the NCC 5.35 ex-Portrush, and similarly Dungannon enthusiasts for the north Atlantic coast could use the 9.40am for another 5 min connection at Cookstown, into Portrush at 1.11pm—a considerably slower journey, though to the locomotive enthusiast the day's outing could have the appeal of six contrasting types of engine.

It was probably goods traffic (so relentlessly removed from the railways 32 years later) which kept the branch passenger service intact, despite the NCC, but caused at the same time a cessation at Markethill, where there was no opposition. At this difficult period the local stations south of Omagh were also encouraged, when a Saturday return service from Omagh market became possible for a short while by attaching six-wheelers to the 'shipper'. Then a new railcar service began to leave Omagh at 4.25pm every weekday for school children and others from this inscrutable area. Two Omagh guards were, week about, kept quite busy on this railcar. Small

56

and dark, Charlie Leonard could often be heard making witty comment and had formerly been a relief man all over the system. Ned McCrory was a different type, a tough character whose complexion was at least suggestive.

This was the period when every line was being considered for suitable minor stopping points to combat 'bus competition. By 1936 Reynold's Cross was breaking up the 6¼ mile Donaghmore-Pomeroy section, with Garvaghy doing the same for the 7½ miles from Beragh to Omagh. For a short glorious period these two platformless places were actually allotted booked times, 6 mins from Donaghmore and 8 mins from Beragh respectively. Garvaghy was given a telephone and trains were not to be allowed to pass Beragh unless the signalman had received confirmation from the gatekeeper that he was ready. One night the Beragh man tried in vain for a long time to get a reply concerning the passage of the Derry goods. He had other work to do, such as cleaning the office grate, so in the end passed the goods through as usual, just after 2.30am. About a half hour later he received this cryptic telephone message from Garvaghy: 'If you need any firewood there's plenty here now'.

By 1938 five more conditional stops, including Garvaghy No.2, were begun between Dungannon and Omagh, two between Portadown and Dungannon and four on the Cookstown branch. But now no time was shown, so it had to be calculated from that at the previous station, this approximation being in a way more in line with the countryman's approach to time. The six-wheelers, now based at Omagh, could be very useful if the railcar developed a mechanical fault, and they sometimes also formed a Saturday night special to the popular greyhound track at Dungannon. On one of these excursions Paddy Campbell killed some people at Garvaghy. The gatekeeper had forgotten about the special and was repairing his boots.

At Beragh the stationmaster was soon deemed unnecessary and Paddy Coyle became 'man in charge', issuing tickets and relieving in the signal cabin. One of the signalmen was John McCusker who lived with his brother, and whose badly strained black moustache suggested chain smoking. With him in the cabin, there was no use any engine crew expecting to pass through at speed. If he adjudged this excessive, McCusker would stand back against the wall and refuse to deliver the staff. Many a difference of opinion he had with Sam Martin, in his usual hurry and confident of making Omagh without delaying an up train. At Carrickmore, signalman Billy Campbell, a Bundoran man, would be rolling about with laughter at the thought of McCusker 'meeting his match'. Now, with so many stopping points, the railcar could be over 20 mins in the Omagh-Beragh section.

With an increase in enginemen personnel due to closures of other sheds, Portadown had additional turns now on the Derry road, working four passenger and two goods in each direction. In the two-crew top link the job with most standing at Portadown was the Derry mail. At first they worked the down run, leaving there at 9.10am and returning with the 12.45. Later in time it was the 11.10 (10.30 ex-Belfast) returning on the up mail, this link's late turn being to take the 12.45 forward to Belfast with a tank engine, returning with the 9.40pm.

The nine-crew second link had only one duty of a non-passenger nature. Apart from one turn to Clones and two on the Derry road, their jobs were mainly to Belfast. More than most, Portadown men constantly complained that the management was mainly engaged, as it seemed to them, in depriving them of every penny possible. Certainly the clerk at Belfast, Sam Robinson, used considerable ingenuity in arranging for suitable services to be run as economically as possible by the locomotive department. In fact on the valued mileage turns, Portadown did rather better proportionally than Belfast, for the top link pair had 151 miles every other week, while it seemed fair to give those in the next link a run to Derry (taking over the 1.30pm at Portadown) every ninth week. They used a Belfast based Q class on this turn, taking over from another Portadown crew who had worked down to Belfast the engine of the previous night's 5.45pm.

Whereas the same glittering Q class could be seen going off to Derry on the mail job every day, a considerable variety of engines and classes could pass through the second link by the time they had gone through all the turns. On the first job, for instance, the 6.38am to Belfast, the engine was usually the same tank which the top link men took when replacing the Q class on the 12.45pm ex-Derry, *144, 148* or *64* being the most likely engine. For the 7.38 to Belfast a somewhat grimy Q class was the most likely and during the 1935-41 period this was very probably *120, 123* or *136*. Another none too well shone engine was that used on the 1.20pm and 8.55pm to Belfast, which returned on the 5.20pm, and Leake's old train, the 10.45pm. This had the only QL seen regularly in Belfast at that period apart from the well polished one used by Clones. *128* and *156* both had long spells on the 1.20pm, which could be a fine sight on a Saturday, well strengthened with six-wheelers. For the Cookstown job, the 9am to Clones and the 12.50pm goods to Banbridge, several types could be used. During this period a PP such as *25, 71* or *77* was just as likely as P class *52, 104* or *72*, PG class *11, 151* or *100* or even, for the Clones job, a big 0–6–0 of SG type.

In 1935 the drivers in this link were a very mixed bunch, in order of seniority as follows: H. Cathcart (ex-Armagh), R. Conn (ex-Derry), J. Beattie (ex-Newcastle), J. Shannon (ex-Armagh), J. Gallagher (ex-Cookstown), T. Rodgers, J. Hoey, W. Gillespie and J. Campbell. The drivers who alternated on the Derry mail job were Andy Barbour and Billy Spence. Fred Lyttle fired for Barbour and even in later days, when he became a driver, he would never (like several other Portadown drivers) make up a minute. He was never known to use his seat but was always on his feet. Frazer fired for Spence, a very fussy and precise little man, very careful of his cylinder oil, and closing the firehole door between each shovelful to keep the air off the fire. Frazer, who patented a headlamp which would not blow out, shone the rails of the mail engine every day with emery paper and kept her in

Driver Bob Conn, with fitter John Spence and helpmate

magnificent condition during the long period he was on this job, for he never became a driver. Still alive, he showed himself an extremely fit man in his day and capable of many athletic feats on the footplate. I never saw him wear a cap.

When Barbour retired in 1936, he was succeeded on the Derry mail turn by Bob Conn, who had been based in Derry in the 'twenties. More like a Spaniard in appearance, Conn had a habit of walking through the train at stations where there was delay, much to the annoyance of both stationmasters and guards. There was no use expecting to travel on the footplate with this man, even if one had a pass obtained from the Chief Engineer himself. His senior partner, Spence, had a mishap on 7.8.37 after completing the final part of the top link's other turn, the 9.40pm Belfast to Portadown. Boy porter R.G. Wright (the present stationmaster at Craigavon West) was in the goods yard attending to a van for Coleraine which had arrived with the 3.40pm goods ex-Dublin, when he was struck by Spence's tank engine (probably *63* or *64*) running light to the shed. Five toes were subsequently amputated. George Wright was in the wars yet again on 3.1.38 when he was badly bitten intercepting a greyhound which had broken loose. When Spence retired he was succeeded on the mail turn by that canny old engineman Joe 'War Loan' Beattie, who knew the value of a sixpence better than most, and who had driven on the Newcastle trains until 1933, coming to Portadown when that shed closed. *132* was a lovely free running engine and one tended to associate her with Spence and the mail. By Beattie's time *135* was on this turn.

The best occasion to see passenger engines stretched to the full on the Derry road was the yearly meeting of the 'Apprentice Boys'. The big Saturday in 1935 was 10 August and Croft with *123* led off with the 5.55am special ex-Portadown. Next came the 5.45am ex-Belfast with Milne and *171*, followed by *192* with Deane on the 6.10. A third Belfast special left at 6.30 with McKeown and *191*, and another at 7am with *172* and Downey. On the block of this was fitted the 7.52 ex-Portadown with Strannix and *136*, after which came another Belfast special, the 7.25 with *122* and T. Thompson. Just before *125* with Hobson on the ordinary 8.25 mail, came *133* with George Steele, piloted from Portadown by Beattie on *130*. To connect with these trains were early morning specials from Newry, Banbridge (via Scarva) and Keady.

135 does not appear here though she ran 41,607 miles that year, but caused some chaos on 27.8.37 with a fractured connecting-rod strap near Strabane. S. Adams was the fireman and Walter Gillespie, the driver, stuck to his post until he had the train stopped. On 26 January of the same year the same engine had failed with the 7.20am ex-Derry. The engine at Omagh, *199*, took the train forward, and *42* worked the 8.35am Omagh-Dundalk.

The Portadown engine I associate most with the Derry mail was *124* and this seems a suitable point at which to elaborate on the three most common types of engine, apart from the 4—4—2 tanks, to be found at Portadown, over forty years. The other two classes I refer to are the SG type 0—6—0 (*178, 181, 182* and *184*, all invariably working from Portadown) and their big sisters, the SG3 type, of which I associate especially *14* and *48* with that shed.

The Q class was easily the 4—4—0 I knew best and travelled most behind. In this case familiarity never bred the slightest contempt, for I tend to regard their rebuild as Glover's miracle, though that is not to suggest that they originally were not good engines. Then they looked rather more like an enlarged PP, but after superheating a refined kind of S class. The raising of the centre line, to permit the use of 8 inch piston valves on top of 18½ ins x 26 ins cylinders, was responsible for this new look. And so for over a quarter of a century these delightful engines tore down the hills and round the curves of the Derry road but unfortunately still retained the original frames, repeatedly patched after fractures. No doubt hard running to Derry was responsible. The Q class boiler, in dimension and tube heating surface, was identical with the S class but its firebox, deepened from the original 1899 one by 10¼ in, was 9 in shorter, which may at times have been responsible for poor steaming compared to the so reliable *170*s.

Shortage of steam was, however, a rare situation on GNR engines of this period. Not only were they well designed but the GNR fireman was generally a skilled operator. As light regular firing was the standard, almost any quality of coal was acceptable on most duties. A big black fire was frowned upon as the action of a lazy man wanting an easy time. Feeding a red fire, well burnt through and with a

U class 199 pays a rather unusual visit to Beragh

lumpy bottom, with periodical four or five shovelfuls mainly along the sides was the standard. Particularly happy were the enginemen with the steaming and pulling powers of the 'big D' engines, as the SG3 were usually called. This D was a power classification which had formerly applied to small 0−6−0s with 5ft driving wheels. As A (works class A and B), B (class PG and QG) and C (NQG and LQG) were obviously in order of tractive power, D had to be right for the new SG3 engines, and LQG when superheated were altered to this also, while SG remained C and 37, 40 etc, though much less powerful, became E. Another kind of classification for the big Ds was, until 1932, evident in a cast iron circle which meant that the SG3 class was not permitted on the Boyne bridge. The tenders which came new with them (type D.1, later fitted to the Qs class) were also supposed to have this adornment. When any engine carried a diamond plate, it meant its route was unrestricted so it could, for instance, be used on that Portadown-Banbridge goods. At 52¼ tons the SG3 engines came just below the renewed S class as the third heaviest engines on the GNR and the heaviest 0−6−0s in Ireland. The high centre line (8ft 5½ in) produced a massive appearance.

The 1920 engines had been a development of the very successful SG2 class, themselves a slightly altered SG class. 175-9, like the S class delivered earlier the same year, had indirect valve motion with rocking bars, but 180-4 and the 1924 engines, classed SG2, had inclined valve motion (less points to oil). Really a goods version of the S and S.2 classes, these fifteen engines had 19 in x 26 in cylinders, a ½ inch less in diameter than the SG3 type, and from 1913 all new 0−6−0s had a 5ft 1 in driving wheel. Though this was suitable for the mixed traffic concept, all thirty engines were mainly on goods work, especially the SG3 class. But the 48½ ton SG type was free running, though hardly as much as some GS & WR and MGR 0−6−0s, and very useful for heavy moderately timed specials. In 1925 SG2 19, just new, ran 30,801 miles for an average coal consumption of 49.7lbs per mile. In the same year SG3 48 ran 47,053 miles, burning fractionally less per mile, but 14 had a high average of 58.9lbs for a total of 17,626 miles. In 1932 14 was down to 45.3lbs and 19 down to 43.5lbs. In the same year 136, the Qs with experimental valves, burned an average of 39.9lbs for a total of 27,918 miles, almost identical with unaltered 130 which ran her highest yearly total, 54,913 miles.

Not the first engine of class SG, as the number suggests, but the fourth, turned out like the others by Beyer Peacock in 1913. Shown here at Stewartstown

It was Adelaide shed which had the largest SG3 allocation, usually at least eight, twice as many as any other, and the same well known engines. Here they were well maintained, and rivalled the push-pull tank and the express engines for cleanliness. *96* and *97* were especially popular engines but the pair of cushions which adorned the footplate of the latter engine, at one period, could scarcely be regarded as a a suitable way of describing firing duties on their two most important jobs, nearly 100 miles of shovelling through the dead of night to Derry or Enniskillen. Looking at the month of August 1935, as well as the first three months of 1936, with a view to assessing the engines most used on the 10pm to Enniskillen and the 11.15pm to Derry, *47* comes out easily on top, but *202*, *96* and *7* also put in considerable mileage. The 11.15 engine did not return until the following night but the 10pm engine was in action again for the 2.45 'shipper' from Enniskillen and so could be turned out for the next 10pm if Adelaide was short of suitable engines, though usually it was held over for its regular crew—who had one of the perquisites of night goods work, about 27 hours at home. During the 126 workings on the two trains for January-March 1936,*47* was 31 times on the 10pm but never on the Derry train, while *202* divided her time equally with 11 times on each. A SG3 was used on every occasion, for both trains, but during the previous August LQG *160* turned up 9 times on the 11.15 and *110* 4 times. *97* also went 9 times to Derry but on no occasion during the selected four months did she go to Enniskillen. In the end it was *97* which, nearly thirty years later, worked the last goods out of Derry and she was the last of the class to be broken up.

The Belfast drivers who nightly (except Saturdays and Sundays) controlled their steeds along the humps and hollows of the Portadown-Omagh line were all senior men in 1936, who had joined the railway around the turn of the century and after World War II were in running for the passenger top link. They included, in order of seniority: Dick Bunting, 'Oily' Billy Godfrey, George McDonald and Matt Thompson, dapper and moustached and later well known for diversifying his fireman's days on the Lisburn locals with tall stories. There was Hugh McGivern who knew his rights to the *n*th degree, that splendid confident big man Waterhouse, Joe McDonald, too stout for a tank engine and due for a premature death like unusually dark Billy Bryan, who was to die in 1945 on *190*'s footplate and whose fireman on the Derry goods was for years Tommy Bateson. Next were Joe Donnelly, Tom Hobson, and Joe Young of evangelical instincts and a rival of fellow Derryman, Jimmy Kelly. Most had an excellent relationship with his regular fireman and Bunting, for instance, would shovel a good bottom of coal into the big D firebox while his mate was oiling. A great authority on the bible, but rather deaf, he was a mild friendly man who gave me countless footplate trips on his favourite *134* a few years later, when he took over the 8.25 passenger job from J. Hobson. Donnelly, stocky with a fresh complexion, was a different type who rarely put himself out to be agreeable to anyone, but on the Derry goods he invariably took a lengthy spell with the shovel en route as he thought it helped him to sleep afterwards. 'Win the war' Hobson, like his brothers, if not exactly a charmer, was a fine engineman whose unhurried style suited the goods work on which he spent most of his life.

Apart from the goods and an occasional passenger special, Belfast crews did not now go beyond Dungannon. Portadown crews tended to dominate the scene there, appearing on the 4.35am Cookstown goods (returning at 11.40am), the 2.40am Omagh goods and the 8.37am local from Portadown, now usually railcar B, as well as two of the four Derry passenger trains, and the Cookstown passenger workings.

The two most interesting periods of the day to observe traffic at Dungannon were just after 9am and 2.30pm, and overbridge 41, at the Omagh end of the station, was probably better for this than the platforms. Before the advent of the railcars in 1934, *30* was the engine I recollect as most regular on the 9.7am arrival from Portadown. Then for a time it was *A* before it was sent to Banbridge and *B* took its place. The 8.50am ex-Cookstown, now allowed the full half hour, was the next to appear and I used to contrast the lively manner in which its big 0–6–0 (most frequently *48*, but often *14, 117* or *201*) would come pitching over the points into the bay platform, compared to the slow crawl of the 7.20 ex-Derry. In fact the mail, due 9.31, came in with more bustle, despite the heavy climb it had just completed. By now the 0–6–0 was turned and as soon as it had passed Dungannon Junction on its way back to Cookstown (a much emptier train than the 8.50 with its fair sprinkling of school children), the railcar commenced the rather unique short run to Donaghmore (Pomeroy on Tuesdays). Prior to the strike D.J. Beattie was in charge there but eventually he was given control of both Dungannon and Donaghmore.

Just beyond the cutting at the Dungannon end of the tunnel was the siding for the linen firm of Dickson & Co. Ltd. This dated back to the previous century and the points were opened from the key on the Trew & Moy–Dungannon staff. Another siding usually served daily was the Gas siding near the up platform. Wagons of coal were set opposite shutes into which it was shovelled. The best

Dungannon goods yard seen from Aughnacloy Road bridge

63

period of the day to do the shunting to these two sidings was after the departure to Portadown of the 10.45am local (later 10.25 to connect with the train to Dublin). The busy period at the station was more spread during the afternoon, due to the 1.30 and 12.45 crossing at Trew and Moy instead of Dungannon. The horse fair at Moy was famous and during World War I traffic from this station reached its height, with hundreds of wagons for horses going off to the war. Often open wagons had to be used, due to the pressure on horse boxes. Trew was merely a hamlet near the station, but Moy, quite a busy village, was about three miles away and indeed only about six miles from Armagh. A delightful entry in the *1932* edition of the Northern Ireland directory stated that cars ran from Williamson's posting establishment in Moy to attend all trains, except the 7.37am and 12.30am, at Trew and Moy railway station. This latter must be the old night mail which would hardly miss the 'car's' non-attendance as it had not run for more than a dozen years previously.

Vernersbridge, a short distance from the Blackwater, which divides Moy from her twin village, Charlemont, was the quietest of the three intermediate stations. The only goods which served the siding there was the 10.10pm ex-Dungannon, the key to open the points being kept in the office of the man in charge as, being double track, there was no staff to which to attach it. The elderly man there in November 1939 (T.J. Anderson) suffered injuries when the horse bolted while he was loading bag meal.

Annaghmore station was probably the one best situated for traffic from Co. Armagh's 'Orchard of Ireland'. By 1930 this seems to have justified building a fruit store and during the season regular specials were run. The usual paths for empty wagons from Portadown were 6.10pm and 7.40pm, booked to return loaded at 7pm to Portadown passenger station, and 8.45pm to the goods one. Right up to the UTA takeover there were two very well known platform foremen at that passenger station: Tommy Cassells, alert, courteous and apparently imperturbable, and Ned Reilly. Ned had been a goods guard there but by 1939 was appointed foreman. He seems to have been rather prone to injury, mainly due to displays of energy such as jumping from No.1 platform. I tend to think of him as having an endless number of heavily parcelled acquaintances arriving at the last minute. For

Qs 136 arrives at Annaghmore

64

them, as they appeared at the ticket barrier on No.1, he was prepared to hold almost any train.

The subway at the Dublin end of the platforms served all four. But the other one omitted the two middle platforms and tended to be used only on 12th July or days with heavy excursion traffic. The GNR's attitude to platforms, and especially the noticeboards on them, compares strikingly with facilities today. *Under no circumstances,* it stated in the rules, were station boards to be without bills! The timetables pasted on them had to be in such a position they could be clearly read by day or night, facilitated by a red line ruled under the appropriate times for the station involved. In addition, timetables published locally by other concerns had to be examined regularly for errors.

One driver who was to depart from the GNR scene before World War II began to lower such standards of service, was James Hobson, until 1937 monopolizing the 8.25am mail, though now working only to Dungannon. By that year he could no longer count upon getting *122*, due to Adelaide's 'common usage' methods. The other Adelaide turn on a Derry passenger train had the 4.45pm as far as Portadown, after also working the 12.50pm to Lisburn. Three senior drivers worked in this link: Lisk, a Dublin express driver prior to 1933, Thornbury, placidly living later to an advanced age, and Hodge, whose rapid loss of eyesight caused early retirement. Their other turns were the 7.10am to Newcastle and the 5.45pm to Portadown. For the Derry jobs Adelaide usually tried each Q as it returned from the 'shops but tended after a few weeks to fall back again on the regular favourites: *125, 133, 134* and *135*.

PORTADOWN — BELFAST LOCAL TRAFFIC

The nine crew link which worked, in turn, the 1.30pm to Derry, was also the mainstay of most of the Belfast-Portadown trains. For instance, of the thirteen weekday trains which served Moira from Belfast only the 8.25, 3.10pm, 4.15, 6.10 and 8.35 were not worked by this link. George Graham followed Jack Campbell into it when Conn moved into the top link. He was considerably talented in mechanical matters but, as sometimes happens with this type of man, had no kind of judgement or aptitude for driving and also could not even be relied upon to turn up at the right time. His nickname, 'the Black Doctor', dated from an occasion when, possibly in an effort to make the peace, he had visited old man Willis when the foreman was ill. Unrecognised by the neighbours, his dark colouring was noted and his identity decided, to be so named until the day he was sacked from the railway. Campbell's father had been land steward for an estate on the Tandragee road but Jack was left out of his will. In later days, however, he came to be well off, with some property, and was a strong, very fit man. Firemen and others used to wonder at this as they'd see him eating his lunch with hands as black as the coal in the bunker. His footplate too was generally in a mess but Jack drove with his head well out.

As the GNR attempted to compete with the 'bus for convenience, the 4½ mile stretch of parallel road and railway between Maze and Moira was also considered suitable for new halts. Platforms were built at Damhead and Broomhedge in 1935. The former, opened at the end of March, was at the level crossing just before milepost 100, and the other, opened on 29 April, was on the opposite side from the cabin and sidings of Broomhedge bridge (274). The two workers' trains, the 6.40 and 7.45 from Portadown, were both put back a few minutes to include stops at these two halts and the new 8.43, which since the strike had replaced, from

SG3 13 passing Broomhedge with down goods

Portadown, the former 7.10am ex-Cavan, also called, as did the 10.14 and 1.20, the 4.22pm ex-Warrenpoint and 4.50pm ex-Cavan stopping by request. This sensibly spaced out service was completed by the 10pm ex-Portadown, and was just as good in the other direction.

Compared with the 'twenties there were now two additional afternoon stopping trains out of Belfast. The 2.10pm called at each of the existing eleven places and it was possibly the presence of the Dublin express not far behind which prevented the new ones being included. However, the 4.15 made up for this with the whole thirteen, run in 58 minutes, one less than the only down train which did this, the 10pm. The 2.10 was worked by the engine of the 9.30 ex-Cavan and the Portadown crew who had taken it over at Clones. Tri-compos like *148, 169* and *356* were ideal for such trains with little demand upon 'superior' accommodation, and I also recall *2;* by now displaced from the Oldcastle branch. Prior to 1928, *356* had been yet another of the K.3 type, but when its lavatories were removed, one 1st class compartment and one 2nd were put in their place to make a useful tri-compo. The 4.15 was the only Portadown train out of Belfast, except, for a time, the 7.40am, to be regularly headed by a bunker-first tank engine. Its two coaches were added to the two of the 2.10 to form the 5.43 ex-Portadown, hauled by the 4.15 engine, now chimney first. During February 1936 *21, 30, 62, 63, 65, 116* and *144* all appeared on this working, with Belfast drivers Boomer and Irwin week about. Always, it seemed, with a cigarette butt in his mouth, Tommy Irwin was a regular source of amusement to his fellow railwaymen. Hours before he was due to book on duty he could be seen rushing across the bridge from Adelaide halt to the shed, and would be fully occupied until departure time swopping around shovels and generally trying to make sure of a good trip.

Two other new trains were the 5.45pm ex-Belfast and the 8.55pm ex-Portadown. The latter followed into Belfast the 6.40pm ex-Dublin, which meant that the express could now run nonstop from Portadown. With the same engine as the 1.20pm, usually Portadown's only QL (*156* for many years), it returned to Portadown on the long standing 10.45pm. Rodgers, however, had *130* for it on 1.4.37 when she lost a tyre near Kilmore. The 5.45, a very smart train, was intended to relieve the mail of its Cookstown and Warrenpoint coaches. Usually hauled by either a 4—4—2

66

tank or a Q class, it was also a useful way to employ the spare S class (*192* on 7.5.37) and even more ideal for a small 4–4–0 (*72* on 12.5.37). It ran to Portadown in 36 mins, calling only at Lisburn and Lurgan and, after stabling the engine, the crew then relieved the Portadown crew of the 7.20pm ex-Derry. *465* had now been the through Cookstown coach for some years but this through facility ceased from September 1937.

Such Portadown commuters as did not have to be into work at 9am could use, in the other direction, the Dublin mail, booked to leave Portadown for Belfast at 8.36am. When this express was running in one of several later paths, due to the mail-boat's lateness, a service was still given by the 'mail special'. Its 34 min timing, which included a Lurgan stop, was easy enough for the compounds or S class but quite sufficiently tight for what Portadown shed could provide. Around Christmas was the most likely time for such local passengers to find themselves with the compartment stock of the special. In December 1935, for instance, there were eight such occasions, *30* and *144* monopolizing the job except on the 9th when *73* had a rare opportunity to get into the upper sixties. The engine was usually returned to Portadown by usefully piloting the 10.30, reasonably heavy with both Dublin and Derry portions. The crew usually came from Portadown's shunting link, their more mundane duty being in the goods yard, with *29, 36* or *57*, by the 'thirties the nearest the AL class got to Belfast. Until they lost their bus services in the north, the GNR provided Portadown, Omagh and Armagh with services from the railway station to the town centre, the Portadown one being as frequent as twenty-eight times per weekday.

SUNDAY SERVICES

Generally speaking this was one aspect where the post-strike situation was an improvement. In the winter timetables of the 'twenties no regular Sunday trains passed Portadown Junction for the Derry road, though there were seven services in each direction between Portadown and Belfast, made up of three Dublin, two Clones, one Warrenpoint and a local which left Portadown at 2pm and returned as a useful 10pm ex-Belfast. In these Moira and Maze were treated quite well, with three services in the down direction and four in the other. In the three summer months, however, things were rather better, with the Cookstown engine making trips to Portadown at 9.5am and 6.50pm. The evening service back at 8.8pm took a connection from the 7.5pm Belfast-Clones and the 7.15pm express from Warrenpoint, and other Warrenpoint trains helped to swell the services to and from Belfast.

The cautious post-strike timetable still had those seven Sunday trains to Belfast and, in addition, even in winter, had one run from Portadown to Dungannon and back, soon worked by the new railcar A. However, an out and out effort to encourage regular Sunday travel to Warrenpoint was soon in evidence in subsequent summers, even though Cookstown shed was now closed. Portadown ran a 8am to Cookstown to form the 9.5 and this returned to Cookstown to produce an afternoon excursion at 1.5pm, which combined at Portadown with the 1.15pm ex-Monaghan. There was also a 5.50pm Portadown-Dungannon to form the 7.20pm, for weekenders returning to Belfast, a service which was still there thirty years later when the whole Derry line closed. By 1938 the early morning Cookstown connection to Warrenpoint had been abandoned, no doubt frowned upon by some churchgoers, but a more enterprising idea had evolved. The Omagh railcar ran to Dungannon at 12.55pm, throwing a connection into the 12.55pm Cookstown-Warrenpoint. It then returned to Omagh, calling at all stations but no level crossings. The more avid Sunday travellers from Dungannon (or even Cookstown) could then catch the 2.30pm to Bundoran (arriving 4.15pm) and get back the same way the same evening. Indeed the folk of Coalisland and Stewartstown seem to have greatly preferred Bundoran to Warrenpoint and this zig-zag route soon became very popular for the smuggling excursionist. The connection from the railcar into the 10.15pm Portadown-Cookstown proved very tight, and often it was near midnight before the empty train could return to Portadown from Cookstown—in which case John Kelly, in the cabin there, would get very excited, throwing his cap on the ground and hanging out of the window shouting, 'You can answer for this delay'. Cookstown's enthusiasm for excursions seems to have been traditional and could be due to its being almost as far from the sea as one can be on the GNR. The summer timetable of 1913 shows regular Sunday sorties by the Cookstown engine to both Bundoran and Warrenpoint. The former was a 3½ hour trip, calling only at Pettigo between Omagh and Bundoran.

EARLY WARTIME DAYS

By 1941 the Belfast-Portadown service had been built up to its most intense ever. In the morning, instead of the traditional local trains from Portadown at 6.38, 7.38 and 8.43, there were eight trains: 4.25am (all stations except Balmoral and Adelaide) 6.15 (all stations to Maze, then a nonstop run in 18 mins to Belfast), 6.40 which ran nonstop from Moira in 28 mins, 7.10, 7.30, 8.23 (nonstop from Lurgan in 28 mins) 8.38 (nonstop in 34 mins) and the 8.43 which ran exactly in its old timings despite the other decelerations mainly due to heavier loads. That 4.25 even ran on Sundays and it was suggestive that the traditional 2pm and a new 2.30pm on Sundays both called everywhere between Lisburn and Portadown. At the small stations, once so quiet on a Sunday, bicycles from Aghalee and Aghagallon would indicate the response from that rural area to large pay packets in the various factories.

It was significant that many of these new trains appeared in the May timetable which followed the air raids on Belfast the previous month. On the morning after the most devastating raid (April 16) Walter Gillespie and fireman P.J. Hoey were booked for the 4.25 ex-Portadown, with 72. Gillespie had been a handsome and jolly little man in his early footplate days but now most fireman found him fairly obnoxious, hoking, poking and complaining, and his eccentric behaviour had made him the bane of foreman Willis's life. Hoey was the son of Jack, driver on the same link. Already, before they left, there was a red glow from the Belfast direction but at Finaghy they heard the 'All Clear'. As they approached, Belfast could be seen to be burning from the Falls to the Castlereagh Hills. Then, as 72 was turned, a landmine went off near the Technical College and the old 4—4—0, which during her forty-nine years had never seen anything like this, even in the 'troubles', quivered on the turntable.

Beyond Portadown, on the Derry road, the situation had changed much less as far as regular trains were concerned. As the mail train now left Belfast at 8.50am, the first passenger to Cookstown from Dungannon was not until 10.05. That curious train of the 'thirties, which had followed the mail in various guises—passenger fitted, mixed—had at last been abandoned for a 10am goods Portadown-Dungannon, which now provided the engine for the Cookstown branch afternoon services. So to reach the villages between Dungannon and Omagh before noon it now had to be by NIRTB 'bus except on certain days, when the 8.50 called.

As Christmas 1941 approached, Derryman J. Kelly, who from many years on the Enniskillen goods knew the line well, with his fireman Ralph McBrien, was

The heavy GNR staff about to be passed to Qs 122 crew at Pomeroy

booked for a passenger relief on Christman Eve. A capable man, with many years
of service on the Dublin expresses, Kelly was a tough character and fond of whiskey.
On many an occasion he had desisted for a few minutes from his habitual barrage
of coughing and spitting for some friendly and penetrating comments about engines.
But this afternoon his mind was preoccupied with a commercial venture. As the
special called at Pomeroy, he leaned out to arrange the collection of some fowl on
his return trip, but at the last minute the price seemed to increase surprisingly and
he moved up the bank with a grim face. Later that evening Pomeroy platform was
unusually gay, with country folk awaiting their Christmas visitors off the last train.
When the goodwill was at its height Kelly's train ran into the up platform and his
friend approached with the birds. The choicest assortment of colourful language
ever heard there then echoed through the little station. As Kelly shouted out in-
sults and got them back in full measure, the smiling band of spectators shrank back,
appalled. But doubtless the old GNR driver felt better that December night as his
train ran down the hill and through all those quiet crossings.

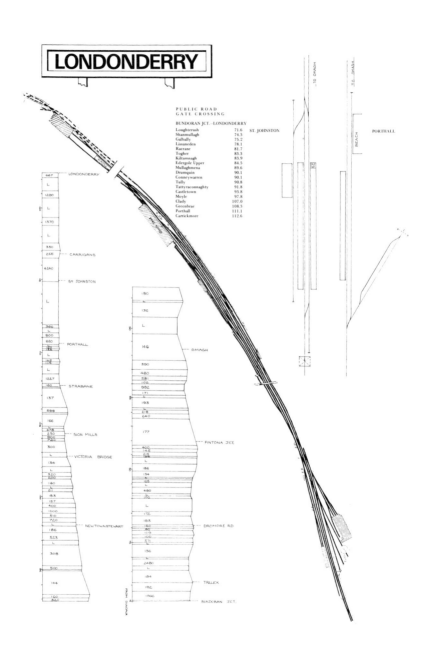

LONDONDERRY

PUBLIC ROAD
GATE CROSSING

BUNDORAN JCT.–LONDONDERRY

Loughterush	71.6
Shanmullagh	74.3
Galbally	75.2
Lissaneden	78.1
Racrane	81.7
Togher	83.3
Kiltamnagh	83.9
Edergole Upper	84.5
Mullaghmena	89.6
Drumquin	90.1
Conneywarren	90.1
Tully	90.8
Tattyraconnaghty	91.8
Castletown	93.8
Moyle	97.8
Clady	107.0
Greenbrae	108.3
Porthall	111.1
Carrickmore	112.6

ST. JOHNSTON

PORTHALL

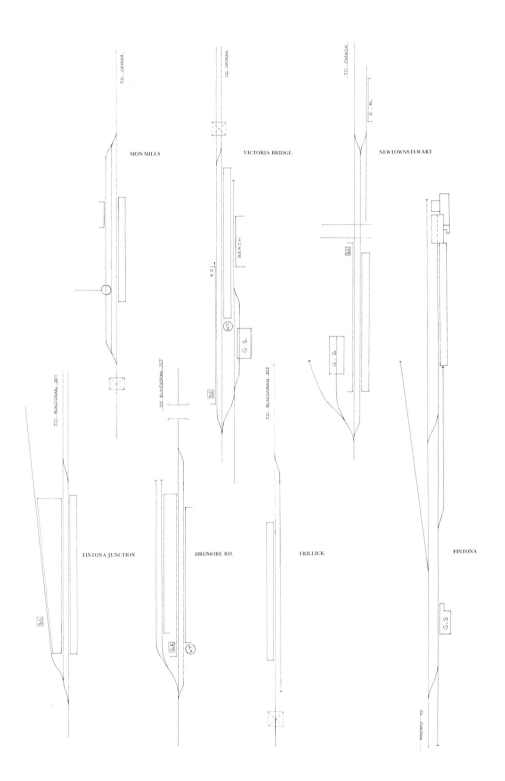

SION MILLS

VICTORIA BRIDGE

NEWTOWNSTEWART

FINTONA JUNCTION

DROMORE RD.

TRILLICK

FINTONA

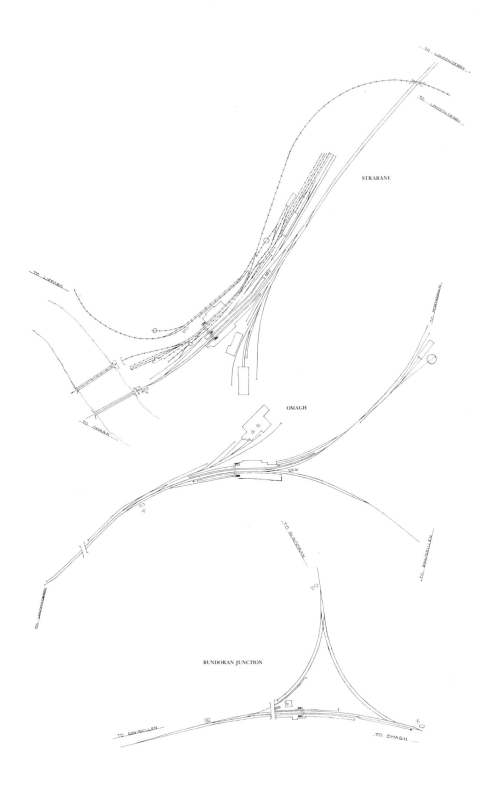

STRABANE

TO LONDON DERRY

TO LONDON DERRY

TO LIFFORD

TO OMAGH

OMAGH

TO PORTADOWN

TO BUNDORAN

TO ENNISKILLEN

TO LONDONDERRY

BUNDORAN JUNCTION

TO ENNISKILLEN

TO OMAGH

LONDONDERRY

Here was the most northerly city in Ireland, the focal point for its three north-western counties. By 1930 even Dublin did not have as many railways or contrasting liveries; and to have four railway termini, all adjacent to the river, was exceptional for a country Ireland's size. Like almost every place where the GNR met other railways, its goods traffic gave it an edge—though the NCC may have dealt with as many passengers, especially since its splendid modernization policy of the 'thirties had done much to entice travellers to Belfast. Considering that they now had a longer journey by nearly 8 miles, the older GNR locomotives until 1942 did operate a splendidly competitive service. George T. Glover—whose responsibility for the locomotives of the CDRJC brought him not infrequently to that area— is said to have looked across the Foyle from a GNR footplate and commented scathingly as a NCC engine steadily blew off steam.

We are concerned in this chapter with the lines of the former Londonderry and Enniskillen Railway as between Derry and Bundoran Junction. Until 1933 the first 40 miles had more stations giving connection to narrow gauge and minor lines of tramway type than any other line in the country, and the enthusiast for such had but to continue on for 27 miles (only 9 by road) when yet another would be encountered in the Clogher Valley Railway. It is an intriguing thought that during World War I a journey of some 54 miles from Fintona to Buncrana could involve no less than two horse trams and two very different railways, the whole having three different gauges. It was only on this part of the GNR that one could observe its small metal mileposts numbered as high as 113-122. For the general public the line had many miles of the best riverside scenery to be seen from any railway carriage in Ireland. It may have been somewhat of a joke in the 1860s but a hundred years later its closure was regretted as few others have been.

The 7.20am ex-Derry was unique among an average of eight weekday departures from Foyle Road station, for it had portions for both Dundalk (via Enniskillen) and Belfast. Its carriage accommodation in 1924 had little main line quality, and unless they were set upon being at the other end of Ireland that day, it was not greatly used by passengers for Dublin. But let us take this 7.20 as far as Bundoran Junction.

Foyle Road's dockside setting was, if anything, even more depressing than that of the NCC terminus across the Foyle, 'Ulster's noblest river'. Its atmosphere, however, if less spick and span, was more homely, and a refreshment room had been evident from Victorian days. At one side of the island platform a train of

QL 127 enters Derry between the Foyle river and Foyle Road

PGs 103 and a stranger, C class 137, at Foyle Road shed 1931

about nine vehicles indicated at that period, by its roof styles, where the Belfast portion ended and the Dundalk one began. Usually there was a six-wheel van at the rear, and then four clerestory vehicles: a bogie van (for years *155*) and 1st/2nd compo *426*, both corridors, and two K.3 class compartment 3rds. The Dundalk portion usually also had a six-wheel van, then compartment 3rd *85*, only member of type K.4, and a brake 3rd of type L.4, often *113*. At some periods there was also tri-compo *20* but more often, to ease the load out of Derry, it was added at Omagh, and could be seen there most mornings around 8.15, being heated by a small 4–4–0 just opposite the South cabin. Finally, next to the engine, there was the through coach to Dublin, a J.4 tri-compo brake which was at that period making the highest daily mileage–351½–of any GNR vehicle.

It gave an intriguing balance to Derry–having two stations on each side of the river, and also being able to depart for Belfast in exactly opposite directions. The NCC narrow gauge to Strabane soon made off away from the river and after our 7.20 had passed Derry's GNR loco depot, near the original terminus at Gallows Strand, it could not be seen (by me, anyway) from the GNR train. For years in Derry's North cabin there was a one-armed signalman called John Hunter. A strap around his neck enabled him to climb signal ladders to deal with the lamps as well as any man.

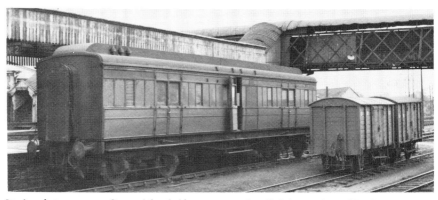

Strabane's two gauges. Covered footbridge connects the adjoining stations. GNR M.1 van 456

Some respect was shown to Derry, as a city, by providing double track for some thirty years over the first 7½ miles to St. Johnston. By 1924 the fact that most of the GNR Derry—Strabane track and all three intermediate stations lay across a frontier was underlined by the presence of a customs official at each, just in case some passenger alighted; otherwise no interest was taken in the train. The 7.20 did not normally call at Porthall, but the other two villages were regular stops in this quiet centre of salmon fishing. Shortly after passing Porthall the line, which had bordered the tidal estuary of the Foyle for 12 miles, crossed the river at 109.4 miles by the 'Foyle' bridge and then ran under the narrow gauge line into Strabane. Here the railhead position for Donegal was one good reason for the GNR line's continued existence.

A GNR 0—6—0, often A class 64, would leave Derry light at 6.10am and work a local goods back at 9.35am, mainly wagons off the night goods from Belfast and Enniskillen. By 1931 the light engine was usually a 4—4—0 to haul a local passenger to Derry at 8.15am. Then the 0—6—0 worked a local goods in each direction and the passenger engine performed the later shunting, after working a 10.10am local Derry-Strabane.

Our 7.20 spent only two minutes at Strabane before taking the staff at the level crossing, and was soon rumbling over the Mourne girder bridge. About half a mile further on there had been a junction to the Finn Valley line during its broad gauge days, and here for the first time our engine faced some collar work, usually receiving rear-end assistance from the shunting engine over a short distance. Sion Mills still remains one of the prettiest villages in Tyrone; a lengthy footbridge which straddled the north end of the station provided safe access to the major source of employment in the district (and a very good customer of the railway)—Herdman's flax spinning mills,into which wagons had access by a 13ft turntable.

That footbridge had been No. 140 (from Portadown, not Dundalk as were the mileposts), and until No. 124 where the main road crossed, after ten miles, to the east side of the line, almost every bridge was a magnificent river viaduct. Twice before Victoria Bridge, and twice after, the fast-moving Mourne passed under the railway. Here there was everything, including a level crossing, staggered platforms.

Heavy traffic at Sion Mills

a viaduct which the engine had to cross and re-cross during shunting, a splendid road bridge over the river, but no township. There was, however, the red engine and carriage of the Castlederg & Victoria Bridge Tramway, but over the years the first train out of Castlederg was usually at 8.15am and so did not connect with the 7.20, except in some timetables when it ran earlier on Fridays and Saturdays. This line was to become the setting for one of the GNR's shortest lived bus services—from 1933, when the railway closed, until 1935, when the NIRTB took over.

Near milepost 100, where there was also an interesting aqueduct, those engaged in planning the L & E line (possibly the great Robert Stephenson himself) seem to have aimed to reduce the number of river bridges by following, instead, the Mourne's twisting course. Hence there was a speed restriction of 30 mph from 101¼ to 100½ and again from 99¾ to 99¼, neither likely to inhibit in the slightest driving in the up direction. At Newtownstewart the road from the village, a ½ mile away, crossed the station by a stone overbridge. Here the river was almost alongside the down platform but it then curved away towards the village to become, after its confluence with Owenkillew, the Strule. The splendid bridge at this point (97.9 miles) was known as the 'Moyle' and further notable river crossings were the 'Blackrock' over the Strule at 96.6 miles and 'Bradford's' at 94.9 miles.

The early halt at 'Old Mountjoy' road overbridge (No. 120), dating from the line's first years but long out of use, was to be reopened in 1928 with most trains booked to call, until 1933. Mountjoy, 92.2 miles, had also a short seven-wagon siding, usually served by propelling from Omagh with the van at the Derry end, around 11am. The points were released by the key on the staff, the traffic being mainly potatoes. Despite five level crossings in 3½ miles (including quite a tongue twister, Tattahannaught), the downhill stretch to Omagh had about the best possibility of 60 mph all the way to Clones—and such was by no means unusual by PP or Q 4–4–0s. The 7.35am ex-Enniskillen was usually in the down platform before the 7.20 ran into Omagh, which meant three trains in the station. This was the only period of the day which had trains about to depart in three different directions.

As far as Fintona Junction the line continued due south, at 85.3 miles crossing the Owenreagh river by a 77ft girder bridge. At the junction the tram should just have arrived after its 11 min trundle, having been into Fintona and out again since its connection into the 7.35. On Enniskillen fairdays (10th of each month), the horse's first half-mile trip was at 6.20am into the 5.15am special ex-Derry. (Fintona itself seemed to me to have much the same kind of sullen antipathy to outsiders as Beragh, also just over 7 miles from Omagh, though the railway staff were friendly enough.) In 1925 Edward Connolly was the stationmaster, with Miss Connolly the clerk, a feature of several stations on the line after 1920 being a female transport

The 'Moyle' bridge near Newtownstewart

PPs shunting at Fintona

official, not so common generally in Ireland. Meehan was the Head Porter and twice a day his domain resounded to an engine shunting: the 3.20pm goods ex-Derry and the 9.30am goods ex-Enniskillen both halted for some 20 mins at the junction while their PG 0–6–0s,accompanied by the Junction signalman,propelled wagons up the branch. When extra traffic warranted it the other two goods did the same, and on Fintona fairdays a cattle special for Derry was often run.

The small 4–4–0s usually galloped along at over 50 mph in both directions between Fintona Junction and Dromore Road. The second word of the latter title

Down train at Trillick with AL class, unusual for a passenger train

was usually omitted by railwaymen though the station was about two miles south of the village which nevertheless sported a 'Railway Hotel'. Trillick was even further away from its station and the line here had to be negotiated with some care by drivers of goods trains. The best practice with up trains was to coast quietly down the 1/136 and remain shut-off until past milepost 73, when the train had almost stopped. Then, with couplings taut, the engine could be steamed strongly through Trillick's deep cutting, after which the regulator was closed again until beyond Ballinamallard.

For years Tommy McAllister and Jimmy Phair were the signalmen at Dromore Road. John Lambert was stationmaster while Dick, one of his sons, later at Fintona, was in charge at Bundoran Junction. Ernie collected tickets at Enniskillen and two other brothers worked at Dundalk. When yet another brother, Fred, arrived at Omagh in the late 'twenties as a sporting fireman it became even more of a family affair. Traditionally the gulf on the GNR between traffic and locomotive departments was considerable and especially evident when delays had to be explained.

AT DERRY

The 7.20 set has already been described as will be the 11.5 in the next chapter. There were also some six-wheelers there for excursions and, usually, a corridor set for the 12.20pm to Belfast. Through the years this returned at various times between 4.15 and 4.45, spending less than an hour at Belfast and arriving there with a healthy tail of piped wagons. In 1924 the set had its superior accommodation in brake compos at each end. *370* and *311* spent many years on such trains but the latter vehicle was switched to the 10.30 in 1934 and replaced by brake 3rd *83*, indicative of the falling off in second class demand. The other two coaches in the set were also centre corridor, the teacar being usually *28* and the other third *147* for a spell. By 1929 these 'light refreshments', served by Sam McSparran, still provided the only catering in Derry-Belfast trains apart from the 4pm mail.

Trains to Belfast from Derry around 7.30am and 12.30pm had been the arrangement for many years. In 1910 they were at 7.30am and 12.15pm, reaching Belfast

187 passing Knockmore Junction with down train, probably the 7.25am Derry-Belfast

at 10.45 and 3.30, the INW service from the former arriving at Dundalk at 11.37. In the summer timetable a stopping 7.15 for Omagh and Dundalk usually preceded what then became the 7.50am. These trains returned from Belfast at 1.50pm and 5pm and all times were slower than those of the day mails (7.30am ex-Belfast and 3.30pm ex-Derry) which exceeded 2½ hours by only 5 and 4 minutes respectively—considerably better than the best NCC time of the period, 2 hours 50 minutes.

For a dozen years the 7.20 was linked with the name of James Hobson at Derry, known as 'the Iron Man' and senior member of a well known GNR family. Prior to 1912 he had had PP class 75 through to Belfast on the 7.20 job, but that year various old bridges between Strabane and Omagh were replaced by lattice girder type so the Q class were permitted, and 124 was one of the engines he drove. Much more unusual was his use of 4—4—2T 187 for a time, when new. From 1915 a QL could be spared from the main line so Hobson got 114, and there is a record of her coal consumption for a fortnight in April that year: 927 cwts for 2,448 miles, rather better than the 44.8lbs to the mile recorded when she was back in the Dublin area. The QL's period on the 7.20 job was about the most active in their history, for 114 ran her highest ever mileage, 56,785, in 1916, and 128 ran 52,444 miles in 1919. 127 was another engine Hobson had on this turn, totalling 59,635 miles in 1917. With the start of the eight-hour day, 1919 was his last year on the Belfast run. Later he had 88 and then 76 as far as Omagh only, shunting there until the arrival of the 10.45am ex-Dundalk which he worked forward to Derry. 88 certainly got a thorough hammering when Hobson took 7 or 8 bogies from Strabane to Newtownstewart.

The other senior drivers at Derry, whose service went back to the 1880s, were the brothers McLaughlin, J. McGranaghan, T. Carlin and W.J. Pentland. Like most other Derry drivers McGranaghan had had a spell at the sub-shed, Omagh, whence he had worked passenger trains to Derry with 70. After a day's work the nearest pub was an irresistible magnet. One old chap often in the vicinity of the station

Derry driver James Hobson. Note nameplate, originally fitted to 76

was wont to tell him he'd seen him 'doing over 80' near Mountjoy and they'd then go off for a drink. James McLaughlin was for years the senior driver at Derry. One morning his younger brother Andy arrived at the shed to work a special, had a heart attack, and died; he had not spoken to James for many years. Cattle specials from the fairs of Tyrone and off the SLNCR line were a great source of employment for Derry engines and men. Early in the morning light engines would leave Derry, often in pairs as required. Some afternoons there were so many trains following each other for the boat at Derry that the North cabin at Omagh would run out of staffs, and a post office official would have to fetch a bundle of them back from Newtownstewart.

A link of four or five worked the Enniskillen goods through to Clones until 1922. One of the goods in each direction worked through the night and the crews concerned could expect to lodge away from home several times a week. They included James Barton and Tommy Hastings, both corpulent men who seemed to thrive on this kind of life, handsome big John Gallagher who lived just opposite the shed at Derry, James Campbell, and Tom Carlin, known to all as 'the Q.T.'. A and B class 0–6–0s had to be used until 1924, when some PG engines became available to work over the restricted Omagh–Enniskillen section. Regular engines during World War I were *33, 62, 67, 80* and *145*. How rewarding it would be if some camera had captured these of an afternoon along that precious riverside stretch, but we do almost as well, thanks to the schoolboy enthusiasm of Sir Cecil Smith at Newtownstewart, as reproduced in this volume. Like other Victorian engines, the A class had soft (hemp) packing, which gave the firemen more work–for it was the fitters who subsequently became responsible for the metallic packing in the super-heated engines with higher pressure. Carlin was fond of oiling the old 0–6–0s in motion, but one day fireman Frank Donohoe, having obtained a comic mask, went down the other side of the engine and stared at Carlin round the smokebox. When the wee driver returned to the footplate he informed Donohoe that the devil was out there, and that was the end of his oiling between stations.

During those firing days and for many years after, until he was on top-link driving, Donohoe had two passions, breeding greyhounds and carving his initials wher-

B class 62 at Newtownstewart about 1913, with 9.30am goods from Enniskillen to Derry

ever he went, be it signal post or platform seat. When Adelaide driver George Cosgrove was transferred as shed foreman from Belfast to Derry he soon began to notice this 'F.D.', and asked what it meant. He was quickly told 'It's those Belfast men, sir. It means 'f . . k Derry'.

At the substantial three-road running shed opposite Derry's South cabin an old bearded Dundalk man called McArdle shunted the engines into their proper order for going out. A spare driving job at the shed was to take a cleaner and bring the 7.20 engine down to the platform for the mileage crew going to Clones. Tom Kelly had W. Donaldson on this one morning when the senior fireman W. Bruce failed to turn up, so Carlin somewhat reluctantly agreed to take the cleaner for the heavy turn to Omagh. A good run was made, and at Omagh Carlin was shouting to the guard, M. Gallagher (usually known as 'Mickey the Hawk'), 'What do you think of that, and with an amateur?'

Kelly had fired for some years to Hobson in the days of the through run to Belfast, and as they passed the shed at Omagh he would wave to a girl who lived nearby; he later married her. Some of his best stories from his earliest driving days began 'As I came against the mail', suggesting top-link work to a stranger, but of course, it was, of course, only the shunting engine. Carlin was famous for being caught 'in possession' of wages greatly in excess of what his wife thought he received. In 1915 the rate was 7 shillings a day, but by the 1922 agreement it had risen to 15 shillings for a senior driver. He explained to her that out of that he had to pay both guard and fireman.

A fireman who joined the same year as Donohoe was Ross Shields, son of a guard of the same name. The father was a tough wee man and a good railwayman, but handwriting was not his strong point. At the end of a run Carlin would receive the journal sheet and screw up his eyes in an exaggerated attempt to read it. Then in front of the infuriated guard he would place it above the regulator as if on a music stand and pretend to play a tune to the implied musical hieroglyph.

Old William Bruce on footplate of Q class 132 at Derry. The fireman with oilcan is Joe Young, later a driver at Belfast

The father and son aspect at Derry was possibly stronger than anywhere else. There was a second generation McLaughlin, Pentland, Hastings, Turner, Barton (two) and numerous Campbells, though not all related. Tom Kelly and big placid Sam Young each had a driver brother at Adelaide. Fireman P. Clifford, five years junior to Ross Shields, had a driver brother, James, at Enniskillen, who ended his days at Derry.

The name of Bruce, famous on the main line, was also well known at Derry shed. Three firemen of the 'twenties belonged to that family but none was to make anything like the stir of the famous Robert of Belfast. The eldest, Billy, slight of build, never progressed beyond the rank of fireman. By 1950 he was gone, and his driver brothers, David and Bob, both died before retiring age. Old William, their father, had been *132*'s driver in 1915 when he worked a military special to Belfast. Later that day the 4—4—0 was 'hung up' with a hot box and he had to take another for the return trip. Within a week he was dead and never saw *132* again. Not a very lucky branch of the family!

Another 1915 incident involved the night mail, on 9th January. As the 9.30pm was leaving, four soldiers climbed the wall in Foyle Road and managed to join the train in motion but, seeing this, stationmaster James D'Arcy had it stopped. When railway constable William Dickson tried to eject the men he was kicked. In court D'Arcy said that the delay 'had disorganised the whole service' (one wonders what he would think of railway working today) and the men were fined ten shillings each and the same amount costs. If this sounds lenient it should be remembered that that sum would have taken them a considerable distance by train at that period.

An incident in August 1917 had more serious consequences. A young shunter named D. McCool suffered a leg amputation after being knocked down during an uncoupling operation in Derry goods yard. This large yard seems to have had its share of painful mishaps, for William Doherty (almost as typical a Derry name as Gallagher) had to go off work after being kicked on the ankle by a horse employed

0—6—0T built out of 4—4—0T 1. On footplate is Joe Hutton and standing on the ground John Henderson, GNR engineman 1902-51

Q class 124 arriving at Newtownstewart with 5pm Derry-Belfast

by Wordie, the carriers. That was in 1921, when *119*, the only 0–6–0T to be 'built' at Dundalk works (out of 4–4–0T *1*),had arrived for the station shunting work and McGranaghan, taken off passenger work, had become her regular driver.

Modern rostering arrangements, such as link working and exchanging of foot-plates began, at Derry, in 1924 when they got their QL back. *126* was the last of this class to be based at Derry, and a link composed of McLaughlin, Pentland and Carlin had her on the 7.20 as far as Omagh, whence an Omagh crew took her on to Belfast. The Derry men would change to an Omagh engine for the run to Clones. Other turns they had, usually with engines *45* and *107*, were the 2.35pm boat train

QGs 153 and compound 85 present a striking contrast at Portadown (platforms 1 and 2).
The compounds were restricted to the main line

as far as Enniskillen returning with the 4.15pm ex-Dundalk, and a pick-up goods from Strabane to Omagh. From 1926 the 7.20 engine became a Qs class, *125* and *134* both having long spells prior to the strike. Small 4—4—0s at Derry 1926-32 included *51, 88, 104, 106* and *129*. By that period 0—6—0s there for fair specials and the Enniskillen goods were *10, 101, 103, 152* and *155*.

As the railway's largest goods engines, the eleven engines of classes PG and QG had had but a short reign (1899-1904). In accordance with Clifford's practice they were goods versions of the PP and Q passenger engines, except that both had the 4ft 6 in diameter boiler, which the PP class did not begin to receive until 1917. After superheating they were the only GNR engines rebuilt to retain slide valves, apart from a couple of shunting tanks, so it was unlikely, after 1932, to be able to travel behind a GNR slide valve engine except these two classes and the 2—4—2 tanks. In rebuilding the QG class the weight was unevenly distributed, with a 15 ton 8 cwt axle load now barring them from restricted sections of line such as the Scarva and Bundoran branches, as well as the Lagan bridge. So now in addition to the diamond plate carried by the PG class and all smaller engines on the side of the buffer plank, to indicate unlimited route availability, the QG had the letter R. As the years rolled on there seemed to be a tendency to ignore this and use them, for instance, to Bangor. Travelling behind PG and QG classes one always waited for the silence that followed as the engines were shut off for pulling up. It was generally regarded as a sign of great strength if a man could adjust the lever on a slide valve engine without closing the regulator.

Also for weight reasons passenger trains between Omagh and Enniskillen during the 'twenties, tended to be hauled by PP class retaining a 4ft 3 boiler or by the lighter P class. The P engines with 5ft 7 driving wheels might more accurately have been classified as JP to save confusion with their four sisters whose driving wheels were one foot more in diameter. They looked much more like the old J class, the GNR's first 4—4—0, and right to the end carried their sandboxes at the splashers, like the J class, though in the final rebuilding *72-3* and *82-3* and the PPs had their sandboxes underneath. When almost due for 'shops *88* and her sisters were just about the worst culprits on the GNR for slipping, but since at other

Ps 104 arriving at Bundoran Junction with 12.58pm ex-Enniskillen. On this train a tail of cattle wagons from Sligo was almost inevitable

times they could pull strongly and run smartly, they proved just as useful as their more graceful cousins of the PP class. Most of them left the Omagh area after 1930 for the Newcastle line on which *104-5* had begun their careers.

There are, unfortunately, no records of the performance of any small engines in the Omagh area prior to the late 'thirties; but J.M. Robbins timed the Q class to Derry in 1924 and his logs of that July provide some insight into the behaviour of a class recently superheated. *120* with 5 bogies and 2 mail vans on the 8.25am mail ex-Belfast reached Dungannon from Portadown in 21 mins 35 sec and then Omagh in 38 mins 10 sec. This exceeded, by a fraction, the best timings of the 'thirties, but in 1924 they were 20 and 42 minutes. *120* then ran to Strabane in 24 mins 20 sec, allowed 25 (cut to 24 by 1938). The same day *121* had 6 bogies and 1 four-wheel van on the 3.30pm out of Derry. Schedule to Strabane was 20 minutes in 1910 and 1924 (cut to 18 after 1932), and the Q took 19. The difficult run thence to Omagh took 26 mins 50 sec, allowed 29; from the summit the last 4½ miles into Omagh were run in 5mins 50 sec. Times on to Dungannon and Portadown were 38¼ and, almost unbelievably fast, 17 mins 25 sec, the 1938 schedule being 20.

While the Derry mail was undoubtedly next in standing to the Dublin expresses, for sheer speed it could never approach that main line where the highest speeds in Ireland were regularly recorded until 1946. 65 mph was about the maximum one could hope to experience between Portadown and Derry but even that was rare and, after 1942, most unlikely. The excellent times made by the Qs class until that period were achieved rather by good climbing and sound judgement on the part of drivers.

OMAGH

The small depot at Omagh, with rarely more than a couple of engines and three or four crews, had probably more character between 1920 and 1940 than most GNR sheds. Possibly this derived from the continuing problem of persuading men to take appointments there. Few thought it worthwhile setting up house if a possibility of getting back to Derry existed.

Prior to 1919 the two drivers there had their own territories, McGranaghan to Derry and Barney Duffy, a Dundalk man, the connection off the 7.20 each day to Dundalk, returning at 4.15pm—for which he usually had *197* in much the same way as *200* spent each night at Enniskillen. With the advent of the eight-hour day, overtime or mileage would have had to be paid for this, so the 133-mile Belfast run became Omagh's job instead. Duffy got the Derry engine *128* for this, then *156* for a short time, until he managed to get a transfer back to Dundalk. W. Wallace came from Banbridge to replace Duffy's successor Turner (of Derry), and to secure quite a reputation at Omagh during his stay there until retirement. Possibly Wallace, a native of Strabane, had never forgotten his experience with *113* on the Cork main line, for he did not rest until he had had this engine transferred to Omagh—and not for the use of any other driver, for *113* came off the 1.30 ex-Belfast each day at Omagh, instead of going forward with a different crew and returning from Derry on the 6.35pm, as *128* and *156* had done. Unlike previous QL engines on this run, *113* was superheated, retaining slide valves, one possible reason for Wallace being permitted a monopoly of a single engine.

Link working began about the same time as *113* went to the 'shops, and her successor, *126*, with the piston valve arrangement for superheating, soon began to be shared between a link of three in Derry (the 7.20 as far as Omagh) and Wallace, who took her forward to Belfast. He was quite happy to permit the other two drivers now at Omagh, Barton and Campbell (from Derry),to have the shunting jobs which

85

P (5ft 6) class 54 with small cab, about 1916

they preferred. Omagh got a shunting engine, for a time old *142* dating back to Ulster Railway days, and now on her last legs. Then *A* class *60* came from the 'shops to replace her, for a long sojourn in the north west. Omagh's other engine had to be a small 4–4–0 for the run to Clones, in charge of Derry men. *54* came on to this job in 1919, still with the small cab, and then *52*, looked after with loving care by cleaners Donaldson and Holland. The only flaw they could see in their glittering engine was a badly scored buffer. One night, however, the two lads observed a really splendid buffer on a ballast engine stabling the night in Omagh, and they set to with an exchange in view. They had not realized that a buffer was so heavy, and then, in the end, it failed to fit the passenger engine. John Holland, that jovial raconteur, laughed off their disappointment. He enjoyed those days in Omagh, working for a pittance, far more than those that followed on the comfortable footplate of a NCC tank engine on Dublin expresses forty years later.

88, now superheated, replaced *52* and then the Omagh passenger engine was *12*, a popular engine known as 'the dozen' which usually came back to this end of the Irish North after each overhaul. By 1930 Wallace's driver colleagues had become Jimmy Sweeney, W. McCaffrey, a nervous rather delicate man, and Joe Hutton, who soon managed to get a transfer back to Derry. His brother was reputed to be a solicitor there, and no one had any doubt that Joe's response to a call to the Bar would have been immediate. Sweeney did set up house in Omagh, only to die after a short time. Omagh fireman were reasonably content as long as they did not have to share a footplate with Wallace, sitting there stolidly on his engine no matter what horseplay was in progress and expecting his fireman to do the same. For a time he had Mickey Gallagher, who knew almost everything about an engine but nothing about rules and discipline and ended his days reduced to coaling those engines at Enniskillen. Frank McCourt was one of his successors and there was also some tension between him and Wallace. He fared even worse when transferred to Dublin, being killed during carriage shunting.

The most celebrated occasion at Omagh station during the 'twenties must surely have been on 22.7.24 when the Duke and Duchess of York, in course of sampling each of the three railways at Belfast (the last time royalty was to do this), made the

86

journey from Belfast to Newtownstewart. Before the five-coach train left Belfast No.3 platform at 4pm, various folk went through the routine of being presented to a future king, the railwaymen in this group including F.A. Campion, the Civil Engineer, G.T. Glover, the Locomotive Engineer and Campbell Wallace, the District Superintendent. Refreshments were served on the train as organised by G.H. Crossley, manager of the GNR's Hotels' Department. *124* was turned out in mint condition for the big occasion, just recently rebuilt. Big George Gillespie was the driver and seeing he was allowed only 30 mins for the nonstop run to Portadown, the newspaper report that the train reached a speed of 75 mph may well be correct. It should be noted that Lurgan, with a greater population than Portadown at that period, by about one thousand, was given no opportunity of partaking in the affair, but 10 minute stops were booked at Portadown, Dungannon and Omagh. At the latter one of the two guide patrol leaders to be presented was Olive, daughter of Thomas Anderson, the stationmaster. Considering the stops, the 125 min schedule to Newtownstewart was quite tight, just about the same as the mail's passing time each morning.

The regular 7.20 guards, who went as far as Clones, were A.T. Loughlin (known as 'Andy the Lash') and M. Gallagher. For the other portion a Belfast guard, who had worked down with the goods, took over. This was often Davie McIlwaine, an inveterate searcher of the train for newspapers and unpopular with the enginemen. From his old Omega watch he noted down their times in his journal without fear or favour and his two favourite words echoing down the train were 'Hurry Up!'

Wallace was not the type of driver to give Davie an opportunity of booking time against him and I now regret that I never thought of jotting down details of some very fast runs with him on that 30 min timing from Portadown to Belfast, due 10.40am. Wallace would keep his fireman hard at work so that they rounded Portadown Junction with a full boiler, for extra coaches were usually added for the final stretch. He had a habit of giving the fire a touch with the pricker and Inspector John Willis, watching from the signal cabin, would indeed be looking for steam blowing off at a station. Firemen on this turn were already irritated to the full by having him on the footplate conversing with Wallace and blocking the fire-box door. So when Willis spoke sharply to the fireman on one occasion about a waste of steam he was told at once to 'Ask him'—which he was, of course, afraid to do.

One morning in the 'twenties the 7.20 was approaching Balmoral at a brisk pace when the engine lost a tyre but did not derail, being eventually brought to a halt conveniently just opposite Adelaide sheds. For about a ¾ mile the 4–4–0 had hopped along in a frightening manner and even Wallace looked ashen afterwards and would not discuss the incident. Almost certainly the engine involved was *126*. This driver's custom until the 1.30 departure was to pay the Loco Superintendent a call rather than enter into the bantering spirit of Adelaide's enginemen. In Hill's office it may have been arranged to end the ten-year-old practice of having the QL type on this run, for a Q class was inevitably used thenceforward until 1950.

Regular 1.30 guards in the 'twenties were Tom Gray, very tall and erect and Bill Strannix, uncle of Sam who had fired for Bob Bruce on the Dublin expresses and was later to become a top link driver at Adelaide. Compartment 3rd *160* was usually attached to the 1.30 as far as Omagh. This was the only K.2, the same length as a K.1 but with the clerestory roof of the K.3, of which eventually there were each 19 examples. Ten compartments in the 55¼ ft K.1 meant very little leg room and they seldom worked through to Dublin or Derry. However, the K.2 and K.3 types had toilets until they were superseded by corridor stock. The space where each

The unique K.2 160

toilet had been was then filled by a seat for two, whose occupants would be just out of sight of passengers at the other side of the carriage. Few who travelled the GNR 1930-60 can have forgotten those compartments where the standard 3rd class seat for five faced two others, one for four passengers and that little nook for two, set further back.

1933–1941

Few locomotive depots can have reacted as strongly as Derry to the GNR's decision to inflict a 10 per cent wage reduction at the beginning of 1933, for Paddy Campbell, greatly respected chairman of many meetings between union and board, was one of the senior drivers there. So it was maybe just as well that Hobson had transferred to Belfast some years previously for, like some other senior men there, he decided to have no part in any strike. In the Derry (No. 2) link at Adelaide he still reached that city two weeks out of three, and with this mileage money he was financially better off than many stationmasters. A week on the 8.25am could earn him £8 whereas the agent at Beragh, for instance, was on a salary of £210 p.a., and there were stations graded lower than that.

So Hobson was one of the drivers prepared, with some help from white-collar staff of the locomotive department, to maintain some kind of skeleton service. On 2nd March, the thirtieth day of the strike, he had his regular engine, *122*, out of Belfast on a train for Enniskillen. At Omagh Market Junction the engine unexpectedly took the branch, taking with her the first two coaches which overturned. The remainder, including a number of vans, took the main line and were badly derailed. Someone had tampered with the points, and the locking bar was later found in the Drumragh River below the bridge there. It was quite a miracle that no one had been seriously injured and indeed a story went that one regular traveller, whose garden adjoined the line there, stepped from a carriage with the remark, 'That is some service!' *122* stayed on the road (downhill at 1/71) and was stopped in the market yard. When the Traffic Manager, James Lockhart, arrived Hobson made light of the incident with 'It's all in a day's work'. Nevertheless three coaches

—tri-compo *20*, which had spent many nights in Omagh, brake 3rd *124* and 100-seater 3rd *419*—had to be scrapped. *122* seems to have incurred some wheel damage for she was given driving wheels and crank axle from QL *114*, whose surprising withdrawal was thus remarkably convenient. Hobson's emergency fireman on this occasion was Joseph Brooks, said to have been an English railwayman, possibly from the GWR, because he was seen firing from the left hand side of the footplate.

The Derry service was slower than most to regain its former frequency after the return to work, and even at the end of the year there was no Derry-Belfast service by GNR between the 7.20am and the 4.10pm mail. When a lunchtime train was at last reintroduced at 12.45pm ex-Derry, the locomotive department had thoroughly recast the workings, though leaving most of the trains at their former times. Derry in fact was not affected, apart from the loss (if one could regard it as such) of the two lodging turns to Enniskillen. From now on the 7.50pm Derry-Belfast goods would be worked by Derry men as far as Omagh, where they exchanged footplates with Belfast men who had left Enniskillen with the 8.35pm goods for Derry. The previous night that crew had left Belfast with the 11.15pm Derry goods, changing at Omagh to the engine of the 11.30pm Derry-Enniskillen goods.

By 1930 bridge strengthening had enabled C and D class goods engines to work over the Omagh-Enniskillen section on these trains. During the first week of February 1937 for example, the 10pm Belfast-Enniskillen goods was worked throughout by SG3 0—6—0s, *20* on the Monday, Wednesday and Friday, returning next afternoon on the 2.45pm 'shipper' via Omagh, *202* on Tuesday, and *7* on Thursday. *202* was renowned as exceedingly free-running, but *7* was an unpopular engine because of a tendency for hot boxes. On alternate nights that week the 11.15pm goods to Derry was headed by *201* and *8*, though quite often it could be a Belfast LQG, such as, at that period, *110, 158* and *161*, a less popular type. C class power on the Derry-Enniskillen goods during this week was represented by *9* and *38* on alternate nights, an interesting way of employing the NQGs. The 10pm goods ex-Belfast did not serve stations Fintona Junction to Trillick so wagons for these stations went forward on the Derry-Enniskillen goods. After

SG3 96 at Fintona Junction, having worked the goods from the town station

1933 the daytime goods, one in each direction between Derry and Enniskillen, had ceased to run.

A regular Derry guard on the Enniskillen goods was wee Sam McKnight, who kept his van like a new pin, even fitting curtains, and presented a very unfriendly face to any fireman hoping to ride home in it after a night out. While shunting was in progress at Omagh the rear wagons and unattended van would be lying up the branch. One fireman, seeing the foreman with a powder compact found in the ladies' waiting room, immediately thought of 'Monkey' and his van. So he liberally perfumed its interior, and when he returned McKnight became convinced that some courting couple had been using it. This was just about the most reprehensible crime he could imagine but it was a delicate matter into which to enquire and the station staff had many a chuckle at his guarded queries.

The marshalling of wagons on the 10pm and 11.15pm ex-Belfast was well organised. Next to the 10pm's van, but at the front of the train from Omagh forward, were the Newtownbutler wagons (a circuitous route), then Lisnaskea and so on until Enniskillen and the Sligo line wagons. Bundoran line wagons came next and finally, depending on the load, a few main-line wagons as far as Portadown, something the 11-15 assisted with also. The 11.15, regularly with brake van 42, had to run to time because it carried the mails, a P van from Dublin being added at Portadown.

P vans (to load to 20 tons) had first appeared in 1930 in the form of three 24½-ton bogie vans with timber body and framing, 779-781. By 1934 six very similar vehicles had been added, so that most six-wheel parcels and mail vans, less acceptable on fast passenger trains, could be withdrawn. The usual practice with P vans was to detach them for loading at certain important stations, to be added later to a following train. Thus the 2.35pm Derry-Dundalk had a P van as far as Omagh, which later went forward to Belfast on the 'shipper'. Strabane's Donegal traffic meant that two P vans were usually attached to the 5.25pm ex-Derry for Enniskillen and then, next day, Dublin. Two survive today on NIR (757 and 788 renumbered 618 and 619), the only GNR bogies still in regular service.

The other goods trains in the Omagh area were handled by Omagh crews, even though one of the 1934 economies had been that the shed no longer had an engine allocation. However, engines from two other sheds were available for much of the day. At 3.45am the Portadown 0—6—0 off the previous day's goods started on its return journey with an Omagh crew. At Pomeroy (usually) the 2.40am goods ex-Portadown was crossed and the crews changed over. For some years a second crew used this engine for a pick-up goods around 12.30pm to Strabane and back. In addition there was the 4—4—0 which arrived with the 8.40am ex-Dundalk and shunted for several hours afterwards at Omagh including, around 3pm, a visit to the Market branch to remove the day's wagons. Early next morning it went to the branch again, before setting off for Dundalk with the connection off the 7.20am ex-Derry, the Omagh crew changing over with Dundalk men at Clones.

Generally one could expect a U class on this Dundalk job except during the summer months. 197 had been at Omagh in her early days and during the week commencing 14th December 1936 we see this again, as she was on the 8.31am to Dundalk on Monday, Wednesday and Friday, 198 appearing on the other three days. However, during the week commencing 15th July 1935, 43 had worked out of Omagh on Monday, 27 on the Tuesday and Thursday, 25 on the Saturday and 74 on the other two days. Each of these engines could be seen at Omagh quite frequently twenty years later.

On 20th July 1934, passing along Castletown bog near Mountjoy with the 5.30pm ex-Derry, 25 broke her left-hand connecting rod, which was forced through the shell of boiler 49 to the firebox. The driver, Mick Connolly, a hard runner and unmistakeable with his big bushy eyebrows, was unhurt but the fireman, jumping off, seems to have sustained minor injury. The PP class, as they bounced along, tended to be more prone to this kind of mishap than most classes and 25 had had a similar kind of fracture six years earlier.

After the 1933 strike Omagh depot found itself with a number of strange faces, of enginemen redundant at their home sheds. Apart from the inevitable Derry men and two firemen already there (Fred Lambert from Drogheda and Jack Campbell from Bundoran), Omagh now had two Newry men, driver Billy McKee and fireman Bob Irwin, and two contrasting firemen from Belfast, wee Mickey Smith who was certainly not daunted by Wallace's attempts at bullying, and Tom Patterson. Most of these men were accommodated at Gorman's in John Street, but that establishment may at times have considered this a dubious privilege, especially on pay nights. It was a regular sight during these lean years to come upon one of this jolly gang entertaining passers-by at the town hall, near the police barracks, by directing the traffic or other horseplay after which, if they weren't arrested, the usual practice was to sober-up on the footplate of the Dundalk engine.

In the morning the job of working bread vans and oil tanks to the Markets branch and then setting them for unloading was easy on the fireman, but shunter James McMaster frowned on any loafing and would stir the crew into action with 'What will the boss say about this? Make a bit of shape or we'll be here all day'. In 1935 McMaster was injured while alighting from an engine and was absent for several months, but he did return to the railway and was later a guard.

Visits to the Market line at Omagh had to be carefully scheduled so as not to interfere with traffic between Beragh and Omagh. This section was famous for breakaways of goods trains and much depended on the guard. One night Tom McMullen was in the van and dropped over to sleep, as he often tended to. Near the Camowen bridge the fireman drew the driver's attention to the fact that the SG3 engine had now only three wagons so they knew what to expect and whistled repeatedly as they passed the Market junction. By good luck, instead of holding them outside, as he often did, the signalman had decided that they could cross the up goods at Newtownstewart, so the 0–6–0 passed through Omagh station with her short train. Soon after and still moving fairly fast came the main part of the train but the station staff were ready for it and, banging hard on the side of the van, woke McMullen who stopped the runaway.

Yet another Derry driver, Sam Martin, now formed part of the four-crew set-up at Omagh. The younger fry at the shed were rather pleased with him because he provided entertainment by arguing with Wallace. Martin did not take lodgings in Omagh and if there was no possibility of slipping off home to Derry in the evening he simply bedded down in the hut at Omagh, something Wallace despised and resented. He would stand over the sleeping Martin writing remarks on the wall above him and even had rotten fish hidden in the floorboards to try to make his sojourn unbearable.

The Strabane goods job was handy for staying overnight in Derry, especially if he could get booked off in time to join the 4.40pm ex-Belfast at Omagh. But on certain afternoons the single line would be infested with livestock specials from the SLNCR or the various fairs, en route to Derry for shipping and therefore more important than the goods. So Martin, boiling with rage, would sit at Victoria Bridge or Newtownstewart waiting for a clear road, when many another man would have been hoping for an hour or two of overtime. Eventually signalman Morrow would hurry along with the staff and Martin would snatch it from him as

91

Driver Sam Martin with fireman Tom Patterson. The shunter is Peter Donnelly and the other man Jimmy Marron

if the delay had been deliberate. Then as they moved off he would give vent to his feelings with some insult at the retreating back such as 'oul flannel feet'. Even when Sam did manage to catch his train home to Derry there was another obstacle in Barney McKinney, ticket collector at Omagh, with strong views about ticketless travellers. More than once Martin dealt with this apparent obsession by spending most of the journey in a bread hamper in the guard's van.

Signalmen at Newtownstewart were Arthur Russell and Alec Arthur, a confusing coincidence of names. Alec was also a farmer and used to tell the railwaymen that he came down to the station for a rest. What he was much more likely to do, however, was appear, during shunting of the store, with a biscuit-tin and suggest 'boring a wee hole' in one of the Guinness barrels. One morning the down goods was held nearly a half hour at the home signal, and when the fireman eventually entered the cabin he found Alec asleep. The porter-signalman (as such were designated during the depression period) jumped up shouting 'I'll be sacked' and promised the train crew 'a wee sheep' for secrecy about the incident. They are still waiting for it.

QGT2 169 shunting at Strabane in 1937

Derry still retained one mileage turn in its top link, a 151-mile day as far as Portadown, replacing the former Clones job of 164 miles. Two schemes were tried. For about a year Derry men went to Portadown with the 7.20am and came back with coaches which had travelled from Belfast on the rear of the 10.30am to Dublin. *120* was their engine during this period but later, when they had *132*, the mileage turn was the 12.45pm ex-Derry, returning from Portadown with the 4.45pm ex-Belfast.

Apart from a Q for the Portadown mileage turn (another Q and a SG3, from Adelaide, were stabled at Derry each night),the largest engines now allocated to Foyle Road were the 0—6—0s for the Enniskillen goods, often NQG class but sometimes SG2 or even LQG. In 1937 Derry also still had *10* and *103*, and *60* was now shunting there instead of at Omagh. By 1935 *119*'s unusual presence had ceased but another shunting tank, *169*, soon arrived. That Belfast could spare this 0—6—2 tank certainly suggests a falling-off in goods traffic. During the 'thirties Derry had also, of course, no less than five of a class which had never been absent in thirty years. As Derry men had only one turn to Enniskillen (the 2.35pm passenger, returning on the 6.52pm), this might seem extraordinarily generous, especially for the 'tight' times of the 'thirties, but right until the closure of Enniskillen shed twenty years later its passenger workings north to Derry continued to be worked by (mainly) PP engines from Derry's stud. So amongst those engines to be seen in, say, 1938, on the 11.15am, 2.35pm and 5.30pm ex-Derry, at least two would be absent from Derry shed each night from the stud of *27, 43, 44, 76, 129*.

From 1929 the Derry foreman in charge of the shed had been big William Gillespie, who had fired on a 4—4—0 tank at Ballyroney around the turn of the century. Possibly the most popular man ever to hold the job at Derry, he was later to receive a large presentation from his men when leaving for Portadown.

A misty evening at Foyle Road where W. Barton has the mail engine under the Craigavon Bridge.

93

About this time came the retirement of dapper Sam Jeffers, stationmaster at Omagh. Handsome and often sporting a monocle, Jeffers had once been in charge of the goods depot at Queens Bridge, a position which frequently involved problems like theft and careless derailments. He had handled them all with splendid phlegm and tact, saving many a man his job. Quiet, deeply religious folk, Sam and his wife were equally popular at Omagh but it seems that on one occasion there he did act a little out of character. On this particular morning he paced the platform and repeatedly looked at the station clock. Similarly the foreman shifted from one leg to the other as he stood beside a van in the cattle beach. A certain undertaker was expected, with a coffin for Lisnaskea. Another of this man's functions in the town's affairs was as conductor of the Omagh Dance Band, but popular opinion had it that he could not conduct himself. The 7.20 ex-Derry was already signalled when his black van dashed into the station yard at a most unfuneral speed. Minutes then passed but still no sign of the foreman so Jeffers went to investigate. He was just in time to witness railwayman and undertaker struggling to fit the corpse with its shroud, which there had been insufficient time to do elsewhere. At the sight the stationmaster felt quite faint and retired to the station house for strong coffee—not alcohol, of course, in his house. He was just recovering when a local coal merchant stormed into the house to inform him that if wagons weren't left at a more convenient spot he'd report Sam to the General Manager. That did it. The previous day Jeffers had had an unsatisfactory interview at Belfast about his impending retirement. He now revealed a hitherto unsuspected vocabulary of four-letter words to describe general manager, coal merchant and undertaker, and it was Mrs Jeffers' turn to require strong coffee.

By now all four carriage sets for Belfast provided refreshments and were composed of corridor stock, centre corridor 3rds such as *16, 147, 316* and *335* on the Derry-based ones, with one of the old clerestory compos *442, 443* or *448*. Tea-car *142* formed part of the 3rd class accommodation of the 7.20 but the 12.45, regarded as more important, now had *254*, described as a buffet car. Both the 12.45 and its 4.45 return had through Dublin coaches between Derry and Portadown, an interesting variety appearing from the time this facility was reintroduced in 1936. The more typical J.4 class was not at first used, but instead through passengers experienced old clerestory vehicles of the same vintage as the compos on the train. So in

Buffet Car 254 of type K.14, usually on the 4.45pm Belfast-Derry in the mid-'thirties

1936 *72*, with a mere 6ft brake compartment, was alternating with the rather similar *445* on the 12.45, *444* replacing *72* the following year. That the management was as unaware of the sublime nature of these Edwardian pieces as regular passengers is suggested by the appearance in 1937 of Derry's first 'steel', J.11 *47*. By 1940 another new carriage, an F.16 compo, was working right through between Belfast and Derry on the mail and now both the 1.30pm ex-Belfast and the 4.10pm ex-Derry had also a through Dublin coach on and off at Portadown. A J.4, *151*, was now available for this, and another, *64*, was alternating with *47* on the 12.45 ex-Derry, until the other two J.11 type were built.

Few cities can have been as splendidly situated as Derry for nearby resorts, and railways to assist citizens to reach them. Each of the other three railways there had an advantage in distance, and even if Portrush had not already had a special kind of appeal for young people, some remarkably good value by the enterprising NCC must certainly have provided it. Though the GNR had long been trying to develop Bundoran's claims, probably both Portrush and Buncrana always had the edge, as far as Derry-city folk were concerned. But even narrow gauge enthusiasts must admit that the GNR's reply of a Sunday 3/6d (17½p) from Derry to Bundoran was pretty mouth-watering. This day lasted from the 9am departure with teacar attached until arrival back in Derry at 11pm, 174 miles for the PP 4—4—0 invariably used. No doubt the standard of refreshment at Bundoran had something to do with the rate of progress of the 9.10pm from there on 29.6.40, for signalman McGuinness at Strabane having to take the staff at speed severely injured his hand. A similar kind of mishap had occurred to John Harte some time previously at the same cabin, though Harte's badly cut head was the result of slipping on an October morning, one of the greatest hazards shunters, especially, had to face on the railway.

A much less generous excursion fare from Derry was 8/3d (12/5d first class) to Enniskillen for the local farming society's show, but this involved the rather superior accommodation of ordinary trains, which also applied to a 7/6d to Belfast from time to time. Big Johnny Henderson was in charge of an 8.55pm return excursion from Belfast on 3.4.37 with 4—4—0 *25*, the other Dundalk-built PP, *43*, having had a similar train on 17th March. On 25.5.37 there was a rare appearance of an S class (still in black livery) at Derry when *191* arrived on the ordinary 1.30pm ex-Belfast, which usually at that period had *135*. But for the return working at 7.20pm *43*, most interestingly, was used instead, and *191* was retained at Derry until the next morning for the heavy excursion to Belfast, driver Joe Hutton.

From Omagh the aforementioned excursions to Bundoran, Enniskillen and Belfast cost respectively 3/-, 3/6d and 5/-. A summer offer, usually on a Wednesday, was a 3/- trip to Bangor by a 12.55pm through train. One could also make a trip to Derry by ordinary train on Saturdays for 3/6d, or by a 7.5am, which ran on fairdays only, for 2/11d.

On seven Sundays of the July-August period Omagh found enough carriages to run a 3rd class only excursion to Bundoran independent of the one from Derry, and the quartet of crews there looked forward to this variation from the more mundane routine. Big William McKee invariably enjoyed himself and was never short of a fireman keen to go with him, for apart from the extra pay and the day out, this could ensure escape from the early turn with Wallace next morning. On the homeward trip from County Donegal the fireman might have to drive as well, if McKee was cuddling the girl from Omagh refreshment room in a corner of the footplate.

During the summer months another Bundoran train, in rather more of a hurry, visited Omagh. This was the Bundoran Express, booked to run from Bundoran Junction, where it left off Dublin coaches, to Omagh in 26 minutes, including a conditional stop at Fintona Junction for through passengers. The through Belfast coach off this train, usually J.4 *43*, was attached to the 4.10pm ex-Derry at Omagh. Derry drivers on the 4.10 were now P. Campbell, W. Temple, as sedate as his arch-bishop namesake, and big John Turner. Turner was an alderman of the city of Derry and would be looking for a pilot to Dungannon because of the extra bogie. Omagh men, with the engine off the 8.40am ex-Dundalk, provided this, but always felt that the condescending Turner regarded them as greenhorns who would do all the work and so would shut off to change his tune. From 1936, however, it be-came a regular summer working for the engine off the 2.35pm Portadown-Omagh local to return piloting the 4.10, now in charge of a Portadown engine.

Traditionally there was no service from Enniskillen to Omagh between the 10.45am and 4.25pm ex-Dundalk, so this Bundoran Express usefully filled a gap in the summer. Its return working was at 5.20pm from Omagh to Clones, a new ser-vice given by the Clones railcar in winter. There was also the 'shipper' at 2.45pm from Enniskillen to Belfast, which provided passenger accommodation as far as Omagh and the chance to travel behind an SG3 0-6-0. At one period the bridges between Trillick and Fintona Junction had been so weak that piloting of any kind had been forbidden but now this pleasant switchback was as unrestricted as the Portadown-Derry stretch.

The twisting up platform at Omagh, with access to street, bookstall, refreshment room and, at most periods, divisional headquarters offices, was, at 733 yards, the longest on the GNR. One morning about this period there was a little entertain-ment on it, though possibly it was only for those who enjoy the embarrassment of others. A valuable greyhound was being sent by passenger train for servicing and one of the porters had been instructed to retain a firm grip on the dog's lead and not to allow it out of his sight. It was a busy morning. The up platform could be quite packed on such occasions and just momentarily this porter fell into absorbing chat with an acquaintance, still, of course, with the lead in his hand. So the station-master's Dalmation, with a reputation for amorous adventures, saw his chance. Country folk pay little attention to such natural events but,even though a bucket of water was hastily put into use,there were doubtless a few questions to answer later.

More serious events, however, were fast catching up with the Great Northern, and the NCC's reaction to a war situation being much more in line with Britain's, the fastest route from Derry to Belfast again became via Omagh. Even in 1941 the down mail, now leaving Belfast at 8.50am, was still booked to reach Derry in 155 minutes, and this often included at least one stop between Dungannon and Omagh. Some of the other times were eased very slightly but the improved service between Belfast and Omagh since 1938, by reason of the railcar connection from Portadown at 9.30pm, was continued. The Clones railcar was already a familiar sight, in the winter timetable, for the 5.20pm Omagh-Enniskillen, and such drivers as B. McGirr and S. McCague soon learnt to handle its twin, *C.3*, on a turn which, leaving Omagh at 4.25pm, threw a connection into the mail at Dungannon. It later in the evening went off to Cookstown, before reaching Portadown for that connec-tion out of the 8.40pm Belfast-Portadown.

Derry folk wishing to travel to Belfast on Sundays seem to have been required, up until World War II, to use the NCC route, but by 1941 Dungannon-Omagh had at last a regular Sunday service which was, of course, in later years to develop into a through Derry service. In 1940 the departure from Belfast was at 8.30pm, due into Omagh (for Enniskillen) at 10.25pm, but there was no balancing service in the up direction. The following year the Belfast departure was put back to 9pm and it also took 115 minutes to Omagh, with Dungannon the only stop actually booked between Portadown and Omagh, but any of the other eight stations could be served if required. This Sunday booking was thus the second fastest in the timetable between Belfast and Omagh.

1941 brought 'double summer time' and its intriguing effect upon the timings of cross-border trains. For instance, the old 7.20, now leaving Derry at 7.15 and reaching Belfast at 10.45am (5 minutes more at each end), was booked to call at St. Johnston at 6.30am. Similarly the 1.30 left Strabane at 4.29 but reached Porthall at 3.36. Strabane's two Saturday night trains from Derry, at 9.30 and 11.15pm, saw many more patrons due to the curtailment of motoring, though the military could not use them. The first returned from Strabane as a passenger service at 10.20pm but the other, empty, at five mins.after midnight was, even in 1941, the only wintertime Sunday activity between Omagh and Derry. The GNR, since the strike, had maintained a policy of not providing a service to bring anyone into Derry before 9.45am.

The line to the west from Omagh did see considerable military activity, being their only rail access to Fermanagh. Few records of those operations remain and in any case most are beyond the period of this book. However, it can be mentioned that William McClain, who was responsible for the horse at Fintona, saw increasing business, especially in 1942 when American soldiers arrived in the area. On most journeys along the short branch one of them would be on the horse's back and a useful volume of tips exchanged hands. About this time the old horse was pensioned off, and there was a circular to enginemen not to sound the whistle near Fintona Junction in case it would frighten the new horse—who was soon to learn the routine and apparently the timetable, for it seemed to know on which journeys it finished by going forward to the stable and on which it went to the other end of the tram.

It should be noted that the Fintona tram, preserved today in Belfast's Transport Museum, was numbered *381*, so no carriage bore that number. A second tram numbered *416*, which may have been to replace *381* or simply act as a spare, was destroyed in a fire at Dundalk on 11.4.13, together with 17 six-wheel coaches and , two bogies. Some say that it would, in any case, have been too heavy for one horse.

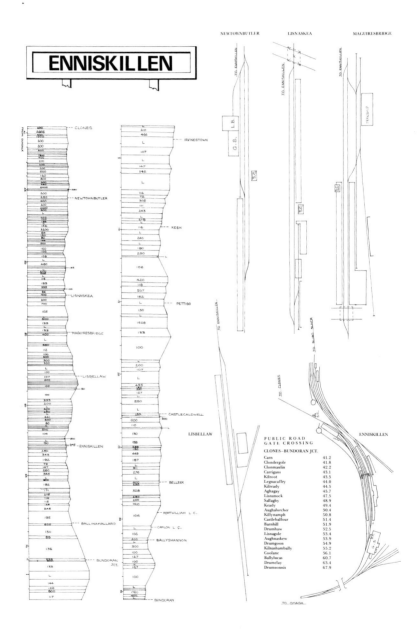

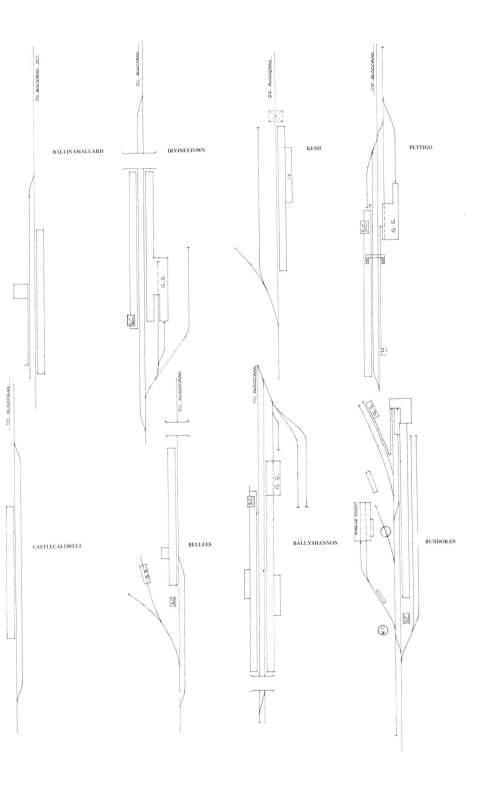

BALLINAMALLARD

IRVINESTOWN

KESH

PETTIGO

CASTLECALDWELL

BELLEEK

BALLYSHANNON

BUNDORAN

ENNISKILLEN

Some readers may be surprised to discover that Fermanagh, that soft grey-green county which seems to be mostly water, is neither the smallest nor the least populated of the twelve into which the GNR penetrated. Two other railways, of lesser importance, provided a modest feeder on each side and Enniskillen, the county town, was the most important railway centre for the area north of Sligo and south of Derry. However, it probably did not quite justify its position on a par with Dublin, Derry and Belfast on the GNR shield, though to many GNR enthusiasts Enniskillen did mean something quite special.

Although a through station, Enniskillen had few through passengers but those who did not alight there saw nothing of the town's rather unique island position or its atmosphere of waterways. Indeed the railway station was very much on the fringe of the town, giving an impression that the railway was trying to serve it and then get away again as quickly as possible. But the historian will know, of course, that two independent lines, from Derry and Dundalk, got there in 1854 and 1859 respectively and were eventually connected by the sharpest curve (330ft radius) on the GNR, restriction 10 mph. The D&E station was the one which lasted nearly one hundred years, the site of the other being henceforward known as the Derry cattle beach. Just beyond, on the Irvinestown Road, some railwaymen's houses were built, their occupants including, by the period of this book, engine driver Dan Sweeney, foreman painter McKinney and guard Jimmy McCombe. Inevitably the passenger station reminded one of Drogheda, with the same cramped curved situation and a locomotive depot at the end of the platform, so that waiting for a train was seldom dull. Frequently there was at both the sound of cattle lowing, but those which arrived off the SLNCR had seldom the stamina of those fed on the rich pasture lands of Meath.

Until the creation of the Border the more important line for passengers out of Enniskillen tended to be towards Clones, as that was the route to both Dublin and Belfast. Leaving Clones the two single lines to Cavan and Enniskillen ran parallel for about a half mile. So continental style operation would have been quite possible, with a train for Newtownbutler passing, on the right, instead of the left, another coming in from Cavan. However, this very seldom occurred, especially with passen-

105 with cattle special, signalled for the Enniskillen route at Clones

ger trains, which, for connections, would all have to be into Clones before the first one departed. Invariably the INWR train (for Enniskillen) left before the one for Cavan. Like most other folk who lived near the line, a Clones mill owner, Joseph Ballagh, knew of this and paid for it with his life on 9.1.15. Walking along the Cavan line about 9pm and hearing a train approach from Clones he must have assumed it was for Enniskillen. On that night, however, there seems to have been some delay at Clones so it was in fact the Cavan train which mowed him down.

Gortgommon was the official name for the crossing a few yards before Newtownbutler station. This quiet but rather pretty village possessed a conveniently sited station which became important from 1922 as the only Northern Ireland customs station between Clones and Strabane. Just beyond the Lisnaskea end of the village the line had one of its few main road level crossings at Aghagay, where the McLaughlins lived, and then came the Gribbens at Lisanock. Salaghy, 1½ miles further, was on a curve where the old road to Dublin crossed. A signal controlled the gates here, 'Newtown' (as it was invariably called) advising the keeper with an alarm bell, with 'Skea' (another shortened form) doing the same for up trains. The next crossing, Keady, (the third so far with a name similar to an actual railway station) was unlikely to be troubled with much road traffic and here it should be mentioned that prior to the birth of the motoring age in the 'twenties the gates of all these crossings were left at night in the railway's favour. Those with vehicle traffic could find the gate keys on the window-sill of the gatehouse.

Aughalurcher was alongside a graveyard and a ½ mile beyond this was Killynamph. After another ½ mile came Castlebalfour, operated in the same manner as Sallaghy and on the main road from Lisnaskea across the Upper Lough to Derrylin—from which it was only about 7 miles to Ballyconnell on the C&LR. At 51.6 miles was the Loughead bridge, possibly the most troublesome to rebuild during the replacement in the 'twenties of the old INWR bridges. Matt D'Arcy of Dundalk had about twenty men on the Loughead project but that cold Fermanagh clay, so little use for growing, swallowed the thousands of tons of concrete supplied for a new foundation. So the temporary closing of the line in November 1920 was a blessing in disguise, and with no interruptions by trains, bridge 134 was at last rebuilt.

After Barnhill crossing, where railwayman Murphy lived, came Lisnaskea station at the west end of this busy town, the property of Lord Erne. Although Moy is often regarded as the most productive horse area of the GNR, it was Lisnaskea about 1910 which had an international reputation for its horses. This reached its peak during World War I when the heavy horse traffic at the station was mainly due to the shows and sales at 'Big Tom' Maguire's place at Munville. So rapidly were horse boxes and even wagons filled that old Sam Connor, shunting driver at Clones, had to be requisitioned for horse specials.

At that period the only regular goods up the line left Derry at 9pm, the crew and engine returning the following evening from Clones at 6.15pm. It was usually around 6am when one of that link of Derry drivers mentioned in the previous chapter reached Lisnaskea, where porter Courtney was killed on 9.9.17. It was thought that he was riding on the shunting pole, which slipped, throwing him under the wheels. After 1920 the Derry goods ceased to run beyond Enniskillen and the stations to Clones were served by the Bundoran goods. This left Clones each morning shortly after the 8.5am school train cleared Newtownbutler.

The crossing over the main road out of Lisnaskea towards Enniskillen was called Drumhaw and the line continued its swing north towards Maguiresbridge, with the lough even less visible from the train. The two-storey house at Lisnagole crossing was the home of Bob Symings, who with Davie McComb replaced in the 'twenties Maguiresbridge signalmen Edward Smith and Frank McGraw. Bill Symings was

101

signalman at Lisnaskea. Aughnaskea crossing came next, the home of ganger Bob Armstrong, whose son Dougie was a World War II addition to Enniskillen shed. On 13.2.26 Mrs Armstrong was injured by a motor car as she ran to close the gates for the 8.50am goods ex-Clones, making better progress than she had calculated. A telephone was later installed here.

Both CVR and GNR crossed over the Colebrooke river just before the two ad-jacent stations at Maguiresbridge, the GNR bridge being a 64¾ft structure. The name of the next crossing, Kilnashambally, might have daunted even the most ex-perienced BBC announcer. The only other crossing before Lisbellaw was home of another ganger, Dick Whitley, a family of the same name being in charge of the crossing near milepost 60, Ballylucas.

My usual reaction to numerous journeys between Clones and Enniskillen tended to be pleased surprise that so many gates did not prevent 50-55 mph for several miles prior to Lisnaskea, with 60 mph quite likely later at Ballylucas. But details of a run from Clones to Maguiresbridge timed by R.N. Clements on 18.2.28 suggest that progress at that period was usually not as lively. *53*, with, presumably, a Derry crew, had at Clones taken over the 10.33am ex-Dundalk, only 4 bogies and 2 cattle wagons, 126 ton tare. Exactly 11¾ mins were taken to Newtown where the train sat 6¼ mins, then 11 mins 55 sec to Lisnaskea for a 65 sec stop and finally 5 mins 15 sec to Maguiresbridge. By 1935 2 mins had been knocked off such a journey, although time at Newtownbutler was unchanged. In the up direction passenger trains seldom sat more than 2 mins there but on wash days, especially, Mrs Mulally, at the station crossing, usually had time to obtain a bucket or two of hot water from an obliging fireman.

At 63.9 miles was 'Hall's bridge'. Renewed in 1923 with six spans, this was the first project in the plan to equip the Enniskillen-Omagh line to take heavier engines. As the line rapidly took itself away from the lough area to Bundoran Junction, there was obviously little traffic to be had from an unending scenario of bushes and untilled lands. Near 'Drumgay' bridge (65.3 miles) a platform was later built at Gortaloughan (opened 23.9.40) to supplement stops by the railcar, begun a few years previously, at Drumclay and Drumsonnis level crossings, one on either side. Occasionally during the petrol-less days of World War II those seeking relaxation at Killadeas on the lough found it convenient to alight for the hotel there, at Gortaloughan, but I'd say it was very seldom used; on a couple of occasions when I myself joined a train there, the driver was obviously quite astonished and did not manage to stop until a little past the platform. At Drumcullion, about 1½ miles

Down train approaching Gortaloughan Halt

further, a temporary halt did for a period in the early 'forties accommodate workers to the wartime seaplane base, the set of six-wheelers running from Derry each morning.

Ballinamallard, certainly not on any road route to Irvinestown, still less Bundoran, had a station quite conveniently sited, after several miles of parallel road and railway. Business was, nevertheless, very light, though the village seems to have been a centre on several occasions for 12th July celebrations when, no doubt, Bundoran Junction had to take the brunt of the traffic. Certainly, about 1928 old *137* arrived at Ballinamallard's solitary 315ft platform with an Orangemen's special of 13 six-wheelers from Clones.

During World War I one of the few passenger jobs which Enniskillen had was the 7.20pm (mixed) to Clones. The engine of this returned light from Clones and thus provided the setting for a disciplinary action by Glover, probably inspired by Inspector McIntyre, which was talked about in the area for more than a generation. In 1917 foodstuffs were scarce, but not in the vicinity of Aughalurcher level crossing, two miles on the Clones side of Lisnaskea. Berry, who lived in the gatehouse there, was employed by the GNR for gate and fencing jobs and had also a substantial farm of land through which the railway ran about a ¼ mile away. It became the custom for the crew on the light engine, which included also the 7.20 guard, to purchase eggs, vegetables and fruit at the crossing. Then Berry retired and the engine began to stop at his farm for the men to buy quite cheaply the same commodities.

But the man at the next crossing, Killynamph, a platelayer, was on bad terms with the Berrys. He reported what he held was happening, and Dundalk investigated, with the result that the two drivers regularly on this turn and three guards were sacked. One driver, J. Long, had formerly been at Belfast, and the other, W. Doherty, is said to have fared quite well afterwards with a taxi business and insurance agency in Enniskillen. One of the guards is said to have become a signalman on the CDRJC at Strabane and another foreman of the SLNCR at Enniskillen, interesting examples of once a railwayman, always one. The signalmen at Lisnaskea and Newtownbutler were also admonished for not reporting delay in the section, and it became a rule that stationmasters were to examine the train books in the cabins. On the face of it such punishments did not quite seem to fit the crime, so there were many tales told of what the culprits had in fact been doing. The most generally accepted one was that the foodstuffs were being exchanged for coal off the engine, not really acceptable, as Berry had more good turf on his land than he knew what to do with. Not unnaturally another story concerned the attractions of his daughters, one of whom normally attended to the gates.

Until then ballast for the line had been obtained from a quarry at Lisbellaw, old wooden wagons being usually kept at Maguiresbridge. By the time the bridges began to be rebuilt a Newry engine was arriving several times a week with stone from Goraghwood quarry. Prior to the Border, bread and newspapers from Belfast came in a 5.15am ex-Clones, connecting with the 11.45pm express goods from Grosvenor Road, a faster service than the GNR could achieve in the 'fifties.

BUNDORAN

What a superb circular rail tour it would have been if, in addition to the pleasant route through mountainous country by the SLNCR to Sligo, the GNR had also reached that town by continuing, as they did later with a good bus service, along the coast and round Ben Bulbin. All the same, tens of thousands must be grateful for the pleasure the branch in its shortened form gave, a holiday line indeed, though many miles from the large centres of population usually necessary to sustain such a branch.

The interesting triangular layout at Bundoran Junction provided a piquant start for the passenger about to commence a journey over the branch. But it was a practical method of taking through trains from both Derry and Dundalk directions whether going to Bundoran or not. It also meant that there was no need to provide a turntable for the branch engine. While neither the North nor West cabin (small and not block posts) might have to be used for an Omagh train for weeks on end in the winter, one or other of the platform porters would be required at least twice daily to operate them for engine turning. Nonstop trains from the south, especially the Bundoran Express, had to negotiate the curving branch platform at 15 mph. On the branch itself there were more sharp curves to add to the problem of the gradients. Most drivers tended to exceed the 30 mph restriction near milepost 2½ but were much more cautious just before Castlecaldwell and then again after Belleek over the Erne bridge.

A railway journey from Enniskillen to Irvinestown was more likely to last a ¾ hour, by the time one had changed trains, so once the motor bus came on the scene there was little local traffic from the station serving the former village of Lowtherstown, but changed by the local family residing at Castle Irvine. The next five miles, well away from main roads, provided very dull travel apart from Lough Bresk. After crossing over the main road at bridge 22 the line then paralleled it for 1¾ miles to Kesh, a much less important place than Irvinestown, with a level crossing one of only three on the 35½ mile branch, where Irvinestown had a fine girder bridge on the road leading from the town.

Pettigo's valley position was in considerable contrast to the two previous stations, but like all on the line except Ballyshannon, it was conveniently situated, just beyond where the Termon river, the border with Donegal, split the village politically. Various 'refreshment' rooms on station road no doubt benefitted in later days from pilgrimage traffic by rail. Two miles past Pettigo the line ran quite near the village of Letter and in later years the railcar used to stop briefly to collect the mail from the village post office. It would also deal with passengers at Tague's crossing on the junction side of Irvinestown and at Johnston's crossing and Castlearchdale between Irvinestown and Kesh.

After 25 rather boring miles from Enniskillen the passenger had now at last some scenic reward, but unless the day was clear enough to make visible the islands of the lough, prior interest may have been in the small 4—4—0 pitching about at the head of the train. After the road, which had crossed Boa Island to avoid

Unusually, an up passenger train in Castlecaldwell loop

Pettigo, began to parallel the railway near the 'Orange Hall' bridge (18.4 miles), the Ross Harbour area provided railway scenery strangely neglected by photographers. In this unpeopled blend of water and trees there was actually a station, Castlecaldwell, considered important enough by the management of 1913 to be the only stop for the Bundoran Express between Enniskillen and Ballyshannon. Like Kesh, Castlecaldwell was not a block post until much later in time, and goods traffic was almost nil.

To Belleek the line was accompanied a short distance to the south by the river Erne. The site of the station was just before the railway ran under the village's main street, near the famous pottery to which there was a siding. The engine of the down goods had to run round its train to deposit wagons of coal at the pottery, from which came more traffic with cases of china. Today Ulsterbus services use a stop near the ruins of the station building and just opposite Daly's pub, a visit to which was occasionally fitted into the goods itinerary.

Ballyshannon, with the Erne flowing through its centre, was easily the most important town on a line which had done better than most in providing convenient stations. The CDRJC station, probably preferred for a journey to Derry, may

John Kerrigan surveys the customs examination and general arrival scene at Ballyshannon

Bundoran's Train Departure Board underlines how well the GNR's furthest-west station served passengers for the north, the north-east and the south-east of Ireland. There were three departures from Bundoran daily, with a fourth (the Bundoran Express) during the summer

have had nearly as much passenger traffic, but firms like W. Neely and John Myles Ltd. kept GNR engines quite busy, while later turf traffic from Frank. H. Morgan flourished for a time. Sidings here and at Pettigo had often to be used to store sets of excursion carriages on busy Sundays, if Bundoran was bursting at the seams.

Bundoran liked to describe itself as a fashionable watering place. The Great Northern Hotel of 1894 could cater for 120 guests and an 18 hole golf course in the grounds was one of its amenities. James Duff, stationmaster in 1918, was quite prepared to apply his energies to the tourist trade, in addition to his GNR duties, and advertized 'Apartments to Let' at 7 Bayview Terrace, while Mrs Duff officiated as Refreshment and Tea Room manageress. Duff was succeeded in the 'twenties by Colhoun, who was later in charge of Lisnaskea and, finally, Dunmurry. In 1913 passenger trains left Bundoran at 7.20am, 11.35am and 5.25pm and this continued, at most periods, to be the pattern. But the goods timings of that period, 10.15pm ex-Bundoran (to connect with the up Derry goods) and 4am ex-Bundoran Junction, were soon altered to daytime workings. Undoubtedly the GNR had high hopes of Bundoran during the Edwardian period, for at the impressive shed building they employed a foreman, a fitter and a man to coal the engines, all deemed expendable by 1922. Charles Clifford may have had a soft spot for Bundoran for his first appointment had been Loco Foreman there with the INWR.

I have no reliable details of an early Bundoran driver with red beard called Mick Ryan, but he had gone by 1915 when the three drivers there were John Campbell, James Doherty and John Cagney. Two well known Bundoran drivers of the 'fifties were at that time cleaning there: Paddy Martin and Jack Kerrigan. It says something for the shed's standing at that period that the passenger engine was the almost new 43, built at Dundalk in 1911. The same PP class, but rebuilt, was there at the close in 1957, sometimes, indeed, 43. Campbell then decided, while still in early middle age, that he was not physically fit for the job and retired. Regularly Doherty would try to talk him into returning but he never did, though living until he was eighty-six. His successor was a Derry man, W. Temple, whose particular speciality was cage birds.

Cagney, small and stoutish, was known as 'John the man', and on the J class engines which preceded *43* on the branch trains he could be seen testing speed with outstretched hand before announcing to his fireman that they were 'going a dinger'. Doherty remained senior driver until the early 'thirties, a position which possibly had a little more standing after 1922 when the shed lost both foreman and fitter, Hand being later in charge of Dublin shed and Ginnity foreman at Clones. Certainly when Inspector Blemings paid his periodical visits he stayed with Doherty, which in itself meant that the rest of the Bundoran enginemen had to be careful.

On a rough winter's night with the foam and a strong wind coming in off Donegal Bay, the brake van and six-wheel carriages would be rocking on their springs. But there were compensations at Bundoran shed: its water was said to be especially suitable for the making of poteen and somewhere convenient a still was in regular use. All suspected that Blemings knew about this but apparently no action was taken so no one was perfectly sure. The large shed seems also to have been used at times as a free-for-all place to bed down at night. Often the cleaners did not know who such people were. One morning Tommy Campbell, a cleaner there and son of the driver on early retirement, nodded casually to a man beside him who was just stirring. The response was 'I've come down to pass you for firing' and true enough it was Fred Morrison, shed foreman at Dundalk and later Locomotive Superintendent at Belfast. Campbell's elder brother John was at Omagh and known to all as 'Saltwater Jack'.

While the more respectable encouraged their wives to keep boarding houses and those less so dabbled in illegal liquor, the really profitable spare time occupation after 1922 was smuggling. Most of the guards were past masters in the art of fooling customs officials at the four posts on the branch. One man seems to have overdone his activities for he was transferred to the Derry-Belfast goods in the same way as certain enginemen with smuggling tendencies at Portadown and Dundalk were not permitted to drive cross-border trains. The guards who remained on the line for years included Tom Hilliard, a splendid shunter, who lived at Bundoran Junction and worked the goods to Bundoran. Guards based there over the years were McCrory, Gallagher whose wife did a brisk trade in their boarding house near the station, and Peter Carty. Talking very quickly and endlessly, Peter could be counted upon to have all the latest news. He had two sons on the GNR.

In 1926 the Ballyshannon agent was W. Duffy, related to the Dundalk engine

GNR motor bus at Killybegs

driver. That he took an active part in traffic operations is evidenced by an accident he incurred in July of that year. As he climbed from the track to the cattle beach he fell against a horsebox, striking his head against the door and knocking himself unconscious. James McDonald came next, brother of two Clones guards. Somewhat of a tyrant to his staff and a splendid figure on the platform with his bow tie and spotless uniform, McDonald was less impressive as a clerk, which as the years rolled on became a stationmaster's main duties. The Ballyshannon Baking Company once infuriated him by paying an account for flour in coin, including five pounds in tiny threepenny pieces. Although the GNR had opened an office and waiting room for their buses in the Market Yard, all the paper work for buses and over a dozen GNR lorries was handled at the railway station, where there continued to be plenty of work, for it was only in Northern Ireland that GNR road services were handed to the NIRTB.

Ballyshannon's humorous signalman, Jimmy Trainor, had an inseparable companion in Pat O'Connor at Castlecaldwell. Pat was still quite a young man when economies made at that quiet station dictated that he transfer to either Donaghmore or Dromore Road. He chose the latter and but a short time afterwards had an accident shunting a cattle wagon there, dying after amputation of both legs.

At Belleek corpulent Maxwell McBrien was the senior signalman and Sam McMulle the other. Big Maxie had a draper's shop near the station but Sam lived out in the country The customs officer there, John Peter Walsh, an ex-RIC man, had the reputation of being the toughest on the line, but the station staff, who had to listen to him, thought he might have been more tolerant about excuses offered by would-be smugglers, seeing his own anecdotes were so wildly improbable.

At Pettigo both Eddie Quinn and, by 1939, P.J. O'Reilly were popular stationmasters. At that period this station, like all others on the branch, was devoid of footbridge, and it was not until after World War II that one was erected to safeguard pilgrims alighting from the Bundoran Express, the up express being due a few minutes later. W.J. Crawford was the tall careful signalman there. His colleague, Quinn, left the signal cabin on 21.6.35 to assist with the loading of cans of cream but, catching his trouser leg in his bicycle chain, fell and broke a bone in his wrist.

Trains could not be crossed at Kesh and when, during the 'thirties, it became a block post, it was not given a signal cabin, the staff being issued from the booking office, like Castlecaldwell. Apart from the Orange Hall, probably the only other public building possessed by the village of Kesh was a courthouse, resounding from the mid-'twenties onwards to complicated battles over (mainly) smuggling offences.

Almost certainly Fermanagh's most interesting case, as far as the railwaymen were concerned, had to do with the wife of the agent at the next station, Irvinestown. She was, apparently, his second wife, and even previously when they were at Newtownbutler, railwaymen at the station there were aware that things were not all they should be in the home of the quiet stationmaster. When stories circulated that the children were so hungry they had to eat the wall paper, action had to be taken and it seems that after they had moved to Irvinestown their step-mother received a gaol sentence.

This was all before stationmaster McGarrity's time at Irvinestown. He was a big strong man with the firm idea (rare today) that the railway came first. When some heavy loading had to be done in the goods yard, he would come shouting for the signalman, Hazlett or Weir, to assist, though the latter, short and stout, was a martyr to arthritis and scarcely able to climb the cabin steps. Under McGarrity's organisation the signalman handed the staff to the crew of a train as it arrived, and then collected the tickets in his cap. The stationmaster would then go over the tickets carefully to ensure that the signalman had excessed passengers who had booked only as far as Bundoran Junction—a regular practice due to uncertainty about a connecting train for the 3½ mile run to the second most important town on the line. Further evidence of conscientious endeavour to save the railway every penny could be seen in his re-usage of every piece of stationery; yet when he passed on, his office was found to be full of virgin balls of twine and pencils hoarded over the years and never used.

Probably no railway journey on the GNR did as well for light refreshment as that from Bundoran to Enniskillen. It was possible to get a cup of tea at both Bundoran and Ballyshannon and Mrs Gray provided this facility for folk waiting at Bundoran Junction, with little to contemplate but that fine flourish of trees within the triangle. At Enniskillen Angela Howard, daughter of the Clones foreman, ran the refreshment room and apparently her sister May was greatly involved in the huge catering arrangements for travel to the Eucharistic Congress at Dublin in 1932.

By 1932 Paddy Flynn, who had once been W. Doherty's fireman at Enniskillen, was driving at Bundoran on the goods turn, Cagney and J. Doherty sharing the passenger work. Paddy Martin, senior driver there in the 'fifties, usually fired for Cagney, Doherty's fireman being Terry Murray who never rose above that rank. One of the cleaners was Paddy Gallagher, tall and thin, another Bundoran driver in later days, when his cap was never a railway one. His predecessor in the shed at Bundoran had been Jimmy Marron, whose eyesight was insufficiently good for him to continue a footplate career, though he became carriage examiner at Omagh. There he still showed a strong partiality for locomotives, and any driver rushing off duty could rest content that Marron would not only put his engine away for him, but enjoy doing the piece of driving involved. It is interesting that the examiner at Enniskillen, Jimmy McGraw, also loved the footplate and usually wore overalls, just on the off chance that when an engine was requisitioned to collect a few wagons from Ballinamallard, he would be permitted to drive for the short run.

The Bundoran cleaners knew full well that in addition to being a timid driver Flynn was a poor mechanical man. So they would laugh at the fussy way he examined their tube cleaning of his regular engine, 0–6–0 68, having in fact done very little work on it except the ends. Until the mid-'twenties the Bundoran. goods men lodged over at Clones and Bundoran alternate nights, the Clones engine, in charge of John Fitzsimons, being usually 79, or occasionally 145, of the same class. Even at Clones Flynn would come down at midnight to make a check on the work of the cleaners there. After an even worse run than usual his fireman, John Kerrigan, would tell Flynn that he wasn't looking too well and the nervous driver would then arrange for a spell of sick leave.

As soon as the big 0–6–0s could work through from Dundalk to Enniskillen, the workings were changed and the Bundoran goods now started from Enniskillen, to which Fitzsimons was transferred. He was a 'big valve' man, the opposite of Flynn, and still crossed Paddy every weekday at Irvinestown. While both goods were there the 11.20 passenger ex-Bundoran made a brief appearance, somewhat straining the track availability. After the 1933 strike, the 6.30am passenger ex-Bundoran and its return working at 8.30am ex-Enniskillen were withdrawn, so one goods worked as a mixed to enable the first passengers of the day, after a 3½ hour run from the junction, to reach Bundoran at 12.40pm. Then in 1935 Bundoran lost its steam working, both goods being in charge of Enniskillen crews. Flynn, transferred to Enniskillen, found he was still suffering from an injury at Bundoran turntable, which had a bad reputation, so was put on the shunting engine. Now second in seniority only to Forster, he managed to get on the middle turn every week so that he could actually travel from Bundoran every day in the summer, lodging in the winter at McGoldrick's and catching the 6.30am only on Monday mornings.

ENNISKILLEN

Through the years activity for the day at Enniskillen station usually ceased shortly after the arrival, about 10.15pm, of the last train from Dundalk, the Derry goods having departed about a ¾ hour previously. Silence then reigned in the garrison town's railway premises until about 4am when the goods from Belfast was due, followed a couple of hours later by the one from Derry. Around 6.30am the first passenger train of the day left for Dundalk, in most carriage arrangements made up of the set which conveniently had arrived in the down platform late the previous night. Even during the late 'twenties these were still six-wheelers; two 3rds, a W.2 van and either *88* or *96*, which had two 1st and two 2nd class compartments, all with lavatory facilities.

Prior to World War I the first passenger train north was the 8.5am, which went as far a Omagh only, making an excellent connection there with the Belfast-Derry mail, which ran earlier at that period and had Enniskillen folk into Derry in 2 hours, a faster service than ever given later. During the 'twenties departure time was usually 7.35am, working right through to Derry in 140 mins. This set, which returned from Derry at times varying from 4.50pm to 5.30pm, was also made up of six-wheelers except for bogie compo *398* of 1892, with similar roof style to *88* and *96*, built the same year. The other vehicles were three six-wheel 3rds and a guard's van, also type W.2.

Having disposed of its early morning passengers in Victorian carriages, Enniskillen staff could relax until the arrival of the 8.5am ex-Clones, allowed 70 mins for the 22½ mile run, as it was a mixed train, instead of an average of 50 mins. The carriage makeup for this was identical with the 7.30am north except that instead of *398*, a six-wheel compo of type R.3 was provided, again with lavatories for all compartments. At first there was no return school train. No doubt such patrons were less in number during the 'twenties and had the boat train, anyway, at 4.44pm. So the 8.5 set worked the 7.30 the following day, balanced by the 5.15pm ex-Derry working through to Clones, again as a mixed. During the 'thirties, the 5.25pm ex-Derry terminated at Enniskillen and there was a 3.10pm school train, with wagons attached.

The Clones crew of the 8.5 had just brought their train to the clattering stop one associates with a mixed, when the first passenger train ex-Derry arrived. The

First/second compo 398 when reduced to third class late in life

110

Ps and PPs crossing at Maguiresbridge

carriages for this have already been described in the previous chapter and they also made up the last train of the day north, the 4.15pm ex-Dundalk. Prior to World War I this train crossed the mail at Maguiresbridge, the only case I can find of carriages occupying the two platforms there at the same time and also making a good connection to Fivemiletown. From 1920 the Kingstown boat was arriving later, so the mail ex-Dundalk began a departure time of 8.45am, which lasted till World War II, crossing the 7.20am ex-Derry at Clones. On its return trip, at 2.35pm ex-Derry, its name of the 'boat train' lasted until the line closed, though strictly speaking a reference to the Greenore route, whose passenger service ceased in the mid-'twenties. Prior to World War I a through DNGR coach ran from Derry to Greenore on the 2.35pm, by 1924 composed only of three clerestory bogies: K.3 3rd, tri-compo *55* (or occasionally *10*) and a van of type M.1, probably *258*.

All through Dundalk-Derry trains had bogie stock by 1920, the 10.30am ex-Dundalk being the next passenger arrival at Enniskillen and a busier train than the 8.45. The van on this was of type L.1, such as *246* and at the other end the through Dublin-Derry coach. For a time *72* was on this, but as more J.4 type were built it was invariably one of these. One K.3 (at busy seasons two) provided the

The first J.4 151

111

main 3rd class accommodation and the compo was, for a lengthy period, either *35* or *36*, very similar to *55* but with more 3rd class accommodation. The 10.30 crossed the 11.10 ex-Derry at Bundoran Junction and the carriages of this were of the same types, each set working alternate days.

The Dublin-Derry through coach had ceased to run via the long INW route by the 'thirties, but Enniskillen still had three through coach workings to Dublin, the vehicle being added at the front quite conveniently, as most trains changed engines in any case. So J.4 type *43, 44, 91, 151* and *217* became very well known to the shunters there. In 1933, for instance, *151* was going out on the 7.35am each morning, leaving Dublin again on the 6.45pm. *43* and *44* were working alternate days, one on the 1.35pm ex-Enniskillen and the other on the 3.15pm ex-Dublin. *91* was based in Dublin, being attached to the 9am ex-Dublin and returning on the boat train. By 1937 *44* was on this 9am job and *91* and *217* spent each night at Enniskillen, one being on the 9.30am back 3.15, and the other on the 1.35pm back 6.40pm. The following summer *91* and *217* were working alternate days on the 11am ex-Bundoran (3¼ miles less than the Derry-Dublin run via Portadown) and the 9.30 ex-Enniskillen.

Over the years Enniskillen's station buildings were usually graced by a few top-ranking GNR officials making their headquarters there, a situation which at times may have been irritating to an independent-minded stationmaster. Prior to and during the 'twenties, for instance, there was the bowler hatted Inspector W.J. McIntyre, in charge of No.4 of the four Traffic Inspector's districts, which covered the Irish North from Carrickmacross to Derry. Then there was W.H.C. Stone, B.A., B.A.I., who had a liking for doing much of his inspection work, as one of the GNR's two district engineers, from the footplate of an engine. Later he was to be the GNR's civil engineer based in Dublin. N.J. Steele (brother of George, the driver at Belfast) and then G.A. Allely were stationmasters in the 'twenties, the latter a strict little man (salary £285 p.a.). Then McIntyre was given the job, followed by Adam Gray.

The men regarded Gray as a 'great outside man'. In other words he was very seldom in his office, liking nothing better than to drive the shunting engine about the yard. Even during his earliest days in charge of Leitrim station he had eagerly awaited the arrival of the daily goods so that he himself could perform the shunts required. When not actually driving at Enniskillen he preferred to watch shunting from a footplate or signal cabin.

From 1922 Enniskillen had also a Loco foreman instead of Bundoran, and when the same year Dundalk produced 25 ton brake van No.54, the old one was supplied for the new foreman as his office. Possibly the fact that the Bundoran branch had to be closed for three months in 1920 had suggested Enniskillen as a more suitable place.

A major source of anxiety for both agent and foreman at Enniskillen was the cattle traffic from west of Ireland fairs such as Boyle, transferred at Coolooney to the SLNCR, who at times performed miracles in working the wagons to Enniskillen. Most of them were then attached either to the 'shipper' or to a special for the boat at Derry. Cattle wagons arrived by SLNCR in goods trains, in cattle specials and attached to passenger trains. The signalmen in the south cabin, who had also control of the 'Sligo' section to Florencecourt, were at times quite appalled at the motley collection of carriages and wagons (cattle and coal) which could arrive without tail-board or lamp, so that the guard had always to be asked if the train was 'clear and correct'.

One of the best known shunters in the 'Sligo yard', rough, tough Bob Gault was one day run down by a SLNCR engine, driven by Tom McGilloway. Gault just walked off and up to the hospital where his arm was amputated. The cattle which arrived off the SLNCR line were often in a sorry state long before they reached Fermanagh. To prevent the weaker beasts being trampled upon by those still able to stand, 'ambulance' wagons were in readiness at Enniskillen for them to be kept separate for the remainder of their journey to the ports. Their tails were pulled, or water was poured into their ears to bring them to their feet and prevent them dying. One day Adam Gray, in an immaculate suit and shirt, was viewing this noisy proceeding when a wagon door burst open and he received the benefit of most of the filth within. As the shunters stared he quickly recovered to say, 'Go on! Laugh! I know you're glad'. But in fact their satisfaction would have been but momentary for few stationmasters inspired morale amongst his staff by energetic example as did this man. He seemed to be everywhere and even such a simple omission as not wearing a uniform cap would be noted at once, as would the unforgiveable fault of missing a door handle improperly turned. More than one man, wondering where Gray had got to and ringing Compton in the cabin for information, received a rude shock when Adam himself answered.

The coal firm of S. Lockington & Company, well established at Newry and Dundalk and in evidence as far afield as Bundoran, had two sidings near the Sligo dock at Enniskillen, where James Maguire sold coal off their wagons. The door of a train arriving at the SLNCR platform on 14.8.28 injured GNR porter Pat Creegan. His ambition had been to be a signalman at Enniskillen like his father, but, as after the 1933 strike the only job on offer there was storeman, Pat gave up the railway. An enthusiastic chorister, he always claimed to have 'discovered' that famous Irish tenor, Josef Locke.

It was usually Tommy (the 'Whacker') Woods who collected tickets at Enniskillen barrier and also made occasional 'raids' on the trains. In the booking office was Miss Troughton, bespectacled and rather frail of physique but a woman of some force of character as well as being a most efficient clerk. The men's view was that 'you daren't look at her' and certainly Paddy Martin came off much the worse when John Holland made a show of having his pay packet in his hand, so Paddy went to the office looking for his. Another well known member of the gentler sex at the station was Kate Murphy at the bookstall. She had formerly had the same job at Bundoran and was to marry driver J.J. Kelly and have a fireman son-in-law, Kevin Love.

Enniskillen down platform with Sam Lee on footplate of Ps 73

Enniskillen regularly used the tracks through the passenger station, and especially the middle road, for marshalling goods trains, just as Drogheda did. The 'shipper' left from the down platform and even in later days, when routed via Clones, this platform was still used. The circular tour for the SG3 of the 9pm goods ex-Belfast (via Omagh) had a precedent during the 'twenties in its tendency to leave signal cabins with unbalanced staffs. During that period *153* and *154*, alternate nights, worked the 9pm forward from Omagh to Enniskillen. Then next evening, with the same Belfast crew, the QG took over the 5.25pm Derry-Clones at Enniskillen and finished with the 9.20pm goods Clones-Belfast.

Goods guards at Enniskillen included John Sheridan, who stuck rigidly to the rules, and Wattie Brown, pale and rather ill-tempered. He rarely did any passenger work and possibly just as well, for he fought with almost every railwayman in the area as well as many customs officers. McKnight or McMaster would probably arrive on the Derry goods. As soon as possible McKnight's van would be shunted against the stop block so that the day's shunting should not disturb his sleep there. Brake vans were possibly his greatest passion and he liked nothing better than to be controlling from the rear a long goods over undulating track. There was no chance of a hot bearing on his van for he oiled and maintained it meticulously. But should a newly painted ex-shops van arrive on the Dundalk goods he might be tempted to try it out that evening. Best known vans to pass through his hands were *49, 64* and *65*. The old *64* of 1894 had been retired in 1924 to act as customs hut at Kesh and her successor was one of five excellent 25 ton vans built in Belgium, one of which (*42*) still survives at RPSI headquarters, Whitehead, Co. Antrim. *49* and *65* were also good 25 ton vans but built at Dundalk.

Passenger guards at Enniskillen included Jack Ellis and Barney McIlroy, both rather fussy and excitable and Billy McKee, just the opposite. To complete the quartet of men most likely to be in charge of the boat train into Dundalk was Herbie Wilson, who lived just beyond Gortaloughan Halt. At the World War I period he had been signalman at Ballyshannon but then went off to France. The 3.10pm mixed to Clones could sometimes exceed 20 vehicles, slow progress for the school children who were its main patrons. A Clones guard had charge of this, often Hughie Kearns. Rather crabbed in manner normally, his reaction to children was quite different. He seemed to know each of them personally, referring to them as 'my wee ducks'.

Best known Enniskillen signalmen were George Henderson, Joe Kirk, a bachelor who lived in Mill Street, and Jimmy Compton who would respond to criticism from the shunters with 'Ye mouth ye!' One day he forgot himself sufficiently to pull points whilst *101* was passing over them but minor derailments were by no means uncommon at Enniskillen. Rather unusual was its bell at the ticket barrier beside the bookstall on the 500ft down platform, often rung by foreman Billy Noble or Ned Flanagan to indicate the right-away, the curve tending to obscure guard or driver's view. Noble had served through the 1914-18 war before becoming a railwayman and his constant worry was delay to any train. When this seemed imminent he would say to the guilty party, 'Sonny, you'll sink the whole place!' At one period brake compo *202* of type J.3 was the carriage usually commandeered to make up a train if the railcar failed. Otherwise it was spare, but Noble would send the carriage cleaners on their way each day with the warning, 'Don't forget *202*!'

The engine shed at Enniskillen, for most of its existence, seems to have been mainly for the job of stabling engines belonging to other sheds. Usually, however, it also had a few of its own, such as, during the World War I period, a J class (*15* and *19* both had a spell there) and a 0—6—0 for shunting. Prior to 1920 *149* was

114

J class 118 in black livery, and unnamed. Prior to 1914 this engine was known as Rose and after 1921, when sold to the SLNCR, it became Blacklion

probably the best known of these but was transferred to Newry in the mid-'twenties. In 1931 it was decided to sell this engine to the chronically short SLNCR, so Enniskillen saw her again, but it took the old 0—6—0 a week to make the journey, spending several days at Clones en route for a boiler maker to attend to leaking tubes. But generally the A class was well liked on the GNR and should have been more useful to Manorhamilton than J class *118/9*, received there in 1921.

Probably never as popular as the A class and decidedly less pretty after rebuilding, in my view, were the slightly larger AL class. The first two of these, *36* and *59*, were constructed by Beyer Peacock in 1893, two years after the last A class, *33*, and by the time the class of eleven was complete, Dundalk, as was the case with several other classes, had turned out some also, *32*, *29* and *55* being their 13th, 14th and 15th locomotive buildings. Rebuilding of the AL class, with 4ft 6 diameter unsuperheated boilers, commenced with *56* in 1914 and they had by now lost their names, which were, like the A class, mainly those of Irish counties. One, however, *29*, was named *Enniskillen*, curiously the only member of this class, except *36*, that I never saw there at any time, but to compensate, there was the SLNCR 0—6—4 tank so named. For the shed's last twenty years at least one of the AL class was an essential part, and the north side of the station was seldom without *32*, *56*, *59* or *140*. Other 0—6—0s there, usually on shed waiting to work the night goods, were prior to 1930, Derry PG and QG types. Later in time these were NQG class and then LQG, as well as a SG3 from Belfast, and another (or LQG) from Dundalk for the early morning goods.

Early in the 'twenties Enniskillen's two passenger engines *42* and *46* seem to have set a standard of cleanliness high even for those halcyon days. Dan Sweeney, the senior driver, had *42* with extended smokebox and still showing signs of green paint. *46*, like *42*, had still the small cab and was the property of driver John O'Toole, a County Louth man. O'Toole, more commonly known as 'Johnny Toal', had something of the same standing at Enniskillen as other great names of the 'twenties, such as Ryan, McBennett, McGuone and Hobson, had at other sheds. At Omagh he had for years fired to Barney Duffy on the Dundalk run and had kept *43* and then *197* in spotless condition. New driving appointments had to be made at Enniskillen after the incident at Berry's so O'Toole, who had joined the railway in 1903 (like the two Sams of Derry, Martin and Young), received his whilst in his early thirties. O'Toole did not wear overalls. No one was likely to get dirty on his engine and his usual dress was a blue jacket and ordinary trousers. Sandy of hair and somewhat

115

excitable, he did not permit his fireman to smoke, and his habit of coming hard against his train could be disconcerting to the shunters—though they admired his usual fast approach past the South cabin followed by a smart stop. O'Toole was said to be a GNR shareholder and to have considerable house property in Enniskillen. He seemed to prefer the company of the Enniskillen carriage examiner, Jimmy McGraw, to any other.

When 42 went to the 'shops to have the extended smokebox removed (the Phoenix superheater had gone as early as 1914) 44 became Dan Sweeney's engine for a spell. The day Dan died he was out exercising his greyhound, known as 'Engine 44'. Indeed to my mind nothing is more evocative of the Enniskillen scene than that PP class, to me always striding 'big' engines; but to a main line guard who once shared my satisfaction with a very smart effort by 44, she was 'a handy wee toy'. Certainly for the next thirty years and more 12, 25 (a great favourite of O'Toole's), 42, 43 and 44 were amongst the best known engines working north of Enniskillen. This seems an appropriate point at which to consider in more detail a class of engine which continued to be built for fifteen years, to become the largest tender type, numerically, on the GNR.

The period of building the PP class corresponds very closely to that of Clifford's own career as Locomotive Engineer, each batch of PP having some minor difference until Glover, to his great credit, rebuilt them into a standard in which the only real difference was that a gradually decreasing few retained the smaller 4ft 3 boiler. Easily mistaken for a PP were those four members of the P class with 6ft 7 driving wheels, but their firebox was 5 in. shorter. For some years their cylinders also were less, but eventually all P and PP engines had the same size as the 4—4—2 tanks and the U and UG classes, 18 x 24 in.

The 1905 pair 106-7 seem to have been built especially for Belfast-Derry services, so probably were never able fully to justify the most dramatic names of any given to the PP engines, Tornado and Cyclone. They were the first to have sandboxes under the platforms; another innovation to become standard was their metallic packing. 45-6, also with names suggestive of a fierce wind, benefitted from another improvement, the strap big end; then, two years later in 1911, came seven more to complete the class. These included the only two of the PP type to be built at Dundalk. Apart from a slight reduction in tubes, 25 and 43 were identical with 45-6 and were named, with scrupulous fairness, after Dublin's and Belfast's great rivers. Beyer Peacock supplied the other five engines, four of them named after the provinces of Ireland as had been old UR 2—4—0s, built by the same firm in 1863. As early as 1914 most had lost these nameplates. Some other aspects did not last long either. All had steel instead of brass tubes, as well as extended smokeboxes. 12 and 42 had, in addition, Phoenix superheaters which could also be fitted to 44,50 and 129. These three had exhaust injectors, but 12 and 42 had feed water heaters with LSWR type steam pumps. Six years later the rebuilding of the 1896/98 batches with 4ft 6 boilers commenced, with the result that 70-1 and 74-7 were banned from the Clones-Omagh line until its bridges had been rebuilt. The superheating policy of the 'twenties was applied to all the PP class, commencing with the 1905-11 engines—of which all except 45 and 107 at first retained their 4ft 3 boilers. When their turn came these two received the larger boiler, which the earlier engines already had. By the end of World War II all were fitted with the larger boiler except 129, which still had the 4ft 3 type when withdrawn.

Most enginemen tended to compare the PP class unfavourably with the U class, stating that the former did not suit the stopping trains which they worked on. But recorders will confirm that the PP class usually made excellent times between stations and kept their feet magnificently. The only drawback to cause the amateur to hesitate about a footplate trip was the unnerving manner in which the PP engines bounced along on their springs. Today, nearly fifteen years after the last of these old ladies (74) hauled a train, I can still hear that steady, rather thin exhaust, especially evocative of those summer occasions when a station foreman could confidently expect them to take double their ideal load of four bogies.

Presumably George Forsyth, O'Toole's fireman in the early 'twenties, had been involved in the Berry affair, for he was not promoted to driver until over fifty. He died about 1930 only a short time after attaining that rank. By then the more junior Enniskillen drivers were two nephews of Dan Sweeney, George and Johnny, as well as Matt Byrne of Drogheda and Tommy Thompson of Belfast. Thompson, like several other young men at Adelaide in 1914, served in World War I and, unlike them, in 1975 is hale and hearty still. S. Downey received mention for conspicuous bravery in 1916, while M. McPoland was killed in action. That same year C.H. Slator, GNR civil engineer from 1939, was awarded the Military Cross and the Royal Engineers had G.T. Glover as a Lieut. Colonel in France.

Until 1933 three Dundalk crews lodged over at Enniskillen each night after working the 4.10am and 12.55pm goods down the Irish North and the 7.55pm passenger ex-Dundalk. By 1930 the Enniskillen top link had three passenger turns. On the first they took the previous night's Derry engine and worked the 7.35am to Derry, returning at 11.15am. On the second, one of their own engines was used to work the 11.20am to Derry, returning at 2.40pm on the boat train. At Enniskillen this was replaced by the 11.15am engine, now in charge of the third crew. They went as far as Clones with it and then came off, turned and worked the 4.15pm ex-Dundalk as far as Bundoran Junction, where they exchanged footplates with the Derry men on the 5.15pm. This returned them to base, a 0-6-0 usually taking the 5.15 forward to Clones.

U class 196 at Enniskillen about 1916. At the smokebox door is driver Quigley of Dundalk and on the footplate Enniskillen's carriage examiner, McGraw. The man to his left is said to be S.C. Little, later General Manager of the SLNCR, and with the shunting pole is shunter John Sheridan, later an Enniskillen guard.

On 28.9.32 a flaw was revealed in this arrangement, but I imagine it was an exception. When *113* reached Clones from Dundalk, with the 4.15, the 2.40 had not arrived; and by the time *73* had come in and turned (allowed 15 mins for this operation), it was 6pm (20 mins late). No doubt the advent of the new compounds was responsible at this period for providing several INW trains with QL class 4—4—0s, as happened again three days later at Enniskillen when *114* took over the 11.15. This engine, despite an overhaul in 1931, was withdrawn at the end of 1932, and one reason may have been her average coal consumption 41.9lbs, compared with the U class. Even *73* in 1932 had an excellent average of 33.7lbs, having been superheated in October of the previous year.

THE POST-STRIKE PERIOD

The timetable of 11.9.33 deprived Enniskillen of little compared with that of the late 'twenties. There was, however, now no passenger service to Dundalk between the 7.35am and 1.35pm (11.15 ex-Derry), for the 7.20 ex-Derry ran only as far as Clones. Similarly, the boat train was the last service towards Clones. Soon the traditional 9.30am service to Dublin was resumed but 4.45pm remained the last train to Clones until the railbus there began to provide a 1.15pm Dundalk-Clones-Omagh and in the evening was able to serve Clones with a very useful 7.40pm. On Saturday nights this shuddering machine actually returned to Enniskillen again at 8.40 so that Enniskillen-Clones folk, having an evening shopping or at the cinema, could return late on a 9.40pm. This railbus also implemented the new policy on many other lines of picking up at level crossings, fourteen in all being available between Clones and Ballinamallard.

The new feature of Enniskillen workings was that the crews there were now going through to Dundalk as well as Derry. The policy of building up this shed had been continued and at least ten crews were required each day. Instead of the pre-strike arrangement of only one passenger train east being worked by Enniskillen men (as far as Clones), they now went through to Dundalk on three trains, the other one, the 9.30, still being worked by Omagh men. The two other turns in the link were the 7.35am to Derry, which they still retained and the 12.40 (10.12am ex-Dundalk) which they worked to Derry, returning with the 5.30pm. Between Derry and Enniskillen a superheated PP was now almost inevitable, a Dundalk U class being usually on east bound trains except the boat train, whose Enniskillen PP returned on the 7.57pm ex-Dundalk. In the summer of 1934 I recall seeing the 4.25pm ex-Dundalk arrive at Enniskillen behind *25*, departing with *27* at 6.52 for Derry, this making a good connection at Omagh for Belfast. While awaiting this train I had noted, to complete the numerical sequence, *26* in the shed, it being prior to the days when foreman Boland looked askance at every shed visitor. Other PPs observed on the 4.25 were *76* (11.9.37) and *107* (12.12.38), but by that period Dundalk quite often turned out a UG on the 10.12, for instance *78* on 14.12.38. *82* was probably the most regular of this class to be used on INW passenger trains, a new type of 0—6—0 for Enniskillen crews and a far from popular one.

During the 'twenties, as this shed gained in importance, firemen from Belfast, Derry, Omagh and Dundalk had arrived to take up driving appointments. Now, due to post-strike redundancies, there were more strangers. In the goods link there was Bob Graham, who was to finish back at Banbridge, 'the scuffler' Gillespie from Belfast and Johnny McManus from Cootehill. Bill Watters from Dublin now worked in the shunting link with Johnny 'Scaldy' Sweeney. The pre-1933 service to Bundoran was restored in 1934 when a new railcar, C.1, replaced *70*. Two firemen who had joined the railway in 1913, J. McCartney and B. Maguire, were appointed to drive the railcar; though in the summer *70*, still kept in reserve in Bundoran shed,

118

came back into daily service. John Fitzsimons and Paddy Martin took up residence there to work the 11am and 5.45pm with *70*, replaced by *52* in 1939. These two trains and their return workings from the junction at 1.25 and 7.30pm were permitted to have four-wheeled vehicles next to the engine, something which the GNR did not allow on their other lines. In the winter, when the railcar catered for passengers, a service was still provided for fitted vans by the 'vacuum' train, worked out of Bundoran at 11am by the engine and crew of the 6.15am goods, Enniskillen-Bundoran. A second crew from Enniskillen took over this engine (often *103*) for the 1.30 'vacuum' back to Bundoran and then took charge of the 3.30pm goods. When egg traffic from Irvinestown offered after the 'vacuum' train had gone, there was an instruction that the 'vacuum' engine, after arriving at Bundoran Junction at 12.32, was to go back the 3½ miles for any which might still be loaded, in time to connect with the 2.45pm 'shipper' ex-Enniskillen. These 7 ton vans (type Y.9)— of which there were nearly fifty still in service even by World War II, many going back to the 1881-8 period—were ideally suited for small commodities, if useless for anything else.

Naturally, with the GNR trying to develop the seaside resorts it had (all less popular than Portrush or Bangor), the Bundoran Express was giving both Belfast and Dublin a good service to Donegal. At that period the accent was on scenery and sea air and not, as became the fashion later, on giving travel facilities to those with a leaning towards religious pilgrimage. The train was still worked from Clones, where through coaches from Dublin (*44* and *279* attached to the 9am) and *43*, off the 9.20am ex-Belfast, were combined, to be hauled invariably by a U class. There was no headboard or even official name at this period but those who have sneered at it being described as an express take no account of the engine's size and the difficulty of producing any kind of high average speed over such a route.

A run on 29.8.32, timed by R.N. Clements, provides very useful proof of how the train's performance at that period compared with later days. *197* had 134 tons and despite 58 mph before Lisnaskea and 60 mph down into Enniskillen, ¾ min was lost on the 32 min timing to a stop there (in the 'fifties it was given 40 mins to *pass* Enniskillen). With staff exchange necessary at four intermediate points, the timing of the 'thirties was obviously quite sharp for 22½ miles, as was the next stretch to Pettigo, 23 miles in 36 mins, including the crawl round Bundoran Junction and at least one other staff exchange. After stopping at Beleek and Ballyshannon, the arrival time in the early 'thirties was 1.53pm, having taken 128 mins from Clones and 4 hours 38 mins from Dublin. By 1938 the Enniskillen-Pettigo timing had been cut by 2 mins and arrival time at Bundoran was 1.35pm, but the overall time from Dublin was just about the same, though now under 2 hours from Clones. The express left Bundoran for Omagh at 3.15, but whereas the engine, denuded of Dublin carriages at Bundoran Junction and Belfast ones at Omagh, returned light to Clones at the early period, in the later 'thirties it was used for the 5.20pm passenger train Omagh-Clones, which even served a few of the level crossings just as the railcar did on this train in the winter. In 1931 the return express had left Bundoran at 3pm; in 1925 it was 2.45pm, running non-stop from Kesh to Omagh. Back in 1913 Bundoran departure time had been much the same (2.40pm) after a 4 hour 47 min run from Dublin.

During the 1933 strike Enniskillen-Clones had been one of the pieces of line left without any service and there was no doubt that as this ceased to be the recognized route to Belfast, due to the Border, it had less passenger traffic than formerly. But as a few good little towns were involved, the GNR made some effort to provide a fair service, especially when the railcars could give a late evening train cheaply out of Enniskillen. They also involved these stations in their famous 'Newell' excursions to Belfast. Mainly during winter and sometimes as frequently as every three weeks, these trips promised a return of the fare by the store in Royal Avenue, if a certain sum were spent there.

Basically the excursion service was given by a 8.10am special from Enniskillen via Omagh which returned at 8pm, with a portion for Derry, worked from Omagh by a Derry engine which came up to meet the special. All other stations in Northern Ireland could be served by ordinary late night trains and the 7.10pm Cavan portion, for instance, left Belfast with a W van for Enniskillen, packed with the day's parcelled purchases, this being attached at Clones to the 8pm ex-Dundalk. So an Enniskillen engine and crew usually worked the special, the crew booking off at Belfast and so making nothing for the day except their 3/6d expenses.

Quite a variety of small 4—4—0s thus paid an unusual visit to Belfast; they included in 1937, for instance, *12* and *42* with J. Sweeney on 24 February and 30 April. P. McKeown had *42* on 10 February and R. Graham had *197* on 17 May, *70* having appeared on 15.12.36. Usually it was up to Enniskillen to find five or six bogies but sometimes the train started from Clones and served the east Fermanagh stations that way, Enniskillen crews taking over *45* for the rest of the day. Even the Bundoran branch stations were encouraged to sample Royal Avenue fare, for the railcar ran back empty from Bundoran to the junction to form a 10.37pm connection from the special, due back at Bundoran at 11.53pm. To Belfast the ordinary 6.30 service made a not entirely perfect connection into the 8.10 special on a winter morning, so Donegal travellers had a very long day. Enniskillen-Newtownbutler folk, by using the 7.25am ex-Enniskillen, were also able to enjoy a similar excursion to Clerys in Dublin.

At Newtownbutler the two best known personalities for many years were almost certainly Johnny McLaughlin and F.C.G. Chapman. The latter man, railway enthusiast and photographer, was in charge of the customs post at the station for almost its entire existence of thirty-five years. Settling in happily at Newtownbutler in 1923, he never seemed to have the slightest desire to return to his native England. Almost certainly he knew as much about railway activities at the station as the staff there.

From trains using the station Johnny McLaughlin seemed an inevitable part of

Johnny McLaughlin at his Newtownbutler 'office'

the scenery there. But that grey soft hat was confusing and even after many journeys one could not be sure if Johnny was a railwayman, a customs official or just a passenger. In fact he had been there since 1917 and I understand that in those early days, as a concession to authority, he did wear a uniform marked 'caller off'. Johnny was present when the customs post was created, but stationmaster Doherty being ill missed the event. Well into his seventies today, he is there still, in a retired six-wheel coach on the deserted platform, filling in customs forms with the utmost expertize beside the handsome station house where lives T.W. Moore, stationmaster there at the closure. Johnny recalls only one derailment in all those years. The 4.20am goods ex-Dundalk was in the loop, crossing the 7.20am ex-Derry, as often happened, though booked to cross at Lisnaskea. Guard Wattie Brown, impatient as usual, shouted to the driver to start shunting, but although the 7.20 was in the platform the points had not yet been altered for the loop and the big 0–6–0 was derailed at them, putting the line out of action for most of the day.

At Maguiresbridge, instead of customs complications, the trans-ship shed between the two gauges kept the staff busy, though less so than at Tynan at the CVR's other end. A good local passenger service was still provided in 1937 to enable folk in the valley to reach Enniskillen. The 8.5am ex-Fivemiletown made a smart 3 min connection, so that one could be in 'Skintown' at 8.54.

If Lisbellaw's business was possibly least of the four, its staff nevertheless kept the station in magnificent trim. Like Trillick, large cement letters alongside beds of roses and sweet pea gave a distinctive touch to the name. Signalman Alec Lindsay had no cabin, the staff being issued from the booking office. Decent, gruff and a little deaf, Alec later had two sons shunting at Enniskillen and he took a special pride in something rather rare today, spotlessly clean toilets. On one occasion he was waiting to present mop and bucket to a passenger who on a previous visit had failed to leave them as he had found them. On another a Yankee visitor had been criticising the poor amenities, as he considered them, at both village and station. He next asked for the toilets and Alec indicated the notice 'Gentlemen' along the platform. 'Pay no attention to that,' he said, 'just go on in.' Henderson's woollen mill was the main source of income for both railway station and village. The station

The 3.10pm Enniskillen-Clones at Lisbellaw

sidings, awkward to operate due to the gradient, were opened from the staffs. In an emergency trains could be crossed by using the loop but it was a cumbersome business as the keys on the staffs, necessary to open the ground frames, were in possession of the approaching trains.

Three-quarters of a mile from Enniskillen, where the road to Tempo crossed over the railway at the Killynure bridge (155), a siding was added during World War II to provide Enniskillen's sorely tried shunters with somewhere to store surplus coal and cattle wagons. Permanent way man Tom Ford kept a plot near the bridge. His brother Paddy was Wordie's carter at the station, handling beer barrels and other bulky loads with consummate skill and strength. Enniskillen's railwaymen did most of their drinking at McNamee's Railway Hotel. Almost certainly one of the best customers was driver Johnny McManus, after whom a pit near the shed was named when McManus fell in.

One of the greatest personalities at Enniskillen was J.J. Kelly who fired there for nearly twenty years, until in the early years of World War II he and Steele surmounted the block in promotion caused by the strike, and became drivers. Kelly's career had ceased almost before it had begun, for after a few weeks at Derry shed, Jimmy, not the most docile of men, had a disagreement with the foreman there and was sacked. So Kelly made his way to Dundalk and put his case to the little Welshman there, A.W. Denniss, the GNR's Running Superintendent, who immediately re-employed him as cleaner. For a number of years Kelly saw very little of Enniskillen, until the occasion of a VIP Grand Tour of the railway—which made a break one evening at the Great Northern Hotel, Bundoran. He was sent from Dundalk to clean *200* for her driver, 'lonely' McGuone, who invariably demanded an almost impossible standard and would stand at his engine watching the procedure. But Locomotive Inspector Andy Moore was so pleased with Kelly's effort that he was given an extra five shillings (more than two days' pay at that period) as well as two days' leave at Enniskillen.

During the 'twenties Kelly had firing spells with both Enniskillen's top drivers. He had *44* looking a treat for Dan Sweeney, and Glover, taking a trip with them, was greatly intrigued with Kelly's lavatory-style attachment to the whistle. In Jimmy's opinion O'Toole was incapable of seeing a joke but some of that martinet's views about a spotless footplate seem to have rubbed off, for wee Willie Johnson, one of the three signalmen there, used to ride on the footplate from Bundoran Junction and as often as he spat Kelly carefully hosed it away. He did admit to me that O'Toole was the best engineman and hardest runner he had ever worked with.

When Bob Forster came to Enniskillen from the closed shed at Armagh in 1933, Kelly at last got the kind of partner to whom he could really warm. Forster, who took on the thankless job of collecting the union dues for the area, was a decent, tolerant, rather childish man. Kelly's sharp tongue on the other side of the footplate provided him with constant entertainment. One day at Culloville wee Barney McElroy, the guard, frantically waved his flag but the train did not move. As he came very crossly up to the engine Forster, sitting there as usual with the ash of his cigarette the major part, chuckled as Kelly said, 'We have to obey the rules up here, you know'. Indeed, rather unusually, the signals were still against them. On 24.10.38 they had QL *113* for the 4.25pm ex-Dundalk and were going well at Doohamlet when the connecting-rod fractured, but fortunately went forward instead of back. Old Bob must have felt he bore a fairly charmed life for he had already survived this rather unusual occurrence with *106*, between Dromore Road and Fintona Junction. I am told that when he died abroad, not so very long ago, he was ninety-two.

Just a few days senior to Kelly, and therefore usually the other top link fireman,

122

A county town's GNR turntable in a rural setting

was William Steele, always called 'Charlie', a brother of the Cavan fireman. When 'Charlie' became a driver a box was necessary to help him reach the regulator for he was unusually small. Another fireman of the 'twenties was Gussie, Kelly's brother, later a very hard runner but a somewhat wild fellow off-duty. Big Paddy McKeown of Dundalk, who both fired and drove at Enniskillen, was one of the few men shed-labourer Mickey Gallagher feared. Gallagher's footplate days at Omagh were over but he had still an enviable mechanical flair and was also noted for his dramatic skill and as a clever imitator of bird calls. Another fireman at Enniskillen for a time, Joe Thompson, did not enjoy his exile from Belfast. 'Any news?' was his query every morning as he awaited the transfer he had requested. There were also among the enginemen no less than three Armstrongs and more were to be recruited during World War II.

George Sweeney's transfer to Derry was said to have been due to his derailing 59 at Enniskillen turntable. Foreman George Henry was absent attending a rugby international on the Saturday this happened but he was bound to enquire about a wagon smashed against a tree. So Sweeney had to do six months firing at Derry on the senior job, the mail, a tough assignment for a middle-aged man.

BUNDORAN EXCURSION TRAFFIC

Sunday pay for the Bundoran shed cleaners was rare enough to be very welcome, but on some of the busiest weekends of each June-September period they may have felt that it was well and truly earned, with half a dozen engines to prepare for return trains in the evening whilst their crews enjoyed themselves in the town. The actual excursion parties made use of the GNR pavilion beside the station, which could accommodate 300 with hot or cold meals, according to which advertizing gimmick was applicable, 'bracing breezes' or 'warmed by the Gulf Stream'. During the 'twenties there was no Sunday Bundoran Express, but the increasing popularity of Sunday trips to this resort is evident in the arrival, during the summer timetable, of trains from Cavan at 11.17am, Derry at 11.58, Clones at 3.45pm and Omagh at 4.15, thus catering both for 'heathens' and mid-morning church-goers.

An interesting example of GNR enterprise is evident in the Sunday 9.30am ex-Belfast, with teacar attached, which for a short period in the early 'thirties was called the 'Tour of the Loughs train'. Here the rapidly expanding 'bus fleet was brought into the act, for after the train had arrived at Enniskillen at 12.30pm 'sun saloon coaches' took the excursionists for a tour of the lower Lough Erne as far as

123

An unusual class of engine to pass Maguiresbridge

Belleek. Thus were folk from farther afield introduced to the delights of Fermanagh, before the GNR lost their buses in Northern Ireland in 1935. The train continued to run by the Clones route and was interesting in that it brought with it a class of engine rare to the Maguiresbridge area, usually Qs class *122* in 1935, for instance.

The scenic element was reintroduced in 1937 when this train now left Belfast on Sundays at 9.50am. By cutting out the Maze and Moira stops and reducing slightly the wait at Clones, the 9.50 was booked into Enniskillen at 12.39pm, faster than any train by the now regular Omagh route. At 12.42 it set off for Bundoran, due 2.15pm, after calling at every station between Lurgan and Bundoran. In addition an extra train from Derry now made the total Sunday traffic into Bundoran six trains. Rather than use an Enniskillen or Clones engine the Belfast one worked right through and during 1937's summer, P class *72* was given a D.1 tender for this duty, which involved a quite exceptional round trip of 269 miles. Seldom less than 6 bogies meant keeping the boiler at full pressure for at least 4½ hours, but the steeper banks of the Omagh route and the nuisance of turning would have been even worse. One Sunday driver Mick Connolly had no less than 8 bogies for the small 4–4–0, which meant pulling up again at many stations en route. So fireman Jimmy Shields had a rough time but after Clones came an unexpected respite. Due to their lateness, a Dundalk special in charge of Vincent Donnelly had got ahead but his engine was steaming badly so *72* waited at every block post. For the remainder of the summer one or other of the first two UG 0–6–0s was used on the 9.50 as this was exactly the kind of work on restricted branches they were intended for, though they too, with 8 bogies, might have been in some trouble along the 'Orange Hall' bank on the way home.

By now there was yet another return train for the Derry direction on six Sundays and the customs men at Kesh had scarcely finished with one until Pettigo expected the next. Strict rationing in the north ensured that every such excursion during the war years was booked out. On one of these in 1940 Jack Shannon and J.L. Kidd were again routed via Clones. Shannon, a Randalstown man, was a nice fellow but somewhat nervous at times. His hefty big fireman had a huge amount of contraband on the footplate, successfully negotiated so far, though there was still Monaghan and Tynan to come, when they ran into Clones. Here the senior customs officer was a well known martinet, of whom most railwaymen had good cause to be wary. So Kidd was quite horrified to see Shannon and this man deep in conversation on the

124

platform as they stood, apparently looking at the engine. He was ready to put everything, at the first sign of danger, into the firebox but held back when he saw, surprisingly, Shannon laughing. A few moments later he learned that the two men had
just realized they had been at school together.

One of the most famous occasions at Bundoran was in the early 'twenties when
the annual staff excursion was directed at that resort, requiring four special trains.
On such a day it is no surprise that the great Bob Bruce, apparently passed for every
road, was in charge of one special, and Jimmy Hobson had another. Much more
junior drivers, Joe Young and George Steele, were in charge only as far as Omagh
of the other two specials, but they travelled forward in the train, naturally. Remem-
bering George many years later as a wonderfully sedate old driver on 87, tearing
down Kellystown bank at 75 mph, I can scarcely imagine him getting very drunk
that day at Bundoran. But that is exactly what did happen and he missed the first
train back to Omagh, which he was apparently booked to work forward. Bruce had
a P class, probably *104*, for the second train and made a very fast run in an attempt
to have Steele into Omagh in time. In fact Joe Young, always a decent if rather excitable man, had worked Steele's turn for him. At that period old 0—6—0s such as
137/8 were regularly received at Bundoran on Sunday excursions from Clones, sometimes with 13 six-wheelers, the limit for this branch.

As far as Belfast traffic to Bundoran is concerned I have mentioned so far only
the regular summer timetable trains. But advertized excursions were also run, mainly
on Sundays, one of which later came to be called 'The Hills of Donegal' as it involved
a 3½ hour run through that county on CDRJC metals, including the enchanting
Barnesmore Gap. Eighty mins of this were occupied with a stop at one of the least
appealing places in the county, Donegal itself, where a brochure promised meals
at reasonable charges at such delectable establishments as the Central Hotel in the
Diamond or Mrs Gallagher's in Main Street, not forgetting Mrs Meehan and her meat
teas in Castle Street. At 10.40am on Sundays a GNR corridor set with teacar
attached deposited these excursionists at Strabane. The engine, usually a Qs class,
then worked the empty train back to Omagh for the attention of an engine more
suitable for the restrictions of the Bundoran branch, which reached Ballyshannon
about 2.35pm, just 10 mins after the narrow gauge special had arrived at the CDRJC
station at the other side of the town. A GNR porter was sent to escort the excursionists across in time for the short run to Bundoran at 3pm, altogether a superb outing
for more than the railway enthusiast. This excursion ran about four times in the
summer and when it did not, a more direct trip, again via Omagh and costing 5/6d,
was usually available on Sundays, due into Bundoran at 11.40am.

WORLD WAR II

For the first couple of years the timetable for the Fermanagh area showed almost
no change, but there was more work for the staff and some tiresome regulations.
Due to Double Summer Time, the first passenger departure of the day from
Bundoran became 5.30am, quite a strain on those involved. One morning when
it was ready to leave and the guard, Peter Carty, had not appeared, the booking
clerk cycled four miles to stir the old man into action. Later in the day the
stationmaster, 'Snowdrop' Cunningham, asked the clerk to explain the entry on the
5.30 journal sheet, 'Train delayed 30 minutes booking passengers', so Carty had to
be contacted for a revised, more accurate version of what had transpired. Once
again Bundoran shed had an engine to light up each morning and Paddy Flynn at
Enniskillen suddenly found that his back injury had made a rapid recovery. So
Paddy Martin, who had been counting on the job, had to give way, on seniority, to

Up train at Kesh

the old driver, once more established at Bundoran shed.

White bread came to be regarded as a luxury south of the Border and young Percy Wray, relieving at Kesh, found his daily journey home to Ballyshannon, where his father was a CDRJC railcar driver, useful as a means of providing his home with some. The Kesh agent had the dubious privilege of also representing the NIRTB lorry service and the customs officer there, Jack Seaney, suspected one of these lorry drivers of smuggling. Thwarted at every turn and deciding to take it out on Percy one day, he stepped into his railcar, asked him his name (which he knew perfectly) and confiscated four white loaves. The next day, however, he returned them, having made the point that he had the authority.

The GNR had now a new General Manager, George B. Howden, previously civil and mechanical engineer; a less impartial attitude towards appointments became sometimes apparent. T.H. Algeo, controlling GNR buses in Dublin, did not have an easy time with P.A. Foley, the District Superintendent, and it was possibly

NQGs 38 being prepared for the night goods Enniskillen-Derry

Howden who suggested he apply for a transfer to the rail section. James Lockhart, Traffic Manager, refused the application on the grounds that Algeo had no railway experience but the brisk and somewhat ruthless Howden overruled this decision and had Algeo installed at Ballinamallard, where he soon proved a very popular stationmaster.

Many other new faces could be seen now on the railway as business increased. They included Tommy Redpath, redundant since 1933, but soon to become one of Enniskillen's most reliable engine drivers. There was also young Arthur Gribben, a master shunter. At Enniskillen he could be seen each night, lamp in hand, making up the goods for Derry and Belfast as well as the one next morning for Clones. Walking between two rakes of double coupled wagons, he would examine the destination label of each, and where it differed from its neighbour one coupling would be taken off to facilitate the actual shunting later.

Enniskillen men now worked the 9.30am (8.35 ex-Omagh) through to Dundalk and there was overtime here, for the return working was not until 4.28pm ex-Dundalk. Johnny McManus, however, probably lost money on such a turn, with so much time at a place where drinking facilities were excellent. He had had his own troubles, losing his wife when their house was burned down. Maybe such thoughts were occupying his mind one day on the 12.40, for at Dromore Road he had to inform the relief signalman there that they had come from Bundoran Junction without the staff, enough for dismissal on the spot. A phone call produced the information that the staff was indeed still sitting on a barrel on the platform, so it was cancelled and the whole matter hushed up. McManus was normally quite cautious about most of the regulations and was, for instance, usually reluctant to part with coal to a signalman. But when he returned that day with the 5.25pm ex-Derry he shouted to his fireman in that Cavan accent, so different from the cheerful singsong of Fermanagh, 'Give that man all the coal he wants'.

1941 saw the end of the CVR, so the little streets of Maguiresbridge ceased to have their 'central' station and the GNR one now had only a couple of signalmen and a 'man in charge'. Gone were the days when there had been a busy tranship

PPs 12 arrives at Dromore Road with train from Derry

127

shed with J.E. Smith head porter, but his son Ned still cycled daily to Enniskillen shed and would in due course become a driver there. The Bundoran branch, on the other hand, seemed to be thriving, with four passenger services in each direction, even in winter. The steam worked 11am ex-Bundoran, taking 103 mins, was still a very slow train with most stops as much as 5 mins. The railcar, however, made one run, the 4.28pm from the junction, in 72 mins, only one min faster than the J hauled 1.12pm of 1910 but 8 mins better than the 1.25pm of 1931.

In 1976 almost empty buses in the Enniskillen area do not encourage us to speculate too much upon how the GNR might fare there today. For cross channel journeys, folk now tend to use Aldergrove where half a century ago it would have been Dundalk for the Greenore steamer. The emphasis seems to be on turning Lough Erne into a paradise for holiday folk with expensive boating tastes. Gone indeed are the days when most of the islands there were inhabited and when, from some, smoke could be seen from a GNR train as it chugged its way through the woods of Castlecaldwell.

LOCOMOTIVE and CARRIAGE APPENDIX

Tables show the 204 engines of 1918 and include, where known, each engine's mileage for that year and the average coal consumption in pounds per mile. Their career after 1941 is not really a matter for this book, but withdrawal dates for all the 1918 engines are given, including the 101 (almost exactly half) which survived until 1958.to be divided between CIE and UTA, together with 51 engines built 1920-37 and another 15 outside our period, 1947-8. The period of the book is also the superheating era, with economies in water and coal consumption. Even though the enginemen thought Glover had ruined some engines, by the time he retired in 1934 a total of 85 engines had been rebuilt and superheated. Of the engines which survived after 1924 the only passenger engines not to be so treated were the BP and JT tank engines. The other engines which continued to use saturated steam were old 0–6–0s, all of which might well have been soon withdrawn, as most of them were, but for World War II. Also shunting tanks except QGTs.

CLASS	Tons	− cwt	Grate Area sq.ft	Cylinders 1918	Later	Driving wheels
0−6−0						
U.RLY	33	−−	13.9 16.1 (14²/3)	17x24		4ft 7 in
C	34	02	16.1	17x24		5ft
D	36	08	18.3	17x24		5ft 1½ in
E	37	00	16.1	17x24		5ft
A	34	06	15.1	17x24		4ft 7 in
B	33	18	15.1	17x24		4ft 7 in
AL	38	11	16.7	17x24		4ft 7 in
PG	*39	10	18.3	17½x24		4ft 7 in
QG	*41	10	19.9	17½x26	17¾x26	4ft 7 in
QLG	*45	03	19.9	18½x26	p/v 19x26	4ft 7½ in
NQG	*45	16	19.9	18x26	p/v 19x26	4ft 7 in
NLQG	*48	06	22.7	18½x26	QLG	4ft 7½ in
SG	48	19	22.9	19x26		5ft 1 in
SG2	48	19	22.9	19x26		5ft 1 in
2−4−0						
D&BJR	32	10		16x22		6ft
INWR	33	03	14.8	16x21		6ft
G	32	10	14.1	16½x22		5ft 7 in
H	33	10	14.8	17x22		6ft 1½ in
4−4−0						
J	35	15	14.1	17x22		5ft 7 in
P	*41	09	16.7	17x24	p/v 18x24	5ft 7 in
	43	10	16.7			6ft 7 in
PP	*41 to 46	12 to 10	18.3	17½x24 (some 18x24)	do	6ft 7 in
Q	*45	15	19.9	17½x26	18½x26 pv	6ft 7 in
QL	*49	10	22.1	17¾x26	do	6ft 7 in
S	52	02	22.9	19x26		6ft 7 in
S2	52	02	22.9	19x26		6ft 7 in
U	44	06	18.3	18x24		5ft 9 in
4−4−0T						
BT	31	10	11.3	14x18	570 galls 1½tons coal	4ft 7 in
BP	42	06	15.0	15x20	700 galls 1½tons coal	5ft
2−4−2T						
JT	45	13	14.1	16x22	1000galls 2 tons coal	5ft 7 in
4−4−2T						
T	*65	02	18.3	17⅛x24 pv 18x24	1700galls 3½ tons	5ft 9 in
0−6−2T						
QGT	55	06	19.9	18½x26	1250galls 2 tons	4ft 7 in
QGT2	60	−	21.3	do	do do	do
0−6−4T						
RT	56	−	16.3	17x24	1350galls 3 tons	4ft 3 in
0−4−0ST						
203	16	−	6.0	10x15	370galls 8 cwt	2ft 8½ in
0−6−0T						
204	28	10	10	15x20	730galls 18 cwt	3ft 4 in

* Heavier after superheating.

G N R   L O C O M O T I V E S   L I S T   1918

No.	Built	Class	1918 Mileage	Coal Consumption lbs per mile	S'heated	W'drawn
1	1887	BT	—	—	0-6-0T (1920)	1935
2	1887	BT	9456	34.0		1921
3	1888	BT	—			1921
4	1888	BT	7311	34.9	n	1921
5	1889	BT	4398	31.9	n	1921
6	1889	BT	21804	31.0	n	1920
7	1891	BT	4292	32.4	n	1920
8	1892	BT	—			1921
9	1911	NQG	32461	59.2	**1930	1959
10	1904	PG	30790	49.7	1925	1964
11	1903	PG	19588	49.8	1924	1959
12	1911	PP	22143	44.2	1930	1959
13	1902	JT +91	3308	79.1 †	n	1963
14	1902	JT +92	155	52.0 †	n	1956
15	1885	J	17843	35.2	n	1924
16	1885	J	31418	42.0	n	1924
17	1885	J	12749	39.8	n	1924
18	1885	J	7663	41.2	n	1924
19	1887	J	14585	41.3	n	1924
20	1887	J	8413	46.2	n	1921
21	1889	J	24937	43.1	n	1924
22	1908	RT	16934	46.0	n	1959
23	1908	RT	25171	42.7	n	1963
24	1910	QL	43751	44.4	1924	1957
25	1911	PP	20697	56.3	1927	1957
26	1880	B	19710	41.0	n	1931

No.	Built	Class	1918 Mileage	Coal Consumption lbs per mile	S'heated	W'drawn
27	1879	B	19981	44.7	n	1930
28	1888	A	29559	44.6	n	1956 d
29	1895	AL	939	45.8	n	1959
30	1877	B	24724	38.4	n	1925
31	1890	A	16581	43.4	††	1949
32	1894	AL	31858	40.9	n	1960
33	1891	A	23875	48.7	n	1959
34	1880	B	4972	35.7	n	1932
35	1894	AL	25582	43.0	n	1959
36	1893	AL	19709	40.9	n	1957
37	1876	E	18161	46.4	n	1948
38	1911	NQG	33629	62.8	1931	1960
39	1911	NQG	25382	59.2†††	1931	1959
40	1876	D ex-D&BJR	30210	48.6	n	1937
41	1872	D 21 do	2212409	56.2	n	1934
42	1911	PP	21831	47.1	1929	1960
43	1911	PP	21233	34.2	1928	1960
44	1911	PP	35203	38.8	1928	1960
45	1909	PP	16565	40.1	1928	1957
46	1909	PP	19828	32.9	1927	1959
47	1883	G	NIL		n	1921
48	1883	G	NIL		n	1921
49	1877	G	13414	38.4	n	1921
50	1911	PP	18918	45.3	1929	1960
51	1892	P 5'6"	25234	39.3	1925	1951
52	1892	do	24063	44.8	1923	1951

**= LQGNs 1945: † = (1920): †† = to SLNCR 1928: ††† = LQGNs 1956:

No.	Built	Class	Works No.	Weight	Renumbered	Withdrawn
53	1892	do	28208	50.5	1924	1951
54	1895	do	31800	36.8	1927	1951
55	1895	AL	8078	49.7	n	1961
56	1896	AL	34896	47.4	n	1960
57	1896	AL	18926	43.8	n	1959
58	1896	AL	31775	45.0	n	1959
59	1894	AL	25982	39.6	n	1959
60	1890	A	12719	42.6	n	1959
61	1883	A	˙9589	60.0	n	1935
62	1877	B	15021	36.5	n	1930
63	1877	B	21878	36.3	n	1930
64	1883	A +67	24393	42.5	n	1937
65	1877	B	16834	44.6	n	1930
66	1879	B+27 then 149	12597	50.0	n	1938
67	1877	B	21296	38.6	n	1930
68	1886	A	33779	52.2	n d	1948
69	1882	A	9897	45.3	n	1937
70	1896	PP	10553	51.3	1930	1957
71	1896	PP	18415	32.8	1930	1959
72	1895	P 6'6"	28502	40.6	1931	1959
73	1895	P 6'6"	40545	40.1	1931	1959
74	1896	PP	43573	46.3	1930	1963
75	1898	PP	22793	41.2	1931	1959
76	1898	PP	27650	39.7	1930	1959
77	1898	PP	29862	42.1	1931	1957
78	1908	LQG +119	34286	62.3	1929	1959
79	1882	A sold to SLNCR1940 +69			n	1959
80	1886	A	27690	36.9	n d	1936
81	1886	A	*	*	n d	1936
82	1892	P 6'6"	+27 42507	38.1	1932	1959
83	1892	P 6'6"	+26 18119	49.5	1931	1957
84	1881	H	29529	39.2	n	1932

No.	Built	Class	Works No.	Weight	Renumbered	Withdrawn
85	1881	H	23936	45.1	n	1932
86	1880	H	5718	51.4	n	1932
87	1880	H	17658	44.2	n	1932
88	1905	P 5'6"	17825	50.1	1923	1956
89	1905	P 5'6"	24422	45.0	1925	1956
90	1898	JT	4108	48.8	n	1957
91	1893	JT	NIL		n	1921
92	1893	BT	3351	40.4	n	1921
93	1895	JT Preserved	36001	43.9	n	1955
94	1896	JT	23875	35.7	n	1956
95	1898	JT	21775	46.8	n	1956
96	1885	BT	*	*	n	1921
97	1885	BT	*	*	n	1921
98	1905	QGT	26238	54.5	1932	1957
99	1905	QGT	23897	57.1	1935	1960
100	1900	PG	16896	54.6	1924	1961
101	1901	PG	39280	47.5	1927	1960
102	1901	PG	24958	41.6	1928	1960
103	1901	PG	29849	42.9	1929	1959
104	1906	P 5'6"	18253	51.9	1924	1956
105	1906	P 5'6"	17427	53.5	1925	1960
106	1906	PP	14489	47.8	1928	1960
107	1906	PP	36510	31.7	1929	1959
108	1906	PP	31933	52.9	1928	1959
109	1911	NQGlater LQG	28816	54.8	1930	1959
110	1908	LQG	20854	60.8	1930	1959
111	1908	LQG	39818	64.9	1928	1963
112	1911	NQG	30595	42.0	1931	1963
113	1904	QL	22475	44.1	=1924	1957
114	1904	QL	15441	44.7	=1923	1932
115	1889	J	26043	32.2	n	1924
116	1889	J	9759	43.7 ,	n	1924

+ = later renumbered

GNR LOCOMOTIVES LIST 1918 *Continued*

No.	Built	Class	Works No.	Size	Rebuilt/Notes	d	Withdrawn
117	1885	J	17499	46.3			1921
118	1885	J sold to SLNCR 1921			n		1928
119	1887	J do	1921		n		1938
120	1904	Q	39780	38.2	1923		1957
121	1904	Q	5036	49.4	1924		1959
122	1903	Q	24108	39.4	1924		1960
123	1903	Q	18614	43.2	1923		1959
124	1902	Q	20754	45.6	1924		1957
125	1902	Q	35451	38.7	1924		1959
126	1907	QL	29766	46.4	1923		1957
127	1907	QL	38971	45.6	1928		1960
128	1907	QL	22746	42.4	1923		1959
129	1911	PP	38099	40.6	1929		1957
130	1901	Q	8034	39.7	1922		1959
131	1901	Q	20057	41.9 **	1920		1963
132	1901	Q	30251	41.8	1922		1963
133	1899	Q	19617	51.9	1919		1957
134	1899	Q	32302	41.4	1921		1951
135	1899	Q	30101	40.2	1922		1963
136	1899	Q	27843	39.8	1920		1959
137	1872	C	28261	43.7 ex-UR	n		1939
138	1872	C	12862	46.3 ex-UR	n	d	1948
139	1877	0-6-0	*	* ex-UR	n		1925
140	1894	AL	11245	40.0	n		1957
141	1894	AL	23847	43.4	n		1957
142	1879	0-6-0	*	ex-UR	n		1925
143	1879	0-6-0	*	ex-UR	n		1925
144	1876	0-6-0	*	ex-UR	n		1924
145	1888	A	18671	36.3 ex-UR	n		1937
146	1888	A	22104	41.9 ex-UR	n		1937

No.	Built	Class	Works No.	Size	Rebuilt/Notes	d	Withdrawn
147	1876	0-6-0	*	ex-UR	n		1925
148	1878	0-6-0	*	ex-UR	n		1925
149	1890	A	17767	47.8	n	d	1931
150	1890	A	13133	40.3	n	d	1961
151	1899	PG	19055	49.0	1921		1961
152	1903	QG	33932	52.5	1926		1961
153	1903	QG	30559	48.5	1928		1963
154	1904	QG	37322	47.8	1928		1962
155	1904	QG	20770	50.3	1926		1963
156	1904	QG	13530	56.6	1925		1963
157	1904	QL	2218	60.7	1924		1960
158	1906	LQG	27359	63.1	1921		1959
159	1906	LQG	22699	50.1	1929		1963
160	1906	LQG	23917	46.5	1926		1964
161	1908	LQG	33689	66.2	1929		1959
162	1908	LQG	32433	51.7	1927		1963
163	1908	LQG	26559	61.7	1927		1959
164	1908	LQG	30212	55.3	1930		1963
165	1911	NLQG	28713	58.7	1929		1963
166	1911	RT (later LQG)	29010	46.9	n		1960
167	1911	RT	23369	47.6	n		1963
168	1911	QGT2	*	*	n		1957
169	1911	QGT2	*	*	n		1957
170	1913	S	*	43.0	b		1957
171	1913	S	*	44.9 **	b		1965r
172	1913	S	*	38.1	b		1965r
173	1913	S	*	45.1	b		1965r
174	1913	S	*	43.7	b		1964r
175	1913	SG	36223	55.2	b		1965r
176	1913	SG	36700	53.4	b		1965
177	1913	SG	43464	56.6	b		1963
178	1913	SG	43958	45.6	b		1961

** = pres'd:

GNR LOCOMOTIVES LIST 1918 Continued

No.						
179	1913	SG	54.9	b	43162	1963
180	1915	SG2	48.4	b	31310	1961
181	1915	SG2	52.4	b	34254	1963
182	1915	SG2	52.8	b	34043	1963
183	1915	SG2	45.5	b	34966	1961
184	1915	SG2	51.8	b	36602	1962
185	1915	T	43.8	1924	32114	1960
186	1913	T	44.5	1923	26132	1960
187	1913	T	48.5	1926	25058	1961
188	1913	T	49.6	1927	24329	1959
189	1913	T	48.7	1926	23846	1960
190	1915	S2	45.1 U	b	32372	1964r
191	1915	S2	35.1	b	*	1960r
192	1915	S2	41.0 U	b	47029	1965r

No.					
193	1871	E	21651	47.7 ex- n INWR	1948
194	1872	E	20840	47.8 ex- n INWR	1948
195	1880	BP	24094	43.0 ex- n BCR	1950
196	1915	U	30549	32.9 b	1961
197	1915	U	50113	32.1 b	1963
198	1915	U	39334	32.8 b	1959
199	1915	U	24908	32.7 b	1962
200	1915	U	34375	31.3 b	1961
201	1866	2-4-0	*	* ex- n B&DJR	1920
202	1874	2-4-0	*	* ex-INWR 1921	
203	1904	0-4-0ST	*	* into stock 1930 1913	
204	1908	0-6-0T	*	* into stock 1930 1913	

r = the renewed engines of 1938-9: n = never superheated: b = superheated as built:
* = records destroyed: d = low chimney for Queens Bridge tunnel later

NEW ENGINES 1919-41   Numbered

SG3 type 0—6—0, built 1920-1. Similar to SG2 type but larger with cylinders 19½x26 and boiler diameter 5ft. 52 tons 10. Axle Load 17.7 tons. Grate Area 22.9 sq.ft

6	7	8	13	14	20
47	48	49	96	97	
201	202	117	118		

T2 type 4—4—2 tank, built 1921
                              1924
3½ tons coal
1800 gallons
(185-9 1700 gallons)   1929

1	2	3	4	5
21	30	115	116	139
142	143	144	147	148
62	63	64	65	66

Superheated version of 1913 engines, the final batch having, for a few years, 200lbs boiler pressure instead of standard 175lbs.
Weight now 65 tons 15 and cylinders 18x24. GA 18.3 AL 17t

Crane tank 0—6—0. First GNR engine with outside cylinders (14x20) 650 gallons
1927 Hawthorn Leslie 45 tons, GA 11 sq.ft, AL 15t. 11 cwt coal

31

More SG2 0—6—0s, but built, like the 1924 4—4—2 tanks and the 1911 0—6—0s by Nasmyth Wilson. All other engines 1913-32 built by Beyer Peacock. Axle Load 16.8 tons

15 16 17 18 19

The compound 4—4—0s, to be described in detail in Volume II 1932. One H.P. cylinder 17¼x26 two L.P. 19x26. 65 tons 1, GA 25.2, AL 21t

83 84 85 86 87

1937 UG type 0—6—0, built at Dundalk. Boiler and cylinders of U class. Driving wheels SG class. 45 tons 12, GA 18.3 sq.ft, AL 15.2 tons

78 79 80 81 82

1938-9. Renewing of S and S2 4—4—0s. Regarded as new engines. Grate area 22.9 sq.ft AL 18 tons now 53 tons 6

173 192 171 172
191 170 190 174

24 Element Superheater	V class SG3
18	S,S2,QL,Q,PP(4ft 6),P,SG,SG2, QLG,NQG,QG,PG,QGTs
16	U,UG,T,T2,PP(4ft 3)

(1) 1550 gallons
3 tons of coal
11ft 6 in wheelbase
20 tons weight

Three tenders surviving from 1890-4 and numbered *30/2/7*. Used on G class and possibly J class also, then probably becoming standard goods tender till 1897, used on A, D and probably AL classes.

(2) 1700 gallons
4 tons of coal
12ft wheelbase

Five surviving (*9, 42/8* of 1883 and *29* & *34* of 1884) Another very similar batch of eight for passenger engines 1884-94: *27, 35, 40, 44-7* surviving.

(3) 2000 gallons
4 tons of coal
12ft wheelbase
25 tons 1 cwt.

1895-6 for P and PP 4—4—0s, *72-3* and *75-7*. Tenders numbered *24, 28, 31, 36, 43*. All surviving.

(4) 2400 gallons
4 tons of coal
12ft wheelbase
30 tons

1892. Two for *88-9* and two for *82-3*, all surviving. Tenders numbered *38, 41, 73, 76*.

(5) 2500 gallons
4 tons of coal
12ft wheelbase
30 tons 11 cwt.

In four groups, classified B1, B2, B3 and B4. 52 tenders 1897-1909, for PP, Q, PG, QG, P, QL, QLG. Type B.1. Similar to above, except for tank. Until 1902 all tenders had two coal rails instead of copings, standard from that time forward, with some older ones similarly treated. B.2 18 built 1910-26. Similar to B.1 except for now having outside springs, but retaining Beyer bunker. Later ones possibly intended for SG3 class, as their tenders were given to Q class as they were rebuilt. 11 converted later to type B.3.
B.3 Same as B.2 except that tank was extended forward below bunker to form shovelling plate. 6 built 1911 by Nasmyth Wilson, 4 being used for *12, 42, 38, 39* which had to have special tenders for Drummond heaters.
B.4 Only slight differences from B.3.
28 built 1913-24 for S, S2, SG, SG2, U classes.

(6) 3500 gallons
6 tons of coal
13ft wheelbase
38 tons 10 cwt.

In two groups, classified D.1 and D.2. 15 D.1 for SG3 1920-1, but later to Q class. 15 more built 1923-37 D.2 Last five had higher coping flared inwards. Some D.1 and D.2 had this later.

COACHING STOCK

In 1918, long after the old vehicles from the railways which made up the GNR had disappeared, the varnished mahogany carriages of this railway had a most fascinating variety of shapes and sizes of over one hundred letter classifications. The tables which follow detail the broad history of the 476 vehicles of 1918, and after that there are details of the 123 bogie coaches built 1919-1941, whose numbers gradually overtook the six-wheelers, 180 of which were withdrawn during the same period. The carriage classification was as follows:

BOGIE COACHES

A.	SALOONS	E.	2nd CLASS	K.	3rd CLASS
B.	DINING CARS	F.	1st/2nd COMPO	L.	BRAKE 3rd
C.	1st CLASS	G.	BRAKE 1st/2nd	M.	GUARD'S BRAKES
D.	BRAKE FIRSTS (in	H.	2nd/3rd COMPO	N.	POST OFFICE
	some cases including	I.	TRI-COMPO		SORTING VANS
	2nd class also)	J.	BRAKE TRI-COMPO		

Also, from 1930, when the O and P types of six-wheelers had been withdrawn

O. 1st/3rd BRAKE COMPO   P. 20 ton PARCEL VANS

SIX-WHEELERS

O.	SALOONS	R.	1st/2nd COMPO	U.	3rd CLASS
P.	1st CLASS	S.	2nd/3rd COMPO	V.	3rd BRAKE
Q.	2nd CLASS	T.	TRI-COMPO	W.	GUARD'S BRAKE
				X.	MAIL & PARCEL VANS

FOUR-WHEELERS

Y. VARIOUS VANS (mainly PARCEL)

Excluding saloons, dining cars and mail vans, there were only 33 bogie corridor carriages in 1918, of which only 13 were 3rd class, all of which had centre corridor. Indeed at that period there was only one side-corridor coach (*139* of type D.1). By 1941 the centre-corridor style was still more common, but there were by now 29 side-corridor carriages, in classes D.1/2/3, F.16, G.6 and K.13/4/7. Also the 'superior' part of the following compos had side-corridor: H.5, I.13, J.6/11, K.18 (had once been 2nd class) and O.1. In the tables all corridor carriages are marked v. Slip coaches SC., and C. Tea car.

As regards the ultimate fate of carriages lasting until 1958, this is indicated at the right hand side of each column just before the actual withdrawal date. Those which went to CIE are simply marked thus, as they never were renumbered, the UTA ones having either their new number or UTA, if scrapped without being renumbered by 1960.

All passenger coaches built after 1918 were of a standard 62ft (including buffers), width 9½ft, except *480* of type M.3 which was 60ft long and *3* of type K.19 which was only 47½ft long. The 'high eliptical' roof was also now standard.

CARRIAGE LIST 1918

No.	Built	Class	Length over buffers	Weight	Later	After 1958	W'drawn
1	1911	A.4	v50ft	25¼t			1951
2	1911	G.2	57ft	25¾t	SC		1960
3	1889	P.2	34ft	13½t			1929
4	1913	K.6	v60ft	28¼t	L.11	452	1965
5	1913	L.5	v60ft	26¾t		CIE	1960
6	1913	K.6	v60ft	28¾t	L.11	CIE	1961
7	1897	C.2	49ft	23¼t	F.14		1958
8	1896	U.1	35ft	13t			1948
9	1896	U.1	do	do			1947
10	1903	I.8	56ft	25t		271	1960
11	1913	K.6	v60ft	28¾t	L.11	CIE	1960
12	1910	K.3	52ft	25¼t		UTA	1959
13	1910	K.3	do	do			1958
14	1905	C.1	v56ft	26¾t			1958
15	1910	G.1	57ft	25¾t	SC	UTA	1959
16	1915	K.8	v62ft	29¼t		318	1965
17	1901	H.1	55¼ft	23¾t	K.30	UTA	1959
18	1915	K.8	v62ft	29¼t		320	1963
19	1910	I.1	v57ft	27¾t	J.7	UTA	1959
20	1911	J.9	54ft	26¾t			1933
21	1885	P.2	34ft	13½t	U.6(1927)		1933
22	1885	P.2	do	do			1930
23	1889	P.2	do	do			1928
24	1889	P.2	do	do	U.6(1927)		1932
25	1909	K.3	52ft	25¼t		CIE	1960
26	1897	F.8	54ft	24¼t		UTA	1959
27	1909	K.3	52ft	25¼t	(tc till 1949)	308	1958
28	1914	K.7	v62ft	30t	U.6(1927)		1964
29	1889	P.2	34ft	13½t	U.6(1927)		1934
30	1888	P.2	do	do	U.6(1930)		1934

No.	Built	Class	Length over buffers	Weight	Later	After 1958	W'drawn
31	1890	P.2	do	do	do 358(1922)		1933
32	1893	P.1	37½ft	14½t	U.8(1927)		1933
33	1862/90	O.1	27ft	11½t			1920
34	1914	K.7	v62ft	30t	tc till 1948	310	1964
35	1903	I.7	57ft	25¾t			1957
36	1904	I.7	do	do			1957
37	1871	O.2	26¼ft	9¾t	Reb.1890		1920
38	1910	G.1	57ft	25¾t		SC CIE	1960
39	1911	F.4	v53ft	26t		UTA	1959
40	1911	K.5	v56ft	27t		CIE	1963
41	1914	K.7	v62ft	30t	tc till 1948	312	1960
42	1897	I.4	56ft	24t		J.10 UTA	1959
43	1918	J.4	v62ft	33t		SC 208	1960
44	1881	R.5	34ft	13¼t			1919
45	1899	I.4	56ft	24t		J.10 UTA	1959
46	1893	U.2	34ft	12½t			1944
47	1889	U.2	do	do			1936
48	1915	K.8	v62ft	29¼t		322	1965
49	1905	F.1	v57ft	26¼t	F.13	CIE	1960
50	1911	A.3	v52ft	29¼t		150 pres'd	
51	1883	R.5	34ft	13¼t	X.6 1923		1930
52	1903	F.5	v53ft	25¼t		CIE	1960
53	1895	R.3	37½ft	14¾t	U.8(1931)		1934
54	1883	R.5	34ft	13¼t	X.6(1923)		1930
55	1903	I.8	56ft	25t		CIE	1960
56	1883	R.5	34ft	13¼t	S.2(1919)		1928
57	1899	I.4	56ft	24t	J.10		1958
58	1896	I.6	54ft	22t			1957
59	1896	I.6	do	do		Sold	1957
60	1883	R.5	34ft	13¼t			1921

No.							
61	1903	F.1	57ft	26¼t		CIE	1960
62	1912	L.4	55¼ft	22½t		475	1960
63	1887	R.6	31ft	12½t	U.9(1927)		1933
64	1881	R.5	34ft	13¼t	'plane truck '18		1920
65	1883	R.5	do	do	X.6(1924)		1929
66	1887	R.6	31ft	12½t			1934
67	1887	R.6	do	do			1934
68	1891	U.2	34ft	12½t			1946
69	1902	I.8	56ft	25t			1958
70	1890	R.1	34ft	13½t			1947
71	1901	K.1	55¼ft	23¾t	K.30		1957
72	1905	I.3	v57ft	26¼t	J.9	CIE	1960
73	1884	R.4	34ft	13t			1929
74	1884	R.5	34ft	13¼t	S.2('21)U.5('26)		1930
75	1884	R.5	do	do	U.5(1930)		1932
76	1911	L.4	55¼ft	22½t		473	1965
77	1885	R.5	34ft	13¼t	U.5(1926)		1933
78	1893	R.3	37½ft	14¾t	U.8(1929)		1934
79	1891	U.2	34ft	12½t			1940
80	1911	L.4	55¼ft	22½t		UTA	1959
81	1885	R.5	34ft	13¼t			1933
82	1890	T.4	32½ft	12¾t	R.4		1946
83	1886	R.5	34ft	13¼t	X.6(1923)		1933
84	1885	R.5	do	do	sold to SLNCR		1929
85	1910	K.4	52ft	22½t		CIE	1960
86	1881	O.6	34ft	10t			1920
87	1915	L.6	v62ft	28½t		456	1964
88	1892	R.2	34ft	12¾t			1933
89	1890	R.5	34ft	13¼t	U.5(1930)		1933
90	1886	R.5	do	do			1925
91							
92	1894	R.3	37½ft	14¾t			1948

No.							
93	1893	R.3	do	do			1933
94	1888	R.6	31ft	12½t	U.9(1927)		1930
95	1888	R.6	do	do	sold to SLNCR		1935
96	1892	R.2	34ft	12¾t			1947
97	1886	R.5	do	13¼t			1932
98	1886	R.4	do	13t	U.5(1928)		1932
99	1898	I.5	56ft	22¾t		CIE	1960
100	1898	I.5	do	do			1955
101	1894	R.3	37½ft	14¾t			1947
102	1898	F.7	56ft	25t		CIE	1960
103	1885	R.1	34ft	13½t			1935
104	1909	K.3	52ft	25¼t		341	1963
105	1887	R.6	31ft	12½t	U.9(1930)		1932
106	1889	T.4	32½ft	12¾t	R.4		1948
107	1895	R.3	37½ft	14¾t			1947
108	1891	U.2	34ft	12½t	Z.1(1939)		1948
109	1890	R.5	do	13¾t			1947
110	1885	R.1	do	13½t			1924
111	1891	R.1	do	do	S.1(1919)		1929
112	1910	L.4	55¼ft	22½t		471	1963
113	1910	L.4	do	do		UTA	1959
114	1886	U.3	34ft	13t			1934
115	1884	U.3	do	do			1932
116	1890	U.2	do	12½t			1937
117	1886	U.3	do	13t			1929
118	1898	K.1	55¼ft	24¼t		CIE	1960
119	1888	U.2	34ft	12½t			1936
120	1901	I.4	56ft	24t	J.10 1928-35	UTA	1959
121	1905	L.1	54ft	22¾t		CIE	1960
122	1885	Q.3	34ft	13¼t	U.4(1925)		1933
123	1907	K.3	52ft	25¼t		CIE	1960
124	1905	L.1	54ft	25¼t			1933

CARRIAGE LIST 1918 Continued

140

No.						
125	1907	K.3	52ft	25¼t	UTA	1959
126	1908	K.3	do	do	CIE	1960
127	1886	Q.3	34ft	13¼t		1933
128					U.4(1930)	
129	1891	Q.3	34ft	13¼t	U.4(1926)	1936
130	1899	H.2	52ft	23½t	K.21	1955
131	1894	Q.2	37½ft	13¼t		1949
132	1894	Q.2	do	do	U.10(1929)	1945
133	1888	Q.3	34ft	13¼t		1947
134	1886	U.3	do	13t		1934
135	1889	Q.3	do	13¼t		1932
136	1899	K.1	55¼ft	24¼t	CIE	1960
137	1911	E.2	v54ft	25¾t		1955
138	1886	Q.3	34ft	13¼t	U.4(1925)	1934
139	1916	D.1	v62ft	32½t	190	1964
140	1894	U.2	34ft	12½t		1938
141	1884	U.2	do	do	sold to CM&DR	1921
142	1882	U.3	do	13t	'plane truck 1918	1920
143	1894	U.2	do	12½t		1945
144	1916	A.5	v62ft	34t	B.5(1927)	1964
145	1893	V.1	35ft	12¼t		1934
146	1884	V.3	34ft	12½t		1930
147	1916	K.8	v62ft	29¼t	324	1969
148	1901	G.4	v49ft	23¾t	CIE	1960
149	1894	U.2	34ft	12½t		1948
150	1904	H.3	v55¼ft	26¼t		1957
151	1916	J.4	v62ft	33t	SC 204	1967
152	1893	U.2	34ft	12½t		1945
153	1884	V.3	do	do		1932
154	1884	V.3	do	do		1932
155	1904	M.1	v52ft	22t	CIE	1960
156	1896	U.1	35ft	13t		1948

No.						
157	1900	K.1	55¼ft	24¼t	CIE	1960
158	1891	U.2	34ft	12½t		1945
159	1904	K.3	52ft	25¼t	CIE	1960
160	1903	K.2	55¼ft	24¼t	333	1963
161	1903	E.1	v54ft	25¾t	CIE	1960
162	1893	U.2	34ft	12½t		1947
163	1893	U.2	do	do		1944
164	1893	U.2	do	do		1944
165	1890	U.3	do	do		1933
166	1884	U.2	do	13t	'plane truck	1920
167	1891	U.2	do	12½t		1943
168	1890	U.2	do	do		1938
169	1900	F.13	49ft	22¼t	G.4	1960
170	1892	U.2	34ft	12½t	CIE	1936
171	1891	U.2	do	do		1946
172	1884	U.2	do	do		1928
173	1892	V.2	34ft	11½t		1947
174	1893	U.2	do	12½t		1948
175	1893	U.2	do	do		1938
176	1893	V.3	34ft	12½t		1938
177	1894	U.2	do	do		1932
178	1890	U.2	do	do		1947
179	1890	U.2	do	do		1946
180	1884	U.3	do	13t		1930
181	1895	U.1	35ft	do		1930
182	1886	U.3	34ft	do		1928
183	1896	U.1	35ft	do		1940
184	1902	L.2	55¼ft	21¼t	UTA	1959
185	1885	U.3	34ft	13t		1934
186	1887	U.3	do	do		1932
187	1890	U.2	do	12½t		1943
188	1886	U.3	do	13t		1934

CARRIAGE LIST 1918 Continued

No.						
189	1888	U.2	do	12½t		1932
190	1885	U.3	do	13t		1928
191	1897	K.1	55¼ft	24¼t		1957
192	1887	U.3	34ft	13t		1934
193	1887	U.3	do	do		1934
194	1896	K.1	55¼ft	24¼t	CIE	1959
195	1886	U.3	34ft	13t		1933
196	1891	V.2	do	11½t		1946
197	1891	V.2	do	do		1938
198	1894	U.2	do	12½t		1948
199	1887	U.3	do	13t		1934
200	1894	U.2	do	12½t		1943
201	1905	J.3	62ft	27¾t	formerly 'motor	1950
202	1905	J.3	do	do	do	1957
203	1905	J.3	do	do	do	1950
204	1907	J.2	65½ft	29¼t	do SC	1951
205	1907	J.2	do	do	do SC	1955
206	1907	J.2	do	do	do SC	1955
207	1907	J.1	vdo	28¾t	do SC	1949
208	1906	F.12	57ft	25t	formerly trailer	1955
209	1906	F.12	do	do	do	1957
210	1906	L.7	do	25¼t	do	1953
211	1906	K.9	55ft	24¾t	do	1957
212	1906	K.9	do	do	do	1957
213	1906	K.9	do	do	do	1955
214	1906	K.9	do	do	do UTA	1959
215	1906	F.12	57ft	25t	do	1957
216	1906	F.12	do	do	do	1957
217	1917	J.4	v62ft	33t	SC 206	1965
218	1884	U.3	34ft	13t		1933
219	1889	U.2	do	12½t		1936
220	1886	U.3	do	13t		1933

No.						
221	1891	U.1	35ft	13t		1936
222	1892	U.2	34ft	12½t		1936
223	1887	U.3	do	13t		1934
224	1885	U.3	do	do	'plane truck '18	1920
225	1896	U.1	35ft	do		1945
226	1891	U.2	34ft	12½t		1932
227	1889	U.2	do	do		1944
228	1889	U.2	do	do		1932
229	1886	U.2	do	do		1934
230	1890	U.2	do	do		1937
231	1892	U.2	do	do		1943
232	1892	U.2	do	do		1945
233	1892	U.2	do	do		1945
234	1886	U.2	do	do		1932
235	1891	U.1	35ft	13t		1938
236	1889	U.2	34ft	do		1936
237	1888	R.5	do	13¼t		1949
238	1888	R.4	do	13t	V.5(1931)	1934
239	1890	U.2	do	12½t		1945
240	1901	M.2	52ft	19¼t	607	1960
241	1892	Q.2	37½ft	13¼t		1947
242	1882	W.4	32ft	10t		1920
243	1883	W.3	32ft	11t		1931
244						
245	1882	W.4	32ft	10t		1920
246	1904	L.1	54ft	22¾t	CIE	1961
247	1905	W.1	34ft	12t	UTA	1959
248	1887	W.3	32ft	11t		1932
249	1896	W.2	32ft	11¼t		1948
250	1890	W.3	32ft	11t		1948
251	1896	W.2	32ft	11¼t		1947
252	1900	K.1	55¼ft	24¼t	UTA	1960

CARRIAGE LIST 1918 *Continued*

No.	Built	Type	Length	Weight	Notes	Withdrawn
253	1894	W.2	32ft	11¼t		1948
254	1888	U.2	34ft	12½t		1929
255	1887	U.3	34ft	13t		1934
256	1887	U.3	do	do		1933
257	1908	L.1	54ft	22¾t	UTA 608	1960
258	1904	M.1	v52ft	22t		1960
259	1892	W.2	32ft	11¼t		1948
260	1892	W.2	do	do		1948
261	1915	K.6	v60ft	34¼t / 28¼t	as 12 wheeler 306 later	1963
262	1888	W.3	32ft	11t		1934
263	1883	W.3	do	do		1931
264	1887	W.3	do	do		1934
265	1882	W.4	32ft	10t		1920
266	1883	W.3	32ft	11t		1935
267	1888	W.3	do	do		1932
268	1884	W.3	do	do		1932
269	1888	W.3	do	do	destroyed	1921
270	1886	W.3	do	do		1928
271	1884	W.3	do	do	to rail dept.	1921
272	1901	M.2	52ft	19¼t	B.7(1940) CIE	1967
273	1883	W.3	32ft	11t		1934
274	1904	W.1	34ft	12t		1957
275	1904	W.1	do	do		1951
276	1890	W.3	32ft	11t		1947
277	1883	W.3	do	do		1933
278	1887	W.3	do	do		1933
279	1883	W.3	do	do		1926
280	1893	V.1	35ft	12¼t		1949
281	1893	V.1	35ft	12¼t		1948
282	1896	Y.3	28ft	8½t	753 1924 652 parcel post	1961
283	1896	Y.3	do	do	754 1924 parcel post CIE	1967
284	1887	W.3	32ft	11t		1936
285	1895	U.2	34ft	12½t		1936
286	1888	U.2	do	do		1939
287	1889	W.3	32ft	11t		1936
288	1893	W.2	32ft	11¼t	601	1969
289	1894	W.2	do	do		1949
290	1888	W.3	32ft	11t		1946
291	1886	W.3	do	do		1935
292	1890	W.3	do	do	CIE	1966
293	1891	W.3	do	do		1947
294	1888	W.3	do	do		1931
295						
296	1894	W.2	32ft	11¼t	602	1965
297	1889	W.3	32ft	11t		1946
298	1894	W.2	32ft	11¼t		1948
299	1895	W.2	do	do		1948
300	1889	W.3	32ft	11t		1948
301	1896	W.2	32ft	11¼t	rebuilt '44 CIE	1959
302	1889	W.3	32ft	11t		1948
303	1886	W.3	do	do		1933
304	1897	W.2	32ft	11¼t	603	1969
305	1897	W.2	do	do		1948
306	1917	L.8	62ft	31t	CIE	1964
307	1917	I.11	62ft	32¼t	277	1969
308	1893	W.2	32ft	11¼t		1946
309	1895	W.2	do	do		1946
310	1889	W.3	32ft	11t	W.2(1945)604	1960
311	1914	G.3	v62ft	32t	200	1963
312	1915	G.3	do	do	202	1965
313	1885	U.3	34ft	13t	'plane truck '18	1920

No.						
314	1882	U.3	do	do		1919
315	1885	U.3	do	do	Sold to BCDR (171)	1922
316	1886	U.3	do	do		1928
317	1883	U.3	Sold to BCDR as 172			1922
318	1896	U.1	35ft	13t	Z.1 (1939)	1948
319	1893	U.2	34ft	12½t		1945
320	1917	E.3	62ft	31¾t	later D.4 479	1960
321	1899	K.1	55¼ft	24¼t	CIE	1960
322	1899	K.1	do	do	CIE	1960
323	1890	U.2	34ft	12½t		1937
324	1883	U.3	Rail service vehicle from			1922
325	1883	U.3	Sold to BCDR as 173			1922
326	1900	A.1	v49ft	24t		1951
327	1902	H.4	56½ft	25¼t	UTA	1960
328	1891	U.2	34ft	12½t		1940
329	1885	Q.3	34ft	13¼t	U.4(5/24)	1928
330	1889	U.2	34ft	12½t		1936
331	1888	U.2	do	do		1934
332	1892	U.2	do	do		1938
333	1891	U.2	do	do		1940
334	1887	W.3	32ft	11t		1934
335	1887	U.3	34ft	13t		1929
336	1895	U.2	34ft	12½t		1944
338	1895	F.6	v49ft	23¾t	formerly UTA diner 301	1960
339	1892	Q.1	37½ft	14¼t	later V.4(1930)	1947
340	1889	T.4	32½ft	12¾t	U.7(1919)	1935
341	1889	T.4	do	do	R.4	1938
342	1887	Q.3	34ft	13¼t	U.4(1930)	1934
343	1887	Q.3	do	do		1934
344	1894	U.2	34ft	12½t		1945
345	1885	Q.3	34ft	13¼t	271(1922)U.4 '29	1936

No.						
346	1882	W.4	34ft	10t	Rail vehicle	1921
347	1893	W.2	32ft	11¼t	CIE	1968
348	1887	Q.3	34ft	13¼t	U.4(1926)	1930
349	1914	L.6	v62ft	28½t	454	1963
350	1905	L.3	55¼ft	22¾t	UTA	1960
351	1912	L.4	55¼ft	22½t	UTA	1960
352	1902	F.3	v56½ft	26¾t	CIE	1960
353	1912	L.4	55¼ft	22½t	477	1964
354	1880	U.5	31½ft	12½t	U.4(1916)	1920
355	1904	K.3	52ft	25¼t	CIE	1960
356	1904	K.3	do	do	later I.12 CIE	1960
357	1917	K.8	v62ft	29¼t	326	1967
358	1883	U.3	34ft	13t	sold to BCDR as 177	1922
359	1883	U.3	do	do	do174	1922
360	1883	U.3	do	do	do175	1922
361	1883	U.3	34ft	13t		1928
362	1883	U.3	do	do		1920
363	1883	U.3	sold to BCDR as 178			1922
364	1884	V.3	34ft	12½t		1933
365	1882	O.3	34ft	15½t	as O.1 37	1925
366	1918	D.2	wrecked at Dromiskin 1933			1933
367	1885	U.3	sold to BCDR as 176			1922
368	1885	U.3	'plane truck 1918 then flat			1920
369	1885	U.3	34ft	13t		1928
370	1917	G.5	v62ft	31¾t	214	1965
371	1885	U.3	'plane truck 1918 then loco dept.			1920
372	1885	U.3	34ft	13t		1928
373	1885	T.2	49ft	18½t	BCR of 1875	1926
374	1885	T.3	do	do	do	1925
375						
376	1887	Y.3	755 (1924)		Parcel van	1929
377	1888	Y.3	28ft	8½t	do	1919

CARRIAGE LIST 1918 Continued

No.						
378	1888	Y.3	756 (1924) Rebuilt 1944 CIE			1966
379	1888	U.2	34ft	12½t		1927
380	1888	U.2	do	do		1935
381	1883	Fintona Horse Tramcar Preserved				1957
382	1889	F.9	42½ft	19½t		1955
383	1890	F.9	do	do		1951
384	1890	U.2	34ft	12½t		1935
385	1890	U.2	do	do		1935
386	1890	U.2	do	do	Z.1(1939)	1948
387	1890	U.2	do	do		1946
388	1891	U.2	do	do		1937
389	1891	U.2	do	do		1939
390	1891	U.2	do	do		1938
391	1891	T.1	36ft	13½t		1947
392	1891	T.1	do	do		1948
393	1891	U.2	34ft	12½t		1939
394	1891	U.2	do	do		1942
395	1891	U.2	do	do		1938
396	1918	E.4	v62ft	32t	burnt C'ham	1922
397	1892	F.10	49ft	21½t		1957
398	1892	F.11	49ft	21t	kitchen car	1957
399	1902	M.2	52ft	19¼t	B7 1940 166	1971
400	1893	A.2	46ft	22¼t	later M.4	1957
401	1916	B.1	v62ft	36½t	reblt '33 CIE	1964
402	1917	B.1	v62ft	36½t	burnt C'ham	1922
403	1896	U.2	34ft	12½t		1943
404	1895	I.10	50ft	20t		1958
405	1895	V.1	35ft	12¼t		1947
406	1895	U.2	34ft	12½t		1944
407	1895	A.6	54ft	25¼t	formerly 401(diner) 306(Amb)A.2(1921) E.5 '23	1957

No.							
408	1896	U.2	34ft	12½t			1947
409	1896	B.4	v59ft	33¾t	12 wh. till burnt926		1946
410	1895	U.2	34ft	12½t			1945
411	1896	U.1	35ft	13t			1945
412	1896	U.1	do	do			1945
413	1896	U.1	do	do			1945
414	1896	U.1	do	do			1946
415	1898	Y.1	28ft	8¼t	mortuary van 751(1925)		1928
417	1898	L.2	55¼ft	21¼t		CIE	1960
418	1898	L.2	do	do		UTA	1960
419	1899	K.1	55¼ft	24¼t	wrecked Omagh		1933
420	1899	K.1	do	do			1957
421	1899	K.1	do	do		UTA	1960
422	1899	K.1	do	do			1957
423	1899	K.1	do	do		CIE	1960
424	1899	K.1	do	do		UTA	1960
425	1899	K.1	do	do		UTA	1960
426	1900	F.3	v56½ft	26¾t		UTA	1960
427	1900	B.3	v60ft	33t			1951
428	1900	H.4	56½ft	25¼t	K.22(1942)	CIE	1960
429	1900	K.1	55¼ft	24¼t		CIE	1960
430	1900	K.1	do	do		UTA	1960
431	1900	K.1	do	do			1958
432	1900	K.1	do	do		UTA	1960
433	1901	M.2	52ft	19¼t		CIE	1961
434	1901	Y.4	28ft	9t	758(1924)	CIE	1962
435	1901	Y.4	do	do	759 do	642	1965
436	1901	Y.4	do	do	760	CIE	1965
437	1901	Y.4	do	do	761	643	1965
438	1901	Y.4	do	do	762	CIE	1960
439	1901	Y.4	do	do	763	644	1971
440	1901	L.2	55¼ft	21¼t		CIE	1960

CARRIAGE LIST 1918 Continued

No.							
441	1902	Y.2	752 '24 pcl van '34	26¼t		641	1965
442	1904	F.1	v57ft	do		CIE	1960
443	1905	F.1	do	do		UTA	1955
444	1905	I.2	v56ft	27½t	later J.8	CIE	1960
445	1906	I.2	do	do	do	273	1960
446	1907	F.1	v57ft	26¾t	later F.13 non v		1960
447	1907	F.1	do	do	non v do later H.6	CIE	1960
448	1904	F.2	do	do	later F.1	UTA	1960
449	1905	K.3	52ft	25¼t		CIE	1960
450	1905	K.3	do	do		335	1963
451	1905	K.3	do	do		UTA	1960
452	1906	K.3	do	do		337	1965
453	1904	M.1	v52ft	22t		UTA	1960
454	1907	M.1	do	do		609	1970
455	1907	M.1	do	do	wrecked Dromiskin		1933
456	1908	M.1	do	do		CIE	1960
457	1905	B.2	v60ft	33t			1950
458	1906	K.3	52ft	25¼t			1955
459	1907	K.3	do	do		CIE	1960
460	1907	K.3	do	do		CIE	1960
461	1907	K.3	do	do		339	1963
462	1907	K.3	do	do		UTA	1960

No.						
463	1912	Y.5	28ft	9¼t	bread 764 645 1924	1971
464	1912	Y.5	do	do	765	1956
465	1912	Y.5	do	do	766 646	1967
466	1912	Y.5	do	do	767	1955
467	1912	Y.5	do	do	768 647	1963
468	1912	Y.5	do	do	769	1953
469	1912	Y.5	do	do	770 CIE	1962
470	1912	Y.5	do	do	Y.3 1944 771	1958
471	1912	Y.5	do	do	bread 772 653 Y.3 1944	1971
472	1912	Y.5	do	do	773 648	1961
473	1915	Y.6	28ft	9½t	774(1924) 649	1971
474	1915	Y.6	do	do	775 650	1971
475	1915	Y.6	do	do	776	1955
482	1887	X.1	36ft	14½t	777(1924)	1936
483	1877	X.3	31ft	14t	779	1925
484	1878	X.4	31ft	13¾t	780	1925
485	1878	X.4	do	do	781	1925
486	1885	X.2	32ft	12t	778(1924)	1931
487	1892	N.2	49ft	20½t	789	1950
488	1901	N.1	54ft	23¾t	destroyed C'ham	1922

ADDITIONS TO CARRIAGE STOCK 1919-41

During these years the GNR carriage works at Dundalk produced a total of 123 new carriages. Only two years were unproductive, the immediate post-strike period 1933-4, but during the others a new coach was appearing on average every other month, a pretty fair rate of replacement. In addition several dining cars were re-built and 17 other carriages altered internally, usually to produce more 3rd class accommodation. The actual result, as regards passengers' seats, was 7 additional firsts and 285 thirds while second class seats declined in total by 262, a trend which finally resulted in two classes only by 1951.

No.	Type B.1 36 tons Seats 18(1st) 23 (2nd)		W'drawn
402	1925	164	1970
	Type B.5 34 tons Seats 14 (st) 22 (2nd)		
144	1927 previously IPN saloon	CIE	1964
	Type B.6 32½ tons Seats 12 (1st) 18 (2nd)		
88	1938 preserved	552	1973
	Type D.1 32½ tons Seats 12 (1st) 24 (2nd)		
345	1920	192	1969
365	1922(D.2) 24st	194	1963
	Seats 12 (1st) 16 (2nd)		
265	1922 D.2 1st	CIE	1965
363	1924 1st	196	1969
	Type D.3 32 tons Seats 40 (2nd)(E.4 till 1935)		
396	1923	CIE	1965
	Type E.3 31¾ tons Seats 80 (2nd)		
337	1920 D.4(1935)	481	1965
377	1921 do	483	1969
367	1925 do	485	1965
	Type F.2 32½ tons Seats 16 (1st) 70 (2nd)		
166	1921	279	1969
224	1921	CIE	1961
313	1921 2nd	CIE	1964
354	1921	281	1969
368	1921	283	1966
371	1921	285	1969
33	1922 2nd	CIE	1964
	Type F.15 32½ tons Seats 24 (1st) 60 (2nd)		
86	1923	287	1969
141	1923	CIE	1961
359	1924	289	1965
360	1925	CIE	1961
	Type F.16 31½ tons Seats 24 (1st) 24 (2nd)		
20	1935	571	1973
21	1935	286	1967
24	1935	CIE	1969
29	1935	572	1973
30	1935	288	1970
89	1939	573	

No.	Type G.6 31 tons Seats 12 (1st) 40 (2nd)		W'drawn
37	1931 1st	CIE	1964
84	1931	238	1965
90	1931 1st	CIE	1967
No.	Type H.5 34½ tons Seats 48 (2nd) 28 (3rd)		
416	1920 K.18(1936)	CIE	1964
362	1922 do	330	1965
60	1923 2nd	CIE	1962
325	1923 K.18 2nd	CIE	1967
317	1924 2nd	366	1968
51	1925 K.18(1936)	332	1965
	Type I.13 31 tons Seats 12(1st) 16(2nd) and 39(3rd)		
269	1929	284	1966
270	1929	CIE	1966
	Type J.4 33 tons Seats 12(1st)12(2nd)and 21(3rd)		
44	1920 SC	CIE	1963
64	1920 SC	212	1965
91	1919 SC	210	1965
	Type J.5 32 tons Seats 10 (1st)14(2nd)and 36 (3rd)		
65	1926	CIE	1961
	Type J.6 29½ tons Seats 12(1st)12(2nd)and38(3rd)		
463	1929	CIE	1964
464	1929	232	1965
465	1929	234	1967
	Type J.11 29 tons Seats 6(1st)8(2nd)and 30(3rd)		
47	1937	CIE	1970
103	1941	258	1970
105	1941	CIE	1973
	Type M.3 28½ tons		
480	1919 380(1947)	612	1963
	Type M.5 28½ tons		
434	1925	CIE	1969
	Type N.3 33¼ tons		
790	1922 (481 till 1924)		1954
	Type O. 29¾ tons Seats 12 (1st) 40 (3rd)		
372	1930	CIE	1962
415	1930	236	1969

Type K.7   30 tons

No.	Teacar with 90 seats			
142	1920	2nd	314	1968
314	1922	2nd	316	1966

Type K.8   29¼ tons
90 seats

373	1928		CIE	1963
374	1928	2nd	328	1968

Type K.10   30 tons
85 seats

110	1925	2nd	CIE	1962
282	1927	2nd	368	1966
283	1927	2nd	CIE	1965

Type K.11   29¾ tons
89 seats

376	1928	CIE	1961
378	1928	CIE	1963
379	1928	CIE	1965
435	1928	370	1970
436	1928	372	1964
441	1929	374	1970
54	1930	CIE	1964
56	1930	CIE	1965
73	1930	CIE	1965
316	1930	376	1971
329	1930	378	1969
335	1930	380	1970

Type K.12   29¾ tons
437 Teacar 80 seats
438/9 Buffet car 60 seats

437	1928	2nd	CIE	1965
438	1928	2nd	396	1968
439	1928	2nd	398	1967

Type K.13   32½ tons
68 seats

74	1932	CIE	1969
111	1932	CIE	1967
117	1932	CIE	1966
128	1932	CIE	1965
146	1932	CIE	1960
172	1932	382	1968
180	1932	384	1970
182	1932	386	1969
190	1932	388	1968

Type K.14   33 tons
Teacars 60 seats
254 (buffet car) 52 seats

254	1932		CIE	1962
279	1932	2nd	CIE	1968
295	1932	2nd	390	1969

Type K.15   31 tons
70 seats

262	1935	402	1970
263	1935	404	1970

Type K.15   31 tons

No.	70 seats	Cont.		
264	1935		CIE	1972
32	1935		400	1973
63	1936		CIE	1973
75	1936		CIE	1973
77	1936		406	1970
78	1937		CIE	1973
81	1937		408	1970
93	1939		CIE	1972
97	1941	buffet	CIE	1969
98	1941	preserved	581	1971

Type K.16   31½ tons
Buffet Cars 40 seats

266	1936	Rest. car	551	1973
267	1936		CIE	1961

Type K.17   31½ tons
64 seats

66	1936	CIE	1970
67	1936	CIE	1972

Type K.19   22 tons
60 seats

3	1936	CIE	1963

Type L.6   31½ tons
50 seats

244	1919	458	1969
245	1919	CIE	1967
315	1924	CIE	1966
83	1925	460	1960

Type L.8   31 tons
108 seats

242	1919	487	1960
324	1924	CIE	1965
31	1926	UTA	1960

Type L.9   31½ tons
49 seats

375	1928	464	1969
22	1931	466	1971
23	1931	CIE	1964

Type L.10   31 tons
89 seats

346	1929	CIE	1966
361	1929	468	1968
369	1929	470	1970

Type L.12   28½ tons
39 seats

53	1937	591	1974
94	1939	592	1974
95	1939	CIE	1972

Type L.13   27½ tons
39 seats

114	1940	CIE	1973
115	1940	593	1973

INDEX OF STATIONS AND HALTS

(Illustrations and Diagrams in Italics)

Back row, left to right: W. McKenna, Clerk; S. Robinson, Clerk; G. Gillespie, Clerk; W. Donaldson, Foreman fitter; W. Robinson, Foreman; W. Boland, Foreman; T. McCool, Clerk; Front row, left to right: W. Marshall, Clerk; G. Hall, Clerk; W. Quinn, Clerk; S. Hill, Loco Supt., S. Coleman, Chief Clerk; W. Brennan, J. Bogle, Clerk. See page 23 onwards. [Adelaide Locomotive staff in 1920 photo (Mrs I. Alexander) identified by J. Boland & I. C. Pryce.]

0–6–4 tank 167 shunting at Duncrue Street, Belfast

Back row (from left): James Armstrong (fitter), W. McKee (fireman), P. O'Hara (painter, J. Dudley (fireman), S. Mehaffey (fireman). Next row: H. McKee (foreman), W. Chambers (driver), C. Eshler (fitter's helper), T. Ballentine (driver), J. Lynch (fireman), G. Fletcher and J. Lang. Next row: J. Kidd (fireman), C. McCann (fireman), R. Dudgeon (fireman), P. Lennon (fireman/Dundalk), C. Hurson (fireman), S. Gillespie (fireman), J. Barbour (fireman). Bottom row: W. Swann (fireman), A. Keenan, J. Hamill (driver/Dundalk), S. Kelly (driver), R. Smith (fireman), W. Arneill (fireman), D. Johnson (fireman), T. O'Hagan. [W. Bateson/Andersonstown News]

Here, unusually with passenger headlamp, is the first SG3 (Beyer Peacock 6040), at Great Victoria Street, Belfast. After the rebuilding of the Boyne Viaduct (Drogheda) in 1932 it was also quite rare to see 6 in Belfast.

150

ANTRIM—CRUMLIN—BELFAST.

STATIONS.	WEEK-DAYS.										SUN.		
	a.m.	a.m.	a.m.	SO noon	SO p.m.	SE p.m.	SO p.m.	p.m.	SE p.n.	SO p.m.	a.m.	a.m.	p.m.
ANTRIM ......dep.	...	7 35	9 25	12 0	1 40	2 0	2 35	5 20	...	...	...	...	...
Millar's Bridge „	...	7 40	9 30	...	1 45	2 6		a	...	...	...	...	...
Aldergrove...... „	...	7 45	9 36	12 12	1 50	2 12	2 44	5 29	7 0	11 2	...	10 5	9 20
Crumlin .... „	...	7 52	9 41	12 17	1 55	2 18	2 49	5 34	7 7	11 7	6 8	10 10	9 26
Glenavy .... „	6 15	7 59	9 47	...	2 1	2 24	2 55	5 40	7 13	11 13	6 15	10 16	9 33
Legatiriff . ... „	6 20	8 4	9 51	...	a	2 29	2 59	5 44	...	11 17	6 20	10 20	9 38
Ballinderry ...... „	6 24	8 9	9 55	12 28	2 9	2 33	3 2	5 47	7 20	11 20	6 24	10 23	9 42
Meeting House „	6 27	8 13	9 58	...	a	2 37	3 5	a	...	a	6 27	10 26	9 45
Brookhill......... „	6 31	8 18	10 1	...	2 14	2 41	3 8	5 51	...	11 27	6 31	10 29	9 48
Brookmount ... „	6 37	8 23	10 5	...	2 18	2 45	3 12	5 56	...	11 31	6 37	10 32	9 52
Lisburn ....arr.	6 45	8 30	10 11	12 41	2 24	2 52	3 18	6 3	7 33	11 38	6 45	10 39	9 59
.........dep.	6 47	8 32	10 17	12 42	2 26	2 55	3 19	6 4	7 35	11 40	6 47	10 40	10 0
Hilden .... „	...	...	...	...		2 57	...	...	...	...	...		10 2
Lambeg .... „	...	...	...	...	2 30	2 59	...	...	7 39	...	...	10 44	10 4
Derriaghy ...... „	6 53	...	...	...	...	3 2	...	...	...	...	6 53	10 46	...
Dunmurry ...... „	...	8 41	...	...	2 34	3 5	3 25	...	...	...	...	10 48	10 8
Finaghy .... „	...	...	...	12 50	2 37	3 8	3 28	6 12	7 45	...	...	10 51	10 11
Balmoral .... „	...	...	...	...	2 39	3 10	3 30	...	...	...	...	10 53	10 13
Adelaide .... „	...	...	...	...	2 42	3 13	...	...	...	...	...	10 56	10 16
BELFAST ......arr.	7 2	8 50	10 30	12 57	2 46	3 17	3 35	6 20	7 52	11 55	7 2	11 0	10 20

a Stops as required to pick up or set down passengers. b Stops to pick up passengers only.
SE Saturdays excepted. SO Saturdays only. WSE Wednesdays and Saturdays excepted.

Revised — Antrim-Crumlin-Belfast timetable — 4th May 1941 (after blitz).

Class PP 77 about to leave Antrim with GNR branch train, about 1920. See page 14
[A. Johnston]

151

A 1937 scene at Dunmurry, where the flag suggests that this is indeed 12.7.37. Ps 54 is propelling empty train back to Belfast from Dunmurry, passengers for Finaghy having alighted on the up journey. [A. Donaldson].

A familiar Banbridge line engine (see page 8) on the 'Fifth Road' at Balmoral with carriages of special train. [A. Donaldson]

STATIONS.	WEEK-DAYS.												
	a.m.	a.m.	SO p.m.	p.m.	p.m.	SE p.m.	SO p.m.	SO p.m.	SO p.m.	p.m.	SO p.m.	p.m.	SO p.m.
BANBRIDGE ......dep.	**8 13**	**10 32**	*12 50*	**2 50**	**5 5**	*6 0*	*6 0*	*6 35*	**7 15**	*8 45*	**9 40**	*10 30*	*11 5*
Lenaderg.............. „	8 17	10 36	*12 56*	*2 54*	*5 9*	*6 4*	*6 4*	*6 39*	*7 19*	*8 49*	*9 44*	*10 34*	*11 9*
Laurencetown......... „	8 21	10 41	*1 3*	*2 59*	*5 14*	*6 9*	*6 9*	*6 44*	*7 24*	*8 54*	*9 49*	*10 39*	*11 14*
Drumhork .... „	8 26	10 46	*1 9*	*3 4*	*5 19*	*6 14*	—	—	*7 29*	*8 59*	*9 54*	—	*11 19*
SCARVA ....arr.	**8 31**	**10 52**	*1 15*	**3 10**	**5 25**	*6 20*	...	...	**7 35**	*9 5*	**10 0**	...	*11 25*

	a.m.	a.m.	a.m.	SO p.m.	p.m.	p.m.	SO p.m.	SO p.m.	SE p.m.	SO p.m.	SO p.m.	p.m.	p.m.
SCARVA ....dep.	**5 50**	**9 16**	**11 42**	*1 25*	**4 32**	**5 30**	...	*6 30*	...	*7 45*	**9 18**	**10 2**	...
Drumhork .... „	5 55	9 21	11 47	*1 30*	*4 37*	*5 35*	...	*6 35*	...	*7 50*	*9 23*	*10 7*	...
Laurencetown......... „	6 0	9 25	11 52	*1 36*	*4 42*	*5 40*	*6 15*	*6 40*	*6 50*	*7 55*	*9 27*	*10 11*	...
Lenaderg............. „	6 5	9 30	11 57	*1 43*	*4 47*	*5 45*	*6 20*	*6 45*	*6 55*	*8 0*	*9 32*	*10 16*	...
BANBRIDGE ......arr.	**6 10**	**9 35**	**12 2**	*1 50*	**4 52**	**5 50**	*6 25*	*6 50*	*7 0*	*8 5*	**9 37**	**10 21**	...

NO SUNDAY SERVICE.

All services are " One Class only " and call at Millmount, Hazelbank, Uprichards' and Martin's Bridge
on request. **SE** Saturdays excepted   **SO** Saturdays only.

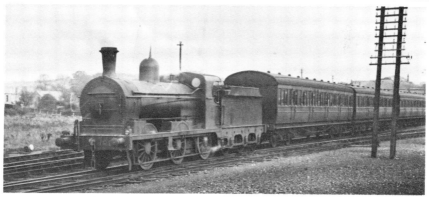

PGs 102 with Dublin excursion via Scarva at Banbridge 15th October 1938. (R.N. Clements)

Lifting train at Laurencetown with PGs 10 [A. Donaldson]

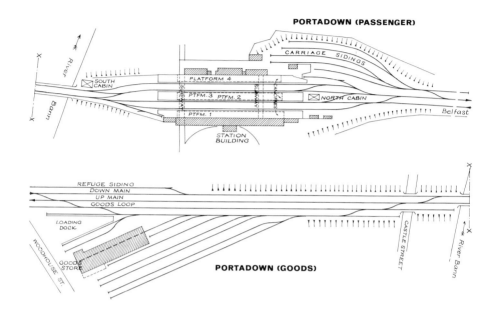

PORTADOWN (PASSENGER)

PORTADOWN (GOODS)

Drawn by D. G. Coakham.

Driver James Hobson and fireman enjoy the prospect of an eight hour day 13 February 1919.
[N. Holland]

4–4–2 tank 64 approaching Dungannon tunnel at Shaw's crossing [A. Donaldson]

QLs 156 with Derry train [A. Donaldson]

PGs 11 Near Old Engine crossing, Cookstown branch, with Twelfth Special.

155

Market Junction Omagh about 1910 [N. Holland]

Qs 136 at Derry with driver George Gillespie and fireman Joe Mason. [A. Johnston]

4–4–2 tank 63 replacing railcar at Sixmilecross.

Belfast-Derry train passes Tattykeernan crossing with Qs 135.

157

Railway bus to Great Northern Hotel at Bundoran Station, about to make its last journey, August 1928. [Mrs I. Alexander]

SG3 49 leaving Enniskillen (see page 100) with Portadown goods. [H.B. Smith]

0–6–0s 9 and 158 at Enniskillen engine shed. SLNCR Lough Gill shunting nearby.

Great Northern Railway (Ireland)
Timetables 1st October 1928

Londonderry, Glenties, Killybegs, Donegal, Stranorlar, Letterkenny, Strabane, Omagh, Bundoran, Sligo, Enniskillen.

Miles	STATIONS.	Week-days													
					L.R.			L.R.		L.R.		L.R.			
		a.m.	a.m.	a.m.	a.m.	a.m.	a.m.	p.m.	p.m	p.m.	p.m.	p.m.	p.m.	p.m.	p.m.
	LONDONDERRY....dep.	..	..	..	7 25	10 10	11 20	12 30	..	2 40	..	4 0	5 15	6 45	*11 0*
5¾	Carrigans .... ,,	..	..	..	7 34	10 20	11 31	..	..	2 50	..	..	5 26	..	*11 10*
7½	St. Johnston .... ,,	..	..	..	7 38	10 25	11 37	..	..	2 56	..	..	5 31	6 58	*11 16*
11¾	Porthall .... ,,	..	..	..	..	10 33	11 44	..	..	3 4	..	..	5 40	..	*11 24*
14¾	**Strabane** ....arr.	..	..	..	7 49	10 38	11 49	12 50	..	3 9	..	4 19	5 45	7 8	*11 29*
53	**Glenties** ....dep.	..	..	..	..	..	7 15	10 40	..	..	..	..	..	4 30	Sats only.
65¾	Killybegs .... ,,	..	..	..	..	..	7 45	..	..	12 0	..	12 0	..	3 45	
46½	Donegal .... ,,	..	..	..	..	..	9 0	..	..	1 10	..	1 10	..	4 55	
28½	Stranorlar......... ,,	..	..	..	..	..	9 58	12 0	..	2 10	..	2 10	..	5 55	
	Strabane ....arr.	..	..	..	..	..	10 35	12 40	..	2 55	..	2 55	..	6 30	
	Letterkenny ......dep.	..	..	..	..	..	9 30	..	..	1 20	..	3 5	..	6 0	
	Strabane ....arr.	..	..	..	..	..	10 30	..	..	2 25	..	4 10	..	7 5	
	Strabane ....dep.	..	..	..	7 51	..	11 51	12 53	..	3 11	..	4 22	5 49	7 11	*11 31*
18	Sion Mills .... ,,	..	..	..	7 59	..	11 59	1 0	..	3 18	..	..	5 56	7 18	*11 38*
19¼	Victoria Bridge ..... ,,	..	..	..	8 4	..	12 3	..	..	3 23	..	..	6 1	7 23	*11 42*
24¼	Newtownstewart .... ,,	..	..	..	8 13	..	12 13	1 11	..	3 32	..	..	6 9	7 32	Stop
30¼	Mountjoy.......... ,,	..	..	..	8 22	..	12 22	..	..	3 41	..	..	6 18	..	
33¾	**Omagh** ....arr.	..	..	..	8 28	..	12 28	1 24	..	3 47	..	4 51	6 24	7 47	..
	,, ...dep.	..	..	..	8 31	..	12 32	..	..	3 52	..	..	6 35	..	..
41	**Fintona** ....arr.	..	..	..	9 0	..	1 0	..	..	4 15	..	..	7 3	..	..
	,, ...dep.	..	..	..	8 20	..	12 25	..	..	3 40	..	..	6 25	..	..
40½	Fintona Jct. .... ,,	..	..	..	8 42	..	12 43	..	..	4 3	..	..	6 46	..	..
46¼	Dromore Road....... ,,	..	..	..	8 52	..	12 54	..	..	4 13	..	..	6 57	..	..
50	Trillick .... ,,	..	..	..	9 0	..	1 2	..	..	4 21	..	..	7 5	..	..
51½	**Bundoran Jct.** ....arr.	..	..	..	9 3	..	1 7	Express Train via Portadown	..	e	..	..	7 8	..	..
87	**Bundoran** ....dep.	..	6 30	..	..	..	11 35		..	..	..	Express Train via Portadown	5 30	..	..
83	**Ballyshannon** ...... ,	..	6 39	..	..	..	11 45		..	..	..		5 39	..	..
79	**Belleek** .... ,,	..	6 48	..	..	..	11 57		..	..	..		5 50	..	..
74½	**Castlecaldwell** ...... ,,	..	6 58	..	..	..	12 7		..	..	..		6 1	..	..
66½	**Pettigo** .... ,,	..	7 12	..	..	..	12 23		..	..	..		6 15	..	..
61¼	**Kesh** .... ,,	..	7 24	..	..	..	12 36		..	..	..		6 28	..	..
55	**Irvinestown** .... ,,	..	7 37	..	..	..	12 49		..	..	..		6 42	..	..
	Bundoran Jct........arr.	..	7 45	..	..	..	12 57		..	..	..		6 50	..	..
	Bundoran Jct. ....dep.	..	7 50	..	9 4	..	1 14		..	..	5 35		7 13	..	..
54	Ballinamallard....... ,,	..	7 56	..	9 9	..	1 20		..	4 30	5 41		7 19	..	..
59½	**Enniskillen** ....arr.	..	8 5	..	9 18	..	1 29		..	4 39	5 50		7 28	..	..
	Sligo ....dep.	..	Stop	..	6 15	..	10 20		..	..	..		3 45	..	..
	Ballysodare ...... ,,	..	..	..	6 27	..	10 35		..	..			3 57	..	..

These had been the standard timings for many years and pertained until June 1932 when very enterprising accelerations were put into force, some of which lasted until 1940.